FOGGED IN

John Day

Copyright © 2020

ISBN 9786749709103 (hdbk)
ISBN 9786749709073 (pbk)
ISBN 9786749709110 (ebook)

CONTENTS

I. INTO THE CULTURE

Two and a half years

1. FOGGED IN.........................3
2. SPRING OF LOVE 34
3. HAPPY DAYS 66

II. DISORIENTED

One year

1. DARKNESS 87
2. UNSETTLED TRANSITION 107
3. DANA HOUSE 120

III. REFLECTING IN A FOG

One year

1. BRIEF INTERLUDE................147
2. MORE NORTHSIDE 173
3. PAST REFLECTIONS...............183
4. BACK TO THE PRESENT PAST.....217

IV. TRANSITIONS

THREE AND A QUARTER YEARS

1. INDEPENDENCE 233
2. LIKE MARRIAGE 248
3. SITTING IN LIMBO 258
4. NEW WORLD 265
5. SURPRISING CHANGE 275

V. SEEKING REALITY

TWENTY-FIVE YEARS

1. MARRIAGE WORLD 291
2. BEGUILING QUAGMIRE 310
3. GOD AND UNDERSTANDING 327

VI. CLARITY

FIFTY YEARS

1. FINDING ORDER 353
2. RELATIONAL ORDER 366
3. REAL ORDER 381

I.

INTO THE CULTURE

Two and a Half Years

1.

FOGGED IN

12/66-3/67

Clarity or Fog

San Francisco has long been identified with the fog that so often embraces it. In a city with dramatic hills bounded by the Pacific Ocean and San Francisco Bay and linked to the greater Bay Area by the iconic Golden Gate Bridge and the Bay Bridge, how could fog be a defining element? It is like a comfortable blanket in the morning, paradoxically cool and warm, that often dissipates between eleven and twelve revealing bright blue skies with scattered clouds before rolling back in again in late afternoon to create its intimate and mysterious effect once more—unless you are a foolish tourist in shorts and a t-shirt expecting Midwest or L.A. weather. The fog keeps the City cooler even in the height of summer. It creates wonderful vistas of the City, partially concealed, the towers of the Golden Gate Bridge poking out into clear sky. I love it because I find it mirrors internal reflection in the way a part becomes the focus, limiting the distraction of the whole. The City fog is rarely so dense that you cannot see and find your way, even if the view is limited and the light dimmed, obscuring a little here, a little there, changing the focal point, and constantly creating new vignettes out of the same physical place. Unless one finds gray weather oppressive and burdensome, unable to see the blue skies behind the fog or clouds, the fog can indeed be comforting and comfortable. I have only rarely found that foggy, gray overcast burdensome.

Unfortunately, when I am fogged in—overcast emotionally or spiritually by my thinking—I often cannot see enough to find my way and have felt burdened. The physical City fog works differently because I have seen the City on a clear day and can understand the vignettes in the context of the whole. Finding understanding internally is much more difficult. I can be lost simply because I am seeing the personal vignettes without the whole context. Without that context, I can easily confuse what is right before my eyes and miss how it fits into a consistent, bigger picture. Searching for that context and order is ultimately a search for meaning. I now find that I have a clearer sense of the whole, the context, and the order. The emotional and spiritual fog is now more like the physical fog, momentary realities that are just part of the ebb and flow of life that can be understood in a greater context. That was not the case when I first returned to San Francisco and the Bay Area as a young adult.

Walking onto the Berkeley campus of the University of California on a brisk and clear December day in 1966, I was stepping into a deeper fog I could not see. I thought everything was so clear. I was sure I was having a religious or transformational experience on that beautiful day, a glorious day. I had only just arrived to complete my transfer registration before heading home for the holidays. I had no idea what Berkeley or the campus looked or felt like.

Berkeley was much more urban than I had expected, with bigger buildings and bustling with activity. That was part of the excitement for me: a different environment from that with which I was familiar. Stepping across Bancroft Way from Telegraph Avenue was like a bridge to this new experience.

Much of this sense was expectation and intention. I was only just setting foot on campus for the first time. Except for the view of Sproul Plaza ahead, I had seen and experienced nothing. Everything was expectation—expectation based on my real, romantic, and spiritual attraction to San Francisco and the Bay Area, expectation for a different educational experience, but, most importantly, expectation based on an attraction to the counterculture just blossoming in that part of the country.

That dramatic and exhilarating experience of joy and confident expectation seemed to occur in an instant as I stepped onto campus that day. I felt like I was where I was supposed to be, where things were happening, in a place that felt like home. If there was a oneness with God, I thought I was feeling it then, even though the attractions seemed to have little to do with God. While the sense of confirmation happened in a moment, the lead up did not. I had been struggling with the move for some time, but simply stepping across the street, the change in feeling and confidence seemed instantaneous. I had a sense of wonder, excitement, and adventure as I walked through Sproul Plaza. I was confronted with its multitude of vendors of ideas: religious, political, topical. I moved past the Sproul Hall Steps, made famous just two years earlier by the free speech movement and Mario Savio, through Sather Gate, which to me looked like a mysterious and ancient artifact, then up a path past a long haired, young man dressed in polka dot clothing calmly sitting on the grass blowing soap bubbles as if he was at a kids' birthday party. Somehow it made total sense, all fit together. It was no ordinary college campus. Here the buildings were older and more impressive than I had previously experienced; the sloping, wooded campus with stately live oaks, paths, and a prominent creek was dramatic. The campus was physically stunning and romantic to me. I felt a sense of physical and emotional comfort.

Some Context

Foundational to this sense of peace, joy, and homecoming was my sense of roots in San Francisco and the Bay Area. Shortly after this time, many came to San Francisco "with flowers in their hair" during the Summer of Love. San Francisco and that time were one for them. My anchoring and attraction were far deeper. Parts of my family had been in the Bay Area since before the 1906 earthquake and World War I. I had lived there several times in my 19 years and continuously between the ages of 4 and 8, when many early memories of the City were formed. They were ethereal but very real: a fair at the Cow Palace, Christmas lights downtown, the Jewish temple on Arguello, the Presidio, and Fort Point. After moving away from California and coming back briefly, we would visit my mother's extended family, most of whom were still living in the East Bay.

Much later when I was starting my junior year in high school, my family moved to the Central Valley of California, the large agricultural expanse between the Coastal Range and the Sierra Nevada Mountains. While living there, I was always feeling out in the "boonies" compared to being in or around the City. We subscribed to the *San Francisco Chronicle*, and I devoured the Herb Caen columns and others that reflected on life in the City. I checked out books of his that were available at the local library, which, like his columns, were part history, part anecdote, part gossip, and all about the City. I read them as if I was living them. His "gossip" columns were different from most columns in that, taken together, over time they painted a complete and vibrant picture of the City. I combined my understanding of the history and my own vague memories of the place with the life in the columns and books to add color. Thus, my image of San Francisco and the Bay Area was not primarily formed of physical experience; however, I ultimately and strangely found it to be very accurate in reality.

I was very lonely in the Central Valley. I think I had been lonely for a long time. I was lonely and fearful or, more accurately, lonely in part because I was fearful. I would have liked to have been more engaged socially, especially with girls, but I was too shy and too afraid to participate in social activities like dances or class parties. When I was younger and living in Colorado, just as I was getting comfortable being more social, we suddenly moved. The kids where we moved in Wisconsin were so much more advanced socially and physically that I never recovered, then, or at the next move, or the next, or the next. Moving was great for geographical anchoring; however, being fearful, it stunted my social growth. Like many, I hoped that when I went to college maybe I could make a break through. I would be away from family, freed from limitations I had set for myself, and the situation would just be different.

However, that was not to be. The school I attended, while academically admirable and in a beautiful environment, did not provide the freedom from self-imposed limitations as I had hoped. I found the whole process of the week planned for incoming freshmen, designed to make us feel good and at home, achieved the opposite for me. No real connecting, dances fit for students far less shy, activities for students far more athletically adept, and yet, so many of these students my age seemed to fit in. I did not. Many of them probably felt the way I did, but I did not know that anymore then than I had in other social relations with young people. I assumed I was the only one who was uncomfortable and out of place.

My classes made me even less happy. While I had thought I was in an appropriate program, I clearly did not understand what it was. I was interested in many things, but my understanding of planning for my future was simple and uninformed. I picked Cal Poly because it was supposed to be a good school not too far away with reasonable tuition. Even though I had done well in high school, scholarships and an ambitious selection process were not on my radar and did not fit my passive, shy persona. My program was rigidly structured with little variety in classes—ostensibly one of the strengths of the school was the focus on practical application of skills in each major. Many of the students were more advanced than I was, and my major often required working late into the night. While I liked my general choice, I lacked focus. Other students seemed to be challenged by the program and fit in; I did not.

Instead of providing a sense of freedom, my separation from home and the comfortable high school environment, in which, even as something of an outsider, I knew the system and could function, was painful. This new system was intimidating in such a way that I was not drawn by the challenge but repelled. My loneliness was now rawer and more exposed. I was alone in the sense of not having anyone I could talk to who might offer a different perspective. I did not know I was not supposed to have it all figured out. That lack of understanding was really a failure to understand a greater meaning in life, a sense of reliable order, or ultimate reality. I had already been searching in my own casual way, but within the safety of home and family the strain at the edges was bearable. Now, the struggle was obvious, and the safety net, inadequate as it had been, was not there at all.

I lived in an older, less expensive dormitory with no common living areas. The door came in from the outside. That helped enforce a separateness which I am glad I had. Luckily, I had a good roommate. Jim was a junior college transfer, so he was at least two years older. He was much more focused on his program, and as I look back, he was the best mooring point I had at that time. He would probably be surprised to hear that; he was like an older brother. He was very experienced sexually, had been from a young age, and shocked me with things I had never heard or known before. He was also Jewish. While I was ultimately to have lots of Jewish friends, at the time I did not have a clue about the Jewish faith. I thought they were people from Bible times, except for the knowledge that as a child I would go with my father to the Presidio and we would pass the synagogue on Arguello, and he would explain that we were seeing lots of people because they had their services on Saturday. My roommate was not like most Jews I would come to know. Even though they were generally secular/cultural Jews with only some celebration of religious observances, he seemed to be just secular.

Shortly after starting school, I met Peter, a slender, very intense student from L.A. who was to become a lifelong friend. He walked stiffly consistent with his intensity, but his eyes invited conversation that was intimate. He was an edge person too, so we could communicate. He lived in one of the newer dorms where there was more of a social community, which made him my primary contact for meeting other people. Nonetheless, I did not really connect much with those "dormies."

I did become friends with a bohemian in my dorm. He was from the north coast and had read extensively in the Beat poets. I had been attracted to the Beats since the seventh grade and locked into this opportunity as a medication for my unhappiness. I read some Ginsburg, Burroughs, Snyder, and Ferlinghetti. I did not connect with much of it except maybe Snyder but soaked up the exposure as an antidote to my boredom and aloneness. This fit right in with my affinity for the mostly gray, depressing lyrics of early Bob Dylan folk albums and early 20th century writers such as Faulkner, Fitzgerald, Hemingway, Camus, Steinbeck, Sinclair Lewis, Erskine Caldwell, and Gertrude Stein. Although I saw it as an exciting exploration then, it was really an immersion in gray hopelessness. I was not depressed; I just could not see where this was supposed to lead. The reading seemed to indicate it was maybe ultimate gray hopelessness. It did nothing to increase my hopefulness, even though I liked the adventure in this new territory. It was certainly better than school.

I continued going regularly to church and was serious about my faith. I drove the VW van that took students to church. I had not been mentored since an earlier conversion experience and did not know how seek help in the most obvious place. I attended youth meetings but connected with no one. To this day, I am amazed at how those in leadership miss connecting with edge people and default to comfortable situations. This was an opportunity for a spiritual connection or growth, relief and nurture, but that simply did not happen.

Television was becoming a greater influence in American culture. It had been a part of my life since grade school, but there was no TV where I lived. The "dormies" had TV in their common areas, but I never went there. Years would pass before I ever had a TV or watched one again.

I cannot remember why or how, but in early December I had tickets to see Bob Dylan in concert in San Francisco with some friends. With this concert tour, Dylan was upsetting fans and critics by moving to an electric rock back-up band on his new album, *Highway 61 Revisited,* that was unlike his other work. Indeed, it was very different from what I had been listening to. Going to San Francisco was still very intriguing to me. I remember I dressed in nice clothes befitting an event at the Masonic Auditorium on Nob Hill only to find that others dressed in a very odd fashion, and some of the guys had very long hair. The concert was great, although the background of the audience and the City were almost as impressive for me. My parents, who had driven us, had to wait in the lobby, they talked afterwards about some of the odd people and how maybe some of the guys were with guys. I was sure that was not true, even though it probably was. I was strongly attracted to this latest evolution of the Beats I had first idolized as I saw the early folk scene and the Beats as parts of this same movement, even though they may have seen themselves as totally different. I went back to Cal Poly, but the grayness was even grayer for me.

Jim moved out in the spring, and the new roommate was not the same. He never attended classes. I am not sure how he stayed in school. Jim moved to an apartment with others I knew, so I did see him some.

That summer I returned home to a job for the county, then, quickly a better job for Mosquito Abatement. A friend from high school and I travelled around the county inspecting property and looking for mosquitos. While this must have been to show tax dollars at work, I am sure those who we discovered with caved in septic tanks and the like did not appreciate the attention. Mostly, my friend and I talked all day. He was different from me—quite comfortable socially—and invited me along to the county fair with a couple of pretty girls from school. I had fun and survived, but that was it. With the money I earned that summer I bought a used '63 VW bug. It was not a '54 Chevy, the iconic car then, but ironically ended up being the iconic car of the counterculture. Late in the summer I went to a Rolling Stones concert in the City. I was mostly interested in the Jefferson Airplane and hippie guys with pierced ears. That was not a thing at the time except maybe for pirates and Hell's Angels.

Nonetheless, I returned to school but to yet another new roommate. He was friendly enough but not someone with whom I could really communicate. I attended classes, read, listened to music, and dreamed of being somewhere else. One week, *Newsweek* ran an article on what was happening in the counterculture in San Francisco, which seemed to be setting the tone for the whole country. The culture was one of free love, more loosely structured music, and psychedelic drugs. One of the signature groups, the Grateful Dead, was featured in the article with their lead guitar player, Jerry Garcia, or as the article called him "Captain Trips," who had taken LSD a ridiculous number of times. As far as I knew from conversations with others and my north coast bohemian friend, none of our schools had much if any drug involvement at the time. Marijuana was a part of Beat culture, then some went farther into heroin, but that was not mainstream even in cutting edge intellectual circles. That was still a few years off. The times were changing as Dylan said. My fascination with San Francisco, interest in the free speech movement, attraction to Dylan and protest music, the experience at the concert in San Francisco, and general unhappiness led me to consider transferring to Berkeley. While that news article and Jerry Garcia, the guitar player, were a tipping point, I had absolutely no idea what Grateful Dead music sounded like. I had heard the Jefferson Airplane during the summer, but they sounded much like the other groups with which I was familiar. Further, I had no idea about drugs, and I also had no idea what UC Berkeley was.

This would be a major decision. I was focused on finishing school as quickly as possible. I am not sure why since I did not know where I was going. I was just doing what I was supposed to do. My program was so tightly structured that I had only taken one elective class outside my major. If I left and then changed my mind, I would be a year behind because of missed classes. I could not face losing a year, even though I had absolutely no goal or plans for what happened when I did finish. It did not make any sense; yet it was a major source of anxiety and fear. Nonetheless, I ordered the application, filled it out, almost did not send it, but then did. I was accepted and would be leaving at the end of the term in early December.

I was nineteen and for the first time had made a major decision of change on my own. For a long time, not just in college, I felt lonely, lost, and without much hope. My situation was not desperate, but it was dull and gray. I could not see how anything would change. I had no exciting view of the future. Now, I thought, life would stop passing me by, and the sun would shine. I would be part of what was really happening, part of a positive and exciting new way of thinking and living. I was incredibly clueless and lost, but I did not know that. I was naively hopeful and enthusiastic. If I had a worldview, I would have thought it was full of compartments: spiritual, political, cultural, and emotional, but could not have tied any of them together into a clear picture of reality. I was buffeted about by everything, and the counterculture seemed like an attractive harbor in the unsettled sea of my emotions.

Like most, when I was young, I had no control over where or how I lived. I lived where my family lived. My family moved a lot, which was emotionally difficult. Maybe I had some control over my emotional and spiritual life but did not understand that at the time because I was young and regularly uprooted. I thought the physical, emotional, and spiritual parts of life were linked in a way that while compartmentalized could not be separated. The move to Berkeley was to be the most dramatic change I ever made—physical, emotional, and spiritual all at once—and was to define how I thought about most things for a long time. I thought I was lost in a fog and had found myself. Yet, I now believe I was getting lost further in a fog of confusion and darkness and would continue being lost for a long time. Ironically, everything seemed so clear, but that clarity was deceiving.

I had no vision, goals, or grounding except in small things: being responsible, going to school, and wishing I had a girlfriend. But I had no aspirations. I was not strong enough to define my environment. My environment had been sending me inward in a dark, foggy way, not in a reflective way. I hoped to piggy-back onto an environment that I thought was better. What I was really doing was looking for meaning, the meaning of life, ultimate reality. I think most of us are doing that in the background and I did not realize I had been doing it whenever I was trying to make sense of my surroundings.

I thought I was more mature, but I was building a false understanding of myself and the world in trying to find happiness but really meaning. I thought a relationship with a girl would make a difference, and I was right. Of course, it would, but that was not where ultimate meaning was to be found. History, literature, religion, and philosophy help connect some dots. For me, religious experience with worship and training in confirmation classes taught by a gifted priest led to a spiritual awakening when I was 12. However, I was young, and shortly thereafter we moved from my mentor priest and parish. I never had a similar replacement. I tried to hang in there on my own but could not connect the dots. My faith was still there but mostly took the form of following rules, legalism, as I was not mature enough to understand how to progress. I went seven years until a counterculture proclaiming answers attracted me. I took a leap of faith and embraced it, but, guess what, that was not the answer either.

Life is a search for meaning—a search for ultimate meaning. If I do this, that will happen and when I string those *this and that* together, the picture makes more sense but does not necessarily get less foggy because all the new elements and their relations become distracting, and then I truly cannot see the forest for the trees. With time, I got more and more confused juggling lots of this and that without thinking about meaning or my worldview, although life is not ultimately about the world or a view of that world.

Back to the Bay

I spent the holidays at home in the Central Valley then returned to the East Bay in late December to set up quarters, at least temporarily, in my grandmother's attic. Her house was less than a half hour drive from the campus. I did not have much money, so this was the most economical accommodation. My parents had saved some money for tuition, but not enough was left for all the living expenses of several years of college. Neither of them had been able to go to college because their own families were so poor. The attic space was fine and gave me a chance to establish a different relationship with my grandmother and some of my relatives. Prior to this time, I had only visited briefly, and at one point while we moved from Wisconsin to Alaska, my family and I had lived on the property together for a few months.

The living situation requires some explanation, as even then it was uncommon. Most people who lived in the suburbs of a metropolitan urban environment like the Bay Area lived in individual houses on individual pieces of property on regular streets in regular communities. We lived in one of those communities on one of those streets, but this situation was different. My grandparents moved to the property in 1926 when the houses were far apart, and they were all on farms. Theirs was a three-acre chicken ranch with an apricot orchard. The one-story house, built just after the 1906 earthquake, sat in a flat area behind a low, white picket fence and six tall English walnut trees. It had horizontal siding and a bay window at the dining room and was built up about four feet with wooden entry steps and a screened in front porch covered with purple wisteria. A creek ran through the property just behind the house. Above the creek, the grade changed, and the chicken houses were terraced up the hill.

By the time I arrived for college forty years later, things had changed. The surrounding community had been parceled up as I described. The farms were all developed as housing. My grandparents' property had changed too, but it was unique. My mother was the only one of the four children to move away and raise her family. Her two brothers and one sister—my uncles and aunt—stayed on the property. In addition, one uncle had started a successful contracting business in the barn; the business was still located on the property even though the neighborhood was otherwise residential. He had, until recently, lived in the converted attic and back portion of the main house where I was now going to stay. My other uncle had a house on the hill above the chicken houses and still ran the chicken business in addition to working for the contracting firm. My aunt had a house across the driveway from my grandparents' house. All three families had raised their total of eleven children on that same piece of property on which they had grown up.

My contractor uncle now owned a house next door and only had his office in the lower room of the back unit which consisted of a room, a bathroom, and small kitchen on the main floor and a bedroom, sleeping area, and half bathroom in the attic up some very steep stairs. The unit was a very small and odd area in which to raise a family with three children, especially since my uncle was quite successful. The attic room was fine for me. It had a low sloped ceiling with a few small dormer windows. I had a mattress on the floor, a makeshift desk fashioned out of an old wooden crate, a desk chair, and a small, portable record player. That was it. I was in heaven.

I had contact with my uncle from up the hill because he came down to have coffee with his mother each morning. He would discuss all kinds of things, from politics and culture to more banal things like the benefits of carpet vs. wood floors. I remembered this characteristic of his from when we had stayed there previously. Every evening, my grandmother and I had dinner with my aunt and her family.

In addition, I would do some odd jobs for money and talk with other cousins when they asked questions. I would also, when possible, participate in the ritual of "coffee time." At three, everyone would gather at the back of my grandmother's house next to where the creek and bridge used to be and have coffee and pastries. The pastry would be homemade, often something with canned apricots from the few remaining orchard trees. Both of my uncles would stop working, and wives and kids who were home would come. The conversation varied day to day. I had always loved listening to my parents when they had guests. This was even better; these were all my relatives relating. When I no longer lived there, I would plan visits for the afternoon just to be a part of coffee time.

I would get up early each morning when it was still dark and cold, as there was no heat in my attic room, take a quick bath as there was no shower, then have breakfast with my grandmother in her kitchen. The kitchen was different from most. The house was old even at that time. the kitchen had two separate rooms. The larger had a small table in the center with a freestanding, metal wood stove to one side. The room also had a wood box, separate sitting chair, and a refrigerator in the corner. The other room was a narrow galley with a counter, sink, and cabinets on one side and a stove and cabinets on the other. The end cabinet had screens to the outside, even then an old feature for cooling. At the end of the room was the narrow back door, which was the one most used to enter the house.

The kitchen was heated in the morning by the wood stove. Even though Bay Area winters are temperate, a house with no heat or insulation makes a stove with a fire a magnetic attraction on dark, cold mornings. I would have eggs and toast and a time of conversation before leaving for the university. Most mornings, maybe all mornings, my uncle from up the hill would come down mid-breakfast for a coffee in a canning jar instead of a cup. This time and its value went beyond the topics of conversation. I loved these mornings, although I did not fully appreciate it then.

I really enjoyed the time with my grandmother. She would have been about 70 at the time. She was of medium height and medium build and wore her long blondish hair braided and wrapped tightly to the back of her head. Her expressive clear blue eyes stood out in her otherwise quiet face. Her standard attire included dresses of light cotton print I associate with movies and posters of the 1930's and black shoes with a thick moderate heal. When I would come home in the afternoon, she would be working at her simple mission style desk in the living room on my uncle's bookkeeping. We might say a few words then, but in the evening, if I was not busy with schoolwork, she was always ready to take a break from watching some public television drama and knitting or putting together a rag rug to converse with me. She was a very shy woman in public, much too shy; she did not go to weddings or funerals because of her shyness. However, with her family she would come alive. She and her many sisters would have birthday parties with all the "*tantes*" showing up, and she had no problem being active in those situations. We would talk about my parents, my uncles and aunts, and whatever else came to mind. In all, we developed quite a good relationship.

A Gathering of the Tribes and More

I was attracted to the counterculture but was unsure how to become part of it. Immediately after moving in, I heard ads for a free concert in Golden Gate Park billed as a "Human

Be-in." Because I had been to San Francisco with my parents over the years and had been to the Dylan concert in the City, unlike with Berkeley, I had a hint of the place, the people, and the experience. However, I had never been to an outdoor concert, much less one with thousands of people in attendance. While this was not like the experience of walking onto the Berkeley campus, this was a new and exciting event within that adventure. My sense of myself, although I thought it was well formed, was more formed of those things I associated with what I held in high regard and not anything I myself did—in other words, my sense of self was actually fabricated of things outside myself. I was smart enough to notice when those people, places, or situations did not live up to my expectations for them, but I followed that path nonetheless. The Human Be-in was full of those people I admired, in a place I thought of fondly, and the event made national news. Something was happening among the youth that was getting a lot of attention. It was a mixture of drugs, sex, music, and politics under the banner of a new lifestyle of love. I was naïve. I bought the message. Others wiser than I was may have been into only one of the elements knowing that the love umbrella was simple minded, but many were like me: idealists.

The free concert had all the national players. Ginsburg, the Beat poet, had a role in organizing the event. I was pleased with myself to be at such an event; I was in the right place. Tim Leary, an ex-professor who was well known nationally for his advocacy of using psychedelic drugs made a rambling statement encouraging the use of psychedelics, listening to the drug induced insights, and becoming a part of a new culture, leaving the old. His mantra of "turn on, tune in, and drop out" was the message.

The park itself was a great environment for the concert. The park reaches from the ocean far up into the heart of the City before narrowing near the Haight Ashbury district. Haight Ashbury was like the central nervous system of the city for many of the hippies and music groups at the time. The park is heavily wooded with many meadows, ponds, and gardens along its length. The street traffic is mostly separated from it. The concert was held in one of the largest outside areas; it was open and warm even though it was January.

I had parked some distance away in the park, and as I walked to the concert, I noticed that many of the young people around me were very different looking. I still had hair that was normal for the times—short on the sides, a little longer on top, and combed to the side—and dressed as I had at Cal Poly in blue denim trousers, a blue cotton work shirt, a dark green corduroy jacket that could be worn to dressier events, and leather work boots. That look was enough different from the norm of dress at the time to have given me some identification in my dress. Now, suddenly, I was among others to whom I must have looked positively establishment. The young men and women wore their hair long and natural, rather than neatly combed or arranged. Their loose clothing was multicolored and textured. Pants were cut low at the hips and flared at the feet, which might have no shoes, sandals, or odd pointy boots. I was so used to not feeling I fit in to be comfortably uncomfortable standing on the sidelines taking in the whole show all around me. All the San Francisco psychedelic groups played. People moved and danced to the music in a free style way with which I was unfamiliar but to which I was attracted not knowing exactly why. Even though I did not fit in, I went home feeling I was a part of the event and a part of something for once.

At the same time, the Vietnam War was ongoing. I sensed the war as anxiety as I listened to radio reports on the way to school, always seeming to list new casualties. I did not have a definitive position on the war. I had been in ROTC but now attended a school that was one of the primary centers for opposition to the war. It seemed far away, but already at least a couple of guys from high school had died there.

Attending classes at the university was exhilarating. After the commute in, the experience started with simply walking on campus and the eclectic cast of characters in Sproul Plaza offering religious and political missives. The lower plaza might have a free concert, and there was always a bazaar of the bizarre. I was energized by it. My background had been so ordinary I thought I had been missing real life. I was too naïve to discern the new and creative from the simply adolescent. The classes themselves were no exception; in truth, they were probably the more substantial experience, though I did not know it at the time. I gave greater accord to the counterculture movement. Because I was uncertain of my future, I took general introductory classes in different disciplines including the classics, sociology, political science, and history. It may have seemed boring to some, but for me each was like a breath of fresh air.

There was so much to see and experience that I felt I was seeing a new and exciting place every day. How could classics be exciting, how could a general class in sociology be exciting, the same with history and political science? Obviously, most of it was me. I transferred the positivity of the campus environment to the classroom. Also, I was taking these classes because I really wanted to take them, not because they were required. I wanted the opportunity to expand my knowledge and get a taste of different disciplines. My previous program had not left room for that. In addition, I had no experience with the way the classes were taught even if they were only routine survey level classes. Each in that first quarter was exciting to me.

My history class was taught in a massive, old auditorium, Wheeler Hall. I could hardly comprehend the size. The class was on the post-Civil War South. The professor, Leon Litwack, who taught this class for years, was unlike any other teacher I had experienced. His presentation and intonation were so powerful that I can still picture specific references from the sources he used. It was a performance of sorts, but it enhanced his ability to convey the information. I was told I would be lost at Cal because the classes would be huge. This class was huge, and I felt I was in the presence of a gifted teacher. I liked the anonymity and the quality. Besides, most large classes, including this one, had smaller sessions with teaching assistants, so it was not all anonymous.

Introduction to classic plays was taught in a neo-classical building just beyond Sather Gate, an apt setting for the topic. If it were not for the teacher, classics might have quickly become tedious. Previously, I only had rudimentary exposure to classic Greek plays and writings. This was not a huge class with extra sessions with teaching assistants. The professor, a thin, energetic man brought life to this work. Reading the works alone, I could never have understood the material. He added all the unwritten background, the color, the sound. He also ensured the interest of the class by pointing out the varied sexual, especially homosexual, references in the plays.

Political science was interesting to me because I did not have a clue what it was. Politics was part of everything going on at Berkeley at that time. The professor was an older gentleman who had held a position in the Roosevelt administration, which seemed ancient to me. As I write this now, about fifty years have passed from that class, and it seems like yesterday. I was fascinated to hear real government experiences from a real person who had been there, rather than just read dates in a book. The theory became real. The class was taught with a large lecture followed by small group classes led by graduate students. The teacher was not as skilled as the history and classics teachers, but the personal anecdotes conveyed a great sense of drama rather than dull principles. Nonetheless, I did not know how they related to something I could use.

Initiative

I took a course in sociology of religion, which was taught in a theater-like lecture hall that held about 100 students. The teacher, Ben Zablocki, had a New York accent, bushy, dark hair, and a beard to match. He dressed casually and would often pull off his wool sweater midway through his lecture, unconcerned that it messed up his hair. He lectured somewhat absentmindedly, sometimes slouching at the front, sometimes sitting on the edge of the stage, and sometimes wandering in the audience. I found him fascinating. He fit my image of the typical Berkeley teacher to a tee—like a beatnik professor from the late 50s. While I cannot admit to understanding all the subtleties of sociology of religion, I can say that his explanations got me past the bulk of the written material and grounded me in what sociology meant. I did not choose to go into sociology, nor did I pick up Weber or Durkheim for casual reading, but I have never forgotten the class or the foundational issues. We were assigned some Bible readings. In reading Mark and the temptations of Christ after his baptism, especially being placed on a tall steeple, I now realize this was a tipping point that led me to set Christianity aside. That unexplainable metaphysical things could happen I had never really questioned before. Now, I saw that I was just not paying attention; *they were foolish*. Instead of moving into great clarity of thinking because I did not understand my faith, I was willingly, even enthusiastically, being led into a mental fog that would last for years.

That class was the setting for my first minor effort at initiative, my first Berkeley infatuation, and my first connection with others in this new setting. We were assigned to report on three religions by attending services or visiting facilities. I was now unsure where I stood with God and religion. Just a couple of months previous, I had driven the van that took students from the Cal Poly campus to our church. I was not walking away because of something specific except that I no longer knew how God, religion, and church related to me. The class was very abstract and intellectual; I am sure I did not understand half of what was conveyed. If it related to my personal spiritual life, I got nothing. The assignment, rather than drawing me to any deeper spiritual understanding, was like classics, political science, and history, teaching me about religion and its structure from a societal point of view. That religion could be something completely different, that it could be more than the sum of its parts, was not part of the class. I did not notice that I was moving into a world or worldview where that other aspect of religion, the metaphysical, particularly in Christianity, was assumed outdated by many when it was simply a different reality.

I was excited by the new world opening up, so rather than look to my church, I tried to think of an alternative religion to explore. I was not interested at that time in a broader scope of religions, like eastern religions that were popular pursuits at the time. What caught my attention was a local radio station that ran a news story about a satanic church in San Francisco performing a wedding. To me that was intriguing, not because I wanted to be a Satanist or even had any idea what that would be, but simply because it seemed to fit the assignment the way I would have liked: looking at a religion from the outside, like it was a house or car, without any sense of the spiritual. That was part of the assignment, but I was focused on the look not the substance. I needed to feel I could try and learn new things. I thought that was the path to a greater satisfaction. I had no illusions about this satanic church being something wonderful, simply an experience; although I was not experienced or confident enough to be discerning about my choice of experiences. I was shy and not at all comfortable speaking in a group, but somehow, I mustered the courage to ask the professor if my idea would qualify for the assignment. He was intrigued enough to want to join in himself. I was feeling even better about this change of schools because of this very modest effort at engaging in my studies and making a provocative suggestion. Even more thrilling—and scary— was that one of the two or three other students who overheard and wanted to join was an attractive young woman. I had noticed her in class before. I still could not think of even approaching a young woman, especially one to whom I was attracted. To have an opportunity to be joined by such a person on an excursion was beyond my dreams. In that kind of situation at least I could talk.

I made the calls to set up the visit, and one evening five of us piled into my VW bug to make the trip to San Francisco. The house was a Victorian like many in San Francisco; unlike others, it was painted black. It was in a normal residential area to the north of the park in the Richmond District. We made our way to the second-floor entrance and were greeted by a woman with long blond hair dressed in black. We were shown into a living room and introduced to the satanic priest, a tall man with a trimmed, pointed beard and shaved head, also dressed in black. The priest, according media reports, kept a full-grown African lion in a back bedroom. For the next hour or so, we asked questions, and he answered much like we were talking to the local Methodist or Presbyterian minister. We could not attend "services" nor did we learn what they did at their services, but we got closer than most to this media phenomenon. The adventure was a success and I have forgotten what my other two religions were.

While after that I could with nervousness in my voice carry on a conversation with the attractive young woman that was all I could do. I had a lot of unreasonable fear and did not know how to get beyond it.

I was lonely. While my grandmother and other family members were available, I was drawn by the attractions of the university and the desire for a companion of the opposite sex. Appreciating what I had, having a long-term perspective and patience were just not possible because I knew I was missing out. I spent some weekends listening to popular music on the record player and daydreaming. I sometimes went to a local music and dance club but simply stood on the side feeling out of place. I did not understand the social rituals and was too shy and uncomfortable to participate. I felt I didn't have anything in common with the people around me. They were into cars and more of a working-class crowd. I did not know how to connect or find a sense of belonging, but I also did not have enough confidence in myself to be an individual. I was being drawn to an individualism that was in truth a group mindset and vain enough to believe it was the mindset for the times. This included the political activism, the music, the drugs, and the new concept of love relationships.

Totally unexpectedly, given my shyness and lack of contact with young women on a casual basis, I was invited by a neighbor from my hometown in the Central Valley to take her to a prom. I accepted, excited and anxious. I was too worried by my lack of experience that made all interaction seem terribly important and therefore difficult because I did not know what to say or do. Even more worrisome, the prom was a dress-up dance, and I did not have any confidence that I could dance. Except for slow dances which followed traditional patterns, the faster songs really did not have as many "steps" to be followed, but even that was daunting. I had only gone to one dance in high school. I enjoyed it, and survived it, but I was on edge the whole time. Nonetheless, I knew I was lonely, I knew I would love to have a relationship with a young woman, and that was enough for me to say yes and move forward in fear.

I knew I had something going for me. I was a college student; she was in high school. In my mind, I also had that I was going to school in Berkeley where things were happening. All of this was to bolster my self confidence in this event that realistically held little importance but seemed of great importance to me. None of this probably mattered to her who, although younger than me, I assumed to have more experience in the relations between young men and women.

While I do not recall all that followed, this I do remember, I survived. I more than survived because before the actual dance, we had some time alone, and we kissed. It was my first kiss. Even though I had looked forward to this, and had imagined what it might be like, I was not prepared for the sublime pleasure of intimate kisses. Unfortunately, the culture of young men and those who seek to affect it focus on aspects of relations between men and women in a manner that totally misses the deep and personal connection that is the subtlest and most powerful aspect. I, like many, noticed the reality, responded to it, but then pulled back into the "real" world. The experience gave me confidence to face the rest of the evening, the social interaction totally unfamiliar to me, the dancing of which I was more than a novice, and the general façade of courtship rituals. I was able to proceed despite my feeling of vulnerability; I was never required to admit to it. In a private moment when I knew I bumbled protocol because of my inexperience, I felt embarrassed but said nothing, which is not what relationships are really about. I was attracted to her but did not really know what to do next. I was not sure why she invited me; I was not sure whether my inexperience had shown more than I was even aware; nor was I prepared to be rejected in pursuing the relationship.

Life, too soon, presented me with a situation that determined my response whether rightly or wrongly. I talked at this time occasionally with a friend from high school who was studying at Stanford. In my mind, I had been making some big steps: changing schools, trying new things, but still defining myself by events. I could not separate what

I did from who I was. I was pleased with the prom date. I thought I could be open with this friend and was used to having what I thought were deep conversations with him. I talked to him about that experience, without the kiss, among other things that were happening.

Avalon Ballroom

Not too much later, my Stanford friend organized a trip for a number of us from my hometown, including my prom date, to attend a concert at the Avalon Ballroom. The Avalon was the second most popular venue in San Francisco after the Fillmore. Although I had attended the free concert in Golden Gate Park and had heard other free music on campus, I had not been immersed in the music culture yet. I had heard of the Fillmore and Avalon but had not been brave enough to venture there on my own. I agreed to go along and, thus, was introduced to the San Francisco music scene by this odd date. The ballroom on Sutter near Van Ness was on the second floor. We arrived after the show had already started. Handing our tickets over at the top of the stairs, I could already hear the music and see parts of the light show in the darkened ballroom ahead of us. While I was self-conscious and aware that the people in this ballroom were different from our group, by being with a group of people, I was able to override my discomfort. I managed to dance, since the music seemed to elicit a free form, anything goes form of dancing. We at one point formed a dancing trail, which I found embarrassing and a clear sign that we were outsiders, but once again, went along because of the comfort of the group. I liked the music and the light show, but I sensed that I was missing something. However, the experience was to prove an introduction to a place I would attend often.

The ride home was one of mixed emotions. As the conversation centered on the evening at the ballroom, I was fine. However, when I noticed my prom date and her interactions with my friend from Stanford, I had a dreadful feeling in my stomach.

Not long after, my friend invited me on a second trip to the Avalon. I was not prepared to learn that he would be going with my prom date, and I could join them with his sister and another couple. While I was totally taken aback, I acted as if nothing had happened. I did not know what I was supposed to say. The concert itself was more comfortable for me this time, but internally I felt distressed and betrayed. When we returned home, I was even more uncomfortable. Some of us sat in the living room rather stiffly. I believe my friend and my prom date were in the family room. I talked to his sister, an attractive young woman, but we had only a casual acquaintance. It was very awkward, especially while processing that my friend took advantage of what I told him, that my date did not really care who she was with and, in fact, probably preferred him because I was not interesting or attractive.

Like a moth drawn to the flame, confused and conflicted, I found myself within the next few weeks calling my friend and planning to visit him at Stanford. He shared a one-story stucco bungalow east of campus with other students who were away at the time of my visit. After general talk and a walk around campus, we went back to his house. He told me that he and the young woman had gone on a real date. He did not talk about her in a particularly respectful tone; he seemed mostly interested in touching her breasts. His boastfulness was bizarre. The dread I originally experienced on suspecting a relationship between them now was more physical, a gnawing anxiety in my stomach. Hearing about it made it worse. I did not communicate my distress as my lack of experience and ingrained fear did not give me any clues as to what was acceptable, and I did not want to make a fool of myself. I did not complain as I knew that I had no claim on her, and maybe was only invited as a place keeper for the prom. Nonetheless, for me, the date with her was a relationship of some kind, even if just a start, requiring definition and boundaries, yes, but I had expected or hoped to see her again. I decided that I had blown it somehow. I would need to conceal my pain, move on, and try to learn from the experience.

Later the same evening my friend brought out some marijuana to smoke, which I had never done. We smoked it, but I did not notice anything, perhaps because it was my first time and I did not know how to inhale properly. He then began playing with a knife and talking strangely, which made me wonder whether this was part of being stoned, but truthfully, I was very uncomfortable. I did not visit him again except for his wedding a couple of years later, nor did I make any effort to contact the young woman. I saw no reason to embarrass myself further. Ironically, when I would run into her in the future, she on more than one occasion would question why we did not go out again. I believe I always avoided answering the question.

Nonetheless, I was able to do certain things on my own. I went back to the Avalon at least once a week for quite a while. I was getting to see the bands I liked and was way more comfortable attending on my own, even if I mostly listened and observed. I started to recognize the regular hippie characters who frequented the Avalon, and that made me feel a part of it.

Towards the end of that first winter quarter, I went down to my old school to visit Peter and other friends including

Jim. I was quite pleased with myself because I thought I was part of something special in Berkeley. I was not really part of anything, but proximity made me feel proud vicariously. They may have even felt a pride in that I had escaped to this new, exciting frontier. On my return, which was right at finals time, my car broke down requiring major engine work. I was forced to get to school without transportation and somehow make it through finals. An acquaintance from high school lived in a fraternity house nearby. I had not previously contacted him because, while we knew one another well enough, we were not friends in high school. He offered to let me stay at his fraternity house for several nights, so I did not have to travel the long distance home. This gave me a good exposure to living in Berkeley, which was appealing to say the least. I liked walking the streets in the evening, walking through the campus when there was no press of a class, and going into the library at night to study. I was also exposed to some of the antics of the fraternity world, though I was not drawn to it. Much of it was arrogant, obnoxious talk about alcohol and girls. The pillows in the house were covered in worse sexual graffiti than a public restroom. While the fraternity/sorority world really was different from the one I was drawn to, the same elements affected both: politics, drugs, music, and sexual freedom.

In my foggy thinking, I was sure the unique benefits of a retreat from my studies and the sharing of ideas with my grandmother and other family members were clearly not superior to living in the university environment. I was already paying room and board. Thus, when my grandmother modestly increased that amount, I realized it was close to what I could pay to be Berkeley. So, I started looking for a place of my own.

2 .

SPRING OF LOVE

3/67 TO 9/67

An Immersion Move

Towards the beginning of the next school quarter, I looked on the student union bulletin board for places to live. I found a bed in an inexpensive share rental and arranged to move. I know my grandmother, although she did not tell me, and I could not have appreciated it except for the clarity and wisdom of these many years, was going to miss me. But I was focused on myself and what I wanted. I thought I knew best.

The bed was in a simple stucco bungalow on the southside of campus on Dana just off Telegraph Avenue, the public street most associated with the university and the counterculture. The house had a second-floor addition that was accessed from the main entry hall. The addition had an outer room, a separate small private room, and a bathroom. The owners, a young Polish couple, were either graduate students or had just started their careers and helped pay for the house with the income from this upstairs space. The addition had two beds in the outer room, one of which was available.

The resident of the private room was a black music student. He had a limp and limited use of his left side from childhood polio. He also had a stutter, had converted to Judaism, and listened incessantly to recordings by Enrico Caruso, a famous Italian tenor popular in the early 1900s. His goal was to conduct music. I would occasionally see him long after moving to new quarters and he always looked much the same.

The other resident, LK, with whom I would share the outer room took longer to get to know, but we would eventually keep in regular contact for many years after. He was a pre-med dropout from the university. He, too, was Jewish. He was relatively tall and lanky. He carried himself in such a way that he projected the image of a bookish fellow oblivious to the world. He was not sophisticated in his manners but was clearly very smart.

LK had his bed and study area in the best corner of the room with a window facing the street. My bed was against a wall opposite the entryway with a little storage space to the left side. The only other notable feature of the space was the view of the blue roof of a pancake house out the bathroom window. Simple as it was, this was my first apartment on my own, and I was thrilled. I was in the middle of the Southside community and close enough to campus that I could walk to all my classes.

One of the first things I noticed on moving in was a framed photograph of the satanic priest from my sociology of religion excursion on LK's desk. I thought it odd that he would be into Satanism. He was not. He was just displaying a photo of his cousin who happened to be getting a lot of media attention. He explained to me that the priest's satanic name was a stage name, that he was just a Jewish boy from Chicago who had worked at many odd jobs including playing the organ in a carnival, and now had this new thing. Religion had nothing to do with it. It was an act. While I was aware that things often were not what they seemed, I was surprised by the serendipitous revelation of these facts so soon after my exciting adventure. I know I was also falsely impressed with myself simply because I had this inside knowledge. This kind of immature, arrogant pride or sense of self-importance, undeserved, was a part of how I defined myself and would continue to do so. LK was unique to me because these things did not seem to affect him. While not moving comfortably in the world of social interactions, he was smart enough to know it did not matter and he did not care. I was smart enough to know it did not matter, but not smart or mature enough to not care. Even though we would move in different social worlds, we got along well, and I learned a lot from living with him and was to find other friendships through my relationship with him.

While LK did not care about these things, his life did not come together as it should for such an intelligent young man. He was bogged down. Dropping out of school bothered him, but more particularly, an arrest for drug dealing troubled him to the point of obsession. At that time, the drug culture had not taken over and certainly was not mainstream. Even in a place like Berkeley, the legal issues were still treated very seriously. The implications of conviction for drug offenses could be career limiting. LK had been arrested because he had shared an apartment with a drug dealer. LK never used or dealt drugs, but the authorities apparently did not care. He had been convicted of a lesser charge; however, he could not let go of the injustice which was, in fact, a black mark on his record. Perhaps, he should not have dwelled on it, but the manner in which his life got stuck was tragic. He knew every detail of the case, who the officers were, the life story of the prosecutor, and the same for the judge. Ultimately, he did get the conviction cleared on his physical record, even if it was never cleared from his emotional record.

In addition, LK told me he was homosexual. I did not have any experience with gays so he was my guide as to this lifestyle. Like with my roommate, Jim, who was very experienced sexually, LK told me things that amazed me. A gay friend of his had danced with a famous actor at a party, one for whom it was not general knowledge at the time that he was gay. I listened as a naïve hick. Ultimately, LK explained the intricacies of the San Francisco gay bath house scene which surprised me. That scene had to modify itself greatly with the onset of HIV-Aids. LK had none of the mannerisms of sophisticated gays I was to come to know.

I loved living close to the university. I walked a lot on campus and on the streets of south side. I would stop to enjoy whatever might be going on in Sproul Plaza. It was different living here and not just commuting. The first few blocks near the campus had lots of shops and lots of interest but turned more residential near where I lived.

My excitement with the university courses and the milieu continued unabated; yet, a subtle shift happened in my studies. Instead of taking basic humanities classes like sociology, political science, classics, and history, I took other classes like psychology, economics, anthropology, and sculpture. I was still expanding my horizons and, at the same time, casually searching for a discipline in which to major. My experience in my previous program was so overwhelming that I thought, in addition to feeling too limited, that I was in the wrong major. The courses this term helped me step into a wider world.

I thought psychology would be more about Freud and theories of the mind, but I found that it was more about basic reactions like how rats responded in mazes. I did not realize the extent to which these specific studies formed the basis for more generalized theories of human action. I remember little of the course except those impressions and the impetus toward a lifelong yearning to understand better why we are the way we are and especially why I am the way I am. I sometimes earned money on the side by participating in experiments. I also remember our teaching assistant, a tall, good looking man, who, oddly at that time, often wore shorts to class and on more than one occasion told us how sexually repressed people from Ohio were. He was from Ohio, although I do not think he included himself in the repressed group. Thus, while I learned psychology was different from my initial impressions, the teaching assistant with anecdotes on relational/sexual issues took us where my interest lay.

With economics, I remember little of the actual class; yet what I took away from the class had a lifelong impact on me. For the first time, I had some sense of the structure on which to hang lessons and impressions from the world of business. I extrapolated from that a better understanding of everyday interactions. I do not think I ever thought I would become an economist; nonetheless, I thought we should all understand the basic concepts. I felt I was growing even with these very ordinary entry level classes.

Anthropology was a little drier. I found the studies of other cultures and theories of need interesting. Margaret Mead's studies of South Sea islanders seemed to play into the counterculture vision of freer sexuality. From classics to psychology to anthropology, sex seemed to be front and center. I found Maslow's hierarchy of needs fit well with my budding secular humanism. The teaching was consistent with the dominant worldview, and I bought into it because I was open to ideas, was not well grounded in other ideas, and thought I was being taught by people smarter than me. I was from the sticks and wanted to hear the truth.

"Just A ..."

While my earlier studies included creative classes, art, or fine arts were not in the mix. I no longer remember what possessed me to sign up for a sculpture class. I was not comfortable exposing myself to potential ridicule. I had felt inadequate in past classes requiring presentations to the class of creative work. Yet, this professor, the material studied, and the work done formed a profound whole rather than just a glimpse of a gifted teacher. It imparted an appreciation and basic understanding of a discipline and a thirst for greater understanding. The professor, Victor Royer, was a quiet, thin man of medium height. He was one of those blonds with very light eyebrows, which combined his demeanor made him seem ethereal, almost not there. At the time, perhaps at all times, many art teachers seemed to derive part of their strength toward their art from eccentricities of personality and presentation. Many artists seemed to need to express an extraordinary personality, manner of dress, style of hair, character of sexual relationships, style of living, or attitude, and many used alcohol and drugs in order to enhance the meaning of their work. Their work in general was modern and abstract. It was not realistic or even necessarily representational. I hoped to understand the work better but found myself convinced that the art and the artist were simplistic attempts at creating an image of uniqueness. Clearly, if you were out of the ordinary, you were creative and what you did and who you were had meaning. I was quite simple.

Ironically, as I began to see this, the professor was not like that at all. He dressed normally, even conservatively, wore his hair in a normal fashion, and in no way injected his personality into his teaching as something necessary to be attached to the thought, concept, or technique being conveyed. He showed his art in galleries, sold pieces, and his bronze sculptures, even to my inexperienced eye, showed technical expertise. Like many things at the time, I did not fully appreciate the lessons learned from him, although the experience was recorded well enough to appreciate and remember when I was ready to understand.

However, the impact of the class was not just the professor and his relationship to his work. His teaching was personal, and the mix of ideas he communicated through the medium of clay was broad. By working through figure, nude figure (totally new to me), and then to abstract representation, I could understand some connection between realistic and abstract modern art. Although still feeling very inadequate, I did gain confidence because of his encouragement and indications to be less intimidated by the work. I was competent with clay. My figurative pieces looked like the subject. I recall specifically that for the final any medium was permitted, even though all our work had been in clay. I, as someone who did not want to talk in front of groups, presented my project, I said, "Mine is just a clay sculpture." Before I could say more about the piece, he said that there was nothing wrong with a clay sculpture. It was not "just a clay sculpture." That comment spoke volumes about who I was at the time and continued to be. Of course, he was right. I had seen that others had used differ-ent mediums and immediately felt inadequate and the need to self-deprecate. It was a comment on me as much as my sculpture. I was just regular—meaning not special—maybe even inadequate, which of course was not true. Just like in many other instances in the class, this professor had posi-tive comments that made me aware of a bigger context I could not see and built me up which, while the specifics have been forgotten, the feeling has not. He could look "just regular," and yet he was an exceptional sculptor. My sculp-ture could use "just regular" materials and techniques, and that was okay. "Just regular or normal" being fine was a les-son I needed to reaffirm. Because of the experience, I have had an ongoing desire to try working with clay again. What I experienced was bigger than "just clay" and of course was more about me than the sculpture.

Since coming to Berkeley, I had steadily grown more attracted to the music and particularly local groups. I had always, like most young people at the time, listened to pop-ular music on the radio and records. I had not grown up in a musical family, and, while I had taken various musi-cal lessons, was not talented in that way. Additionally, the music of the times, as had been true for several years ear-lier, was an integral part of the social fabric of the youth culture. I wanted to be a part of that culture; I wanted to belong. The style of music led and defined that segment of the counterculture. At the time, the Bay Area was one of the epicenters for this psychedelic phenomenon, and many venues played live music: free concerts on campus, evening concerts at the student union hall, free concerts in San Francisco's Golden Gate Park panhandle, and regular ones at concert halls. One of these, the Fillmore, held con-certs every weekend and eventually gained international fame. I preferred the Avalon because it felt more familiar. It was also less mainstream, which appealed to me. As I mentioned, I began going at least one evening probably every weekend.

The Dead were not often headliners, nor were the Airplane. They were more likely to play the Fillmore. However, Quicksilver and Big Brother were often at the Avalon. I also saw the Doors, Sparrow (to become Steppenwolf), Canned Heat, the Charlatans, and many more. The Avalon was my spiritual home at the time. The weekend was something I eagerly awaited. In my loneliness, I did not feel lonely there.

Are You Experienced?

At the beginning of the term, I signed up with one of the university cooperatives for food only. These cooperatives were very much like dormitories; the only differences were that you worked some, and they were cheaper. In joining the co-op, I came to know one student resident better. He was a tall, lanky young man with curly black hair and a passive manner. He had a nonchalant way of expressing himself. It was a common style at the time, but also one I came to associate with those who were a little lost. Some people called it "laid back" or "spaced out." I thought he was quite impressive. I had never run into so many people who were not like me, and I just assumed they must be better than me, more experienced than me. Plenty of other people at the co-op were even more far out. Still, something was different that drew me to him. We could converse like old friends.

It was not long before I came to understand that he experimented with drugs. Except for my non-experience with my Stanford friend, I did not know much beyond what I had read in newspapers and magazines. After a few discussions, I came to believe that a psychedelic experience was not dangerous and that important insights could come of it. It did not occur to me that he could be an unreliable or inexpert source. He procured tabs of LSD, which we took in his room at the co-op. That night, there was a concert scheduled at Pauley Ballroom above the student union, which we planned to attend. While I felt somewhat apprehensive, I did feel safe because he was with me. He had a girlfriend who came along with us that evening. We chatted casually as we walked the few blocks up to the concert. I found that I was not experiencing any difference from having taken the drug and wondered whether this experience would be like the previous one.

As we reached the ballroom, paid our admission, and went in, I was starting to notice some different sensations in my body. At that moment, entering the darkened ballroom full of people, pounding with loud electronic music, flashing lights on multiple screens, my friend said, "Find a chick and have a good time." Then he disappeared into the crowd with his girlfriend. *What?* I would have liked to have had a girlfriend like his to share the experience. But step into a completely foreign environment under the influence of a powerful drug and change who I was? I could not start a conversation with a young woman in most benign situations. Oh, well, I was on my own.

Drug-induced experiences are very personal, and the aspects that seem like they would be of interest to others are often only interesting to the person having the experience— perhaps because in some ways they are inexplicable. Taken farther, some of the things accomplished during a psychedelic experience would seem to be of such incredible importance, but in the light of day and unaltered consciousness, they were ordinary or unremarkable except in their lack of quality. These could be examples of music, conversation, art, or writing—examples that were inspired it seemed by a spirit of God, but that made no sense outside of the context of the drug. Of course, my experience was different!

I was alternately anxious and excited. I really did believe I would be okay, despite some horror stories, because I trusted my friend, but I was also noticing that my body and senses were reacting in ways that I might not be able to control. As a shy person afraid of standing out in any way or being foolish, loss of control was a big deal. The ballroom was a plain, rectilinear space with a high ceiling. Being of modern design, it was not ornamented like the Avalon; yet, with the music, people, and light show, the space had been transformed into a new, colorful, and lively world. The floor was open so that people could listen to the music while standing, sitting, or dancing. There were only a few chairs at the edges. The light show and people visually defined the space, and the music was the unifying element. The projected images of the light show took on meaning beyond the images themselves. As in an unaltered state, the image draws the mind into a complex series of thoughts and connections. I was feeling all those connections at once. Instead of the awareness of the image as the reality and the thoughts a response to that reality, the image was a catalyst for the thoughts, which became the total reality. The sound of the music was tied inextricably to the images. Each song was long and focused not only lyrics but instrumental solos, usually guitar, and haunting vocals. The internal reality was that deeper experience of the music. Each note and movement of the group fit with the performance. Because I was hard of hearing, I had never experienced music like this. I was drawn into the notes and along the notes and into the actions of the entire performance. It was all I could do to sit on the floor and marvel at all the sensory input I was receiving. I was not scared; in some ways I was freed from fear, as I was sure I understood and was feeling what was really happening. Nonetheless, even though I was surrounded by maybe a hundred other young men and women, I was not sufficiently freed to "find a chick and have fun." The dancing followed that flow of the guitar riffs, drumbeats, and the heartbeat thump of the bass. Dancing was a collection of informal movements of feet and hands, while following the underlying beat flowed with the lead instrument like a wave. The legs and feet, arms and hands followed in an undulating pattern. Much of the clothing suddenly took on new meaning as it was clear that the loose, multi-colored, thin fabrics flowed easily too. The fabric, dancing, music, and lights were part of a seamless whole. I understood this new counterculture scene differently now. Of course, I was too new to everything to understand the arrogance of experience as well.

Some discomfort crept into the positive impressions of the evening. Those impressions were accompanied by a sense of electrical pulses in my body. The discomfort was not physical. The discomfort was internal with confusing impressions contrasted against this rushing, overwhelming experience and the desire to still think and maintain some control. I started to notice that some of the young people dancing were hideously made up. Further, I was certain I saw guys dancing with guys and guys making passes at guys, even acting in a sexually suggestive manner. I knew LK was a homosexual, but I had not been exposed to homosexuality except in that intellectual manner. I also knew that I did not have a girlfriend and had studied enough psychology to think I understood latent homosexuality, so my mind was spinning, rushing like an express train with psychedelic input and confusion. At one and the same time, I continued to experience the sights and sounds, held myself in control, and struggled with these dark thoughts creeping in.

The overwhelming sense was still one of freedom, release, joy, and sensory pleasure. Being drawn into the visuals and the music—not just looking at them and listening to them—was so much more than I could have imagined. The experience was powerful.

As I walked home, the heightened sense of my surroundings was still there, but, besides leaving behind the artificial environment of the concert, I could tell the effects of the drug were abating. By morning, I still felt something which was more than just the memories of the experience. That memory alone, though, was now another point for me to feel a sense of belonging to something and therefore feeling more important myself. I felt I understood now what this counterculture movement was and all the beauty of it: love, music, nature, color, freedom, political justice. It all made sense.

Although I had never been attracted to young men sexually, I was troubled by my experience. I had those doubts about myself that I suspect many inexperienced young men have, and I expect many inexperienced young men can be led astray from their true inclinations because of this lack of sense of self. Those who are sensitive enough to be reflective and introspective will question themselves. Having no experience with regular relations with young women, even friendships can cause doubts despite the individual's yearnings for a woman. I was not sure how to handle this but was presented with answers very soon. Within the next week, I saw some of the same people I had seen that evening, and the truth was before my eyes. I had not seen some vision of my inner consciousness projected on the experience by the effects of the drug. I had seen or been a part of a gathering that included a significant number of gay people. It was the type of gathering where they felt freer than in the light of day to express themselves, so my fright was partly heightened awareness on my part and partly bolder expression in dance, make-up, clothing, and communication on their part. I was only seeing what was real and not the effects of a bad trip. I was relieved and felt more confident.

Because of the cost and restrictive schedule of eating times, I shortly thereafter stopped eating at the co-op and cooked for myself on a small electric hotplate in my room. LK had a small refrigerator that he let me use for perishable items. I began attending more regularly the Avalon concerts in San Francisco. While I was still alone, I had gained confidence from my experience at the ballroom on campus. I often walked at night, stopping in the bookstores and record stores. Many of these would play contemporary music, often with some form of incense, often patchouli, filling the space with other-worldly smells. I found that now, even though I was not high, that experience was accessible whether at a concert or elsewhere simply from having had the experience.

Also, because it was costing a little more to live, my savings only covered my tuition for a while, and my parents could only send a small amount of money each month, I began looking for work. Perhaps because of my wish for freedom and my limited needs, I did not look for regular employment. I knew that the university maintained an office of small jobs. It was basically a call bank for short term odd jobs like cleaning, yard work, moving services, or painting. In addition, the afore mentioned psychological testing fit into this kind of work. I really was a believer in the lifestyle of not needing a lot and not earning more than I needed. I wanted the freedom to continue my adventures. I enjoyed the contact with people, the ability to do practical, if simple, jobs for people, and the sense of earning my way. I was very happy with my broad program of study, my living situation, my financial security, and the milieu of Berkeley and San Francisco. I was still alone, but I had a lot going on to keep me occupied and excited about life.

More Experience

That spring, I experimented on two other occasions with LSD. I had still never been high on marijuana, even though this was the most common psychedelic in the culture. I did not belong to any *avant garde* living situations, like a commune, drug house, or with musicians in a band. I was just an individual student on the edges of this cultural phenomenon. I had read much about people experimenting with drugs, and I took it literally. Most who took drugs were looking to achieve an altered state of consciousness and the sensory effects of that state. "Experimenting" gave it an air of legitimacy, but that was really it. Drinking alcohol and that altered state were not referred to as experimenting. Nonetheless, because of what I had read and my nature, in addition to the sensory experience, I wanted to know if I could accomplish anything else.

On my second trip, I set a goal to rid myself of one of my lifelong food phobias. I had never been able to eat tomatoes. Something in the texture caused me to gag. As a child, I can remember being forced to eat just one cherry tomato and having to down several glasses of milk to hide the tiny pieces just to accomplish the task. At a day camp

I attended as a boy, I told the counselors I was allergic to tomatoes so I did not have to eat them in the salad. I could eat tomato sauce but would always leave any part of the sauce that might have chunks of cooked tomato. I would never have tomato on any sandwich or hamburger. So, on the way home from campus, I stopped at the market and bought a large, ripe red tomato. My intention was to eat it like an apple. It did not occur to me that if some other deep-seated psychological scar was the source of my antipathy to tomatoes that I might open myself to a bad trip with this experiment. I also did not consider the fact that this time I was experimenting completely on my own. The last time I had at least started with my friend and his girlfriend even though I ended up alone in a crowd. Because I had survived that rather unsafe testing ground for my first experience in an environment meant to expand the effects, I was fairly certain I would be okay on my own. As I could feel the effects of the drug coming on, I listened to some music and thought a little more about my silly experiment, but further on in the experience felt a sense of freedom kick in that allowed me to look at the tomato, take a large bite out of it, chew it, enjoying it all the while, swallow it, and eat the rest in a similar manner. I stepped through a doorway never to return. I have always been able to eat tomatoes ever since in their many forms. While I felt a sense of freedom that allowed me to follow through, I know that I would never have felt freedom to try flying off a building or any other unsafe escapade. The nature of the feeling was within the realm of the reasonable. It's too bad I never tried beets; I still have trouble eating them. This trip was much milder than the previous one. Perhaps, the dosage was different. Who knows what if any controls existed on that; certainly it was dangerous. Perhaps, the environment of the music, light show, and people contributed to the greater intensity of that first trip—or simply that it had been my first trip. The tomato experience was very mellow.

On another occasion several weeks later, I decided to see if the drug would enhance my ability to make decisions on a clay sculpture. I listened to some music, still in my room, and started work on a clay sculpture for art class. I found myself able to make decisions more confidently than ever before. I was not tentative; I knew that even if I made a decision that later did not appear to be the best that I could correct it, as opposed to never making a move in the first place. Unfortunately, this is where drugs and people have produced some very awful results. The writing, painting, sculpture, conversation, construction, whatever is produced often looks like nonsense the next day. I do not know how to explain this. However, I was encouraged by my success. That clay sculpture was the one I presented for the final I mentioned previously. I still have it, and it still makes sense to me. The subtle experience this time, which later included walking about the south side of campus, stopping in shops, and experiencing the normal pulse of that environment convinced me that this counterculture of music, love, and drugs was onto something very powerful.

I could explain my school experience as being the sum total of my classes, the environment, the odd jobs, and the whole '60s counterculture. Of course, for someone else in the same physical place, Berkeley, the experience at the same time could have been completely different. They may have been very intellectual or political and seen the culture from that perspective only. They may have been into their major program of study so seriously that none of this was more than background noise or a minor dimension of parties and weekends. For me, the time and the events were all of one piece, one I thought was noticed by many. The music was getting broader play; the culture was getting more media attention; parts of it were being adapted for marketability to all young people. I could see that and reveled in being a part of it.

Sea Change

During this time of more frequent visits to the Avalon, I had a life changing experience one weekend. My pattern was to go, enjoy the music and the light show, hang around the edges intrigued by some of the strange people, then go home with a sense of pleasure and satisfaction. Some of the music groups were very popular locally and would become even more popular nationally; yet, for a small sum, I could see three of them perform on the same night. While I was happy, I was still alone. Other apparently unattached young women attended the concerts, but I had no skills or confidence to approach any. I had not graduated to trying that as an experiment, and after my first experience at the concert on campus, was maybe a little worried about what drugs might reveal about the people or me. So, I contented myself with enjoying it all from the sidelines.

Somehow, though, on a particular weekend evening, my eyes caught a young woman's or maybe hers caught mine. I could tell something was happening, but I was not sure what. Her look lingered longer than could be explained as a glance. I was very nervous, I was not experienced, I did not know what I was supposed to do, but I looked back at her again. I mustered up enough courage to stand closer to her during the next song. She did not move away; perhaps she had even moved closer, too. I also managed to say some unmemorable thing, probably about the music, but it was enough to spark a conversation. I had an electrical sense of excitement and a kind of apprehension not strong enough to scare me away. My heart was beating faster, and my adrenalin was poised to help me focus.

Typical of these concerts, most of the floor in front of the stage was devoted to couples dancing during the songs with the edges formed of those standing and watching either because they were resting, did not have someone to dance with, or perhaps were in an altered state. In the ante rooms, others would be mingling, sitting, eating, or drinking. The young lady and I were part of the watching background. Our conversation continued during the songs until, instead, our attention was drawn more to each other than the music. Her eyes and face were open, expressive, and unrestrained in a refreshing exuberance, not overreaching or offensive. Her face was slender with bright, expressive eyes, a mouth framed by delicate lips ready to expose her upper teeth in a full smile and light laugh at the slightest provocation, and a slim nose, perfect for her face. She wore glasses as I did. I noticed that she had a lithe, attractive figure and long, light brown hair worn straight in the style of the time. I was thrilled and nervously expectant. I assume she was as well, but I never asked. While I was still inexperienced in love, I found the conversation easy. I could sense that I was speaking with someone who was interested in speaking with me. I did not even worry about whether I would find myself intimidated by her or, worse, find she was embarrassing to be with. The electric contact overrode any hesitancy, and by blind faith I assumed ours was a special encounter. The more we talked the more I felt a relationship of some kind developing, no part of our conversation led to an awkward dead end, each part led to an expanding interest in music, what we did, who we were. The ballroom was no longer an event but a backdrop, even though that evening's groups included some who would become icons of the music of the times. All that mattered to me was Daphne.

Daphne had come to the concert with a girlfriend with whom she was spending the night. She was seventeen and a senior in high school; her parents would not have allowed her to attend, so the girlfriend provided a way for her to avoid asking for permission. By the time the music ended at 2:00 in the morning, we had talked enough to want to continue the conversation, so Daphne's friend drove home alone, and I gave Daphne a ride back. We drove through the City into the suburban tracts of the peninsula south of the City. We talked until about 4:00 in the morning. We kissed that night, which only confirmed the mutual path we were on. The kiss was different from the kisses with my hometown friend who, even though younger, seemed more experienced than Daphne. Yet, none of those comparisons mattered because with Daphne I felt I was with someone who in many ways was in the same place I was. The tension I felt when with my younger friend was almost totally non-existent with Daphne even though I was no more experienced than I had been. We knew very little about one another, even though our conversation had been questions and answers focused on getting to know more about one another. Nonetheless, we were, even then, looking forward to getting together again.

I drove home in the very early hours of the morning just before sunrise as happy and carefree as I had ever been. Daphne was attractive, spirited, interested in the culture of the times, and me. My life had a new dimension and direction. I was no longer lonely.

I still had the same interests and the same activities in my life, but the addition of Daphne and our common ground would focus me in a different way than had I met someone like her in one of my courses. Music and the culture were the foundation of our meeting, not academics and the campus. I was not on any special, defined path within the counterculture or school. I was going to school because it was what I thought I should be doing. It would lead to a degree, a job, and a family. No one had ever taught me the how or why, and I did not know, I just accepted it on faith. With the counterculture, I understood the path to be "go with the flow." Right now, that seemed to be working.

I was not aware that I could have set my course and controlled the results more than I had. But, I did not care because I was happy. I liked where I was living, where I was going to school, and my courses. I liked the culture in which I found myself, and I maybe had a girlfriend. I could have been taught to be a different person, but for the person I was, I could not have controlled anything to have achieved a higher level of unified positive joy if I had tried.

I called Daphne during the week, and we got together for a concert again the next weekend. After that, we got together most weekends. I now felt I had a balance in my life. I lived in my own place, had classes I liked, worked my odd jobs, was moving toward a goal, even if ill defined, and I had a girlfriend. Though simple, I thought I understood what a love relationship was, although I did not think of it in that way. I just thought of the good feeling and the desire to continue that good feeling. Daphne and I enjoyed one another's company as we explored mutual interests in music and the counterculture scene. We got to know one another better and better as the weeks went by. We saw ourselves as a couple without ever having asked it. At least for now, finding a kindred soul to share the psychedelic culture with was enough. Even though a part of the culture was free love without restrictions of relationships, for me having one relationship was enough.

Another Family

I met and got to know Daphne's parents. My now regular education in Judaism continued. Daphne was Jewish, and while a momentary thought may have crossed my mind as to whether my Christian heritage in any way conflicted with that, it would have only been a moment. By now I was not quite as limited in my understanding of other heritages, and the tone of the counterculture was that none of that mattered anyway.

While I had now had two Jewish roommates, I had never experienced Jewish family life. Daphne's family lived in a very normal suburban house on the peninsula near where I had lived as a child. The towns were similar, as well. As with all the peninsula towns, each starts in the flats by the Bay along the El Camino Real—the Kings Highway—name during Spanish rule in the region. The commercial area and older homes tended to be in that area. As time went on, particularly after World War II, the homes kept moving up the hill to Skyline, the boulevard running along the ridge. Daphne's parents lived in a home closer to the upper boulevard than to the El Camino. While they were different from most parents I knew, this difference was not because they were Jewish, and yet in a way it was. Her father had left Germany just ahead of Hitler's attacks on the Jews and made his way to the United States. He was a thin, quiet, somewhat passive man of greater sensitivity than most fathers I knew. He made prosthetic devices for veterans at a veteran's facility in the City. He was a man comfortable and serious about his work, relaxed in his leisure time, and at least as far as I was aware, unambitious for more. Her mother had grown up in New York and was more intense than her husband. She worked in a secretarial capacity for the county district attorney and was more likely than her husband to engage in a focused discussion on issues. As service work, she was one of the leaders of a local group that provided financial support to disabled people in Israel. This brought them in contact with other Jewish families that probably by position and income may have been financially above them, but in gifts for this service work were challenged at best to be the equal of Daphne's mother. She was of medium height and build with a demeanor and posture of exhaustion from work, but with alert eyes ready for activity. Daphne's parents were what I have come to know as cultural Jews; they did not regularly attend synagogue, though they had a seriousness about their heritage from her father's experience in Germany and her mother's work for Israel. I have seen that same seriousness in other Jewish families that seems to reach back 3,500 years and carry common experiences of the whole people forward, more than I have ever seen with Christians.

Daphne and I grew more attached to one another as the spring moved towards summer. We continued going to concerts at the Avalon; we went to a music festival on Mount Tamalpais in Marin County north of the Golden Gate Bridge. It featured many groups over the course of a few days in an outdoor amphitheater on that iconic mountain. Later, because of that experience, we went on hikes on Mount Tam. More often we would go on drives down the coast west of her parent's house. We also went to events at her high school. Daphne and I sent love letters to one another. She liked to playfully address hers to various pet names or pseudonyms for me.

When together, we shared wonderful glances and smiles with a lot of fun and laughter and kissing and caressing. We were not, however, sexually intimate yet. Nonetheless, with the approach of her high school graduation and eighteenth birthday, we planned together to take that step. We planned a late night out with her parents' permission and traveled to my un-private abode. The romance of our normal time together was somewhat lost in the expectancy and anxiety of our unspoken but mutual understanding of the significance. The tension of worrying about someone walking in on us only added to the pressure. I was too tense and as it happened, before we could even collect ourselves, LK came home. We recovered as gracefully as we could; he pretended not to notice. Afterwards, as we walked together on campus, I felt chagrined and somewhat embarrassed by the awkwardness. Yet, the bond between us continued to grow. I no longer felt I was an inadequate and backwards young man. Little did I know that even humble pride sets up stumbling stones for a fall. But, that must be a long way off. Daphne and I were as happy and in love as I believed two young people could be.

Northside

Soon after Daphne's graduation and the approach of summer, I moved from the Dana house. I had gone home for the summer the past two years, but now I wanted to stay close to the City and to Daphne. I figured that with odd jobs and a less expensive place to live, I could get by. While my parents sent some money during school and I still had some savings for tuition, I did not expect support when I was not in school. I looked first in San Francisco with Daphne and some other friends, but that shortly ended as we found nothing inexpensive enough. Then we paid a real estate agency in the Haight Ashbury district for referrals, but the options were so horrible we could not even consider them. One just a half block off Haight in an old Victorian appeared to have plumbing that did not work and had either human or animal feces on the floor in various rooms while people lived there. I was seeing evidence that the counterculture was already off-track, but I did not properly record this experience and simply put it in the file of "to each his own." Yet, that was the start of what came to be known as the summer of love. Unsuccessful in my search, I returned to the bulletin board at the student union. I found a room, or rather, a laundry porch, on the north side of campus on Oxford Street. Because of inflation, costs lose their meaning over time, but the space was very inexpensive even then at $17 per month. So, I started my first summer on my own and ended my time of returning home, except for visits.

The north side was a completely different environment from the south side. It was quieter, less student infested, more professorial, with a feeling of older times. Oxford was a main arterial through the residential area and aligned with the western, or down slope, edge of the campus. It was still separate from the heart of the north side farther up the hill; neither was it part of commercial Berkeley that began on Shattuck Avenue to the west. It was a relatively quiet area. The house I found was a Victorian with one unit on the lower floor and one on the upper floor. The living room of the upper unit was used by the young man with the lease, a bedroom was shared by two other tenants, and I had the small 5' by 7' covered laundry porch that led to the backstairs.

The residents of this house were an odd assortment starting with me—an idealistic student hippie in love, excited about a summer on his own, and with few cares. The young man who held the lease on the apartment was quite a bit older than I was. He worked as a carpenter and often had his girlfriend stay over. One of the residents of the shared room was also older and had just returned from being a teacher in Mississippi. He had been or was still a part of the civil rights movement, and his whole being revolved around that movement. He was not interested in nor did he understand drugs and the psychedelic music. I noticed he seemed unhappy. I was interested to hear his experiences because I only knew the civil rights movement from what I had read; yet, he had such an overriding seriousness and joylessness that I know something was missing, which I am not sure he ever found. His roommate was a student about my age from an east coast school who was in Berkeley for the summer. He was political, and we often discussed politics. He had a deep distrust of our system, of government, of business, of everything really. Nonetheless, he was not joyless like the teacher. He made extra money selling the local countercultural newspaper on the street and had a penchant for pacing the apartment back and forth in deep thought. We had one other resident, though in reality I think he simply crashed there and was not paying rent. It was the kind of casual arrangement typical of the psychedelic culture. Our crasher was a type of person with which I was unfamiliar. Skinny, barefooted, with long frizzy unkempt hair, he was a hippie but also a speed freak. He took methamphetamines, which made him talk incessantly, and it was usually all nonsense. The teacher could not stand him because of his gibberish, because he slept in his bed without permission, and because he vomited in it, as well. I thought he was odd but was not put off by him as this was the kind of openness we were to have, so I just went with the flow—but then again he never vomited in my bed. The crasher was planning to move up to Mendocino County and grow carrots. I doubt he ever made it. I also do not believe Mendocino was great carrot country.

I did not spend a lot of time at the house as I was often working or spending time with Daphne. Nonetheless, I was present enough to learn from my housemates. From the speed freak, I learned the ease with which a sensible person could become a totally tragicomic figure from the overindulgence in or addiction to drugs—though at the time I only saw the comedy of it because I was so immersed in the culture. He was making his choices, and he added to the flavor of my experience. The intense young man and I had many philosophical discussions. I still loved to have those kinds of discussions at that time. I was still exploring a new world and interested in everything without judging dead end streets. Talking was a great past time, particularly because we did not have television. His father ran a company, and he had worked with blue collar workers. While he was not radical, he was progressive in his ideas about the structure of our society and thought changes had to happen. I thought so as well but never got very caught up in the political side of the culture. Though he experimented with drugs, he was not particularly into the music scene. We were like two sides of the same counterculture coin in that way. I started noticing that I was missing a something I could not put my finger on that the more political of those around me seemed to have. The first was a seriousness and intensity about how the political was the critical organizing principal in life, the point from which all else flowed. The second was an inability to pursue in an intellectual manner a discourse too deeply on politics, not because I was not intelligent enough to understand, but rather, part of me just intuitively said something was wrong even though I was not capable of debating that something. More importantly was a sense of anger that could be felt from someone who did not express much joy, much fun, rather a general brooding. My friend, although nice, was all those things. I'm sure, although I know he liked me, that he thought Daphne and I were just empty-headed hippies having fun and oblivious to what was wrong all around us. The teacher was similar. He was brooding, apparently unhappy, perhaps angry underneath, and intellectually able to defend his worldview without ever seeing its limitations. His life was defined by the civil rights movement, as mine seemed to be defined by the counterculture. The politics of civil rights was it. We did not fit in, what was happening in Berkeley did not fit in, and our speed freak did not fit in with his worldview.

It was a good summer. Daphne and I did not go to the major music festival in Monterey, the Monterey Jazz Festival. It was too establishment for us even though most of our favorite groups were there, and it became an iconic festival defining the times. We had been to the one on Mt. Tamalpais in Marin County, and that was good enough for us. It was more rock and youth focused, whereas, Monterey had more jazz and older, more sophisticated people. Nonetheless, we were in the environs that weekend looking for the so-called nude beach, which I am glad we did not find as I was not ready to be nude in public.

We considered ourselves so much a part of the culture that one of the popular songs about San Francisco set us into howls of derisive laughter as it seemed so overtly commercial and plastic yet attempted to capture the scene and the attraction of the City("If you come to San Francisco be sure to wear some flowers in your hair."). We felt unduly proud that we were not part of whoever was listening to that nonsense. Ironically, seven years later, eons in the future in the way things changed, I would meet my best friend for life who was attracted to San Francisco by that song: same song, same time, dramatically different perceptions.

We continued to regularly go to weekend concerts at the Avalon. One of our recurring dates was to go to the airport which was nearby and walk the concourses people watching. That kind of easy access to airports is long gone. We took all kinds of driving trips around on the weekend then usually ended up staying at her parent's house. They would allow me to stay in the family room and accepted me as another member of the family.

During the early summer, her brother returned from his tour of duty in Vietnam. He was the first person I knew personally who had served there. The daily casualty figures were anxiety provoking because sooner or later a draft might include me. As I said earlier, I was already confronted with the first reports of young men from my high school class who had been killed in the war. I could not properly comprehend or resolve that we had all been in school, were not yet twenty, and, yet, they had been killed in a war. Daphne's brother was a tall, thin man born to talk and sell. Shortly after returning, he had a job, a nice car, an apartment, and seemed to always have a girlfriend when he wanted. He did not belong to or care about the culture in which Daphne and I were immersed. He was already past that and ready for the work world even though he had not gone to college. Daphne and I, along with one of her friends, took him with us to the Haight to purchase some

LSD. We would not normally have done that, but perhaps, to look experienced to him, we did. He was apoplectic. I think that was the last time we ever did something together.

After graduation that summer, Daphne started an entry level administrative job with Macy's, one of the main department stores on Union Square in San Francisco. I would come in to meet her; we would often walk in the downtown and grab inexpensive food to eat on the Joice Street steps off Bush near Grant. We were both thrilled with our experiences. We were too confident of our special insight into the meaning of life as translated by our culture, optimistic and naive at the same time. On a visit to an older cousin of mine in the Bernal Heights neighborhood, we were met at the door by her husband, a lawyer. I was dressed in odd garb and had on a train conductor's hat, totally normal for our sort but totally odd. He made no comment except that my cousin was not home, but his look spoke volumes. It was not shocking to him, just silly.

Daphne's parents, on the other hand, were very tolerant of our youthful enthusiasm for odd dress and music even though they were very middle class. Nor did they seem to mind that I was not Jewish. Daphne and I were by that time obviously very closely and romantically involved. They treated me as one of the family. Our relationship with them was such that we respected their authority and that their home was theirs not ours. Even though we were part of a youth culture that was not very respectful of authority and pushed boundaries of normative behavior, not just with hair and dress, our relationship with them was very traditional. We shared time together, meals together, and Daphne and I helped around the house. Even though our culture would have seemed farther from them than their son's, who was "straight" and moving toward a regular job,

I think we had more communication with them and on a deeper level. I did not realize at the time how significant this relationship with them was. I would have thought of a concert or other legendary event as significant and not of the contact with Daphne's parents as much more significant.

During that summer, the Six Day War took place in the Middle East. The City newspapers were on strike, so the news was provided by the local public television station. However, I believe most of the visual coverage of the war may have been from the major networks. I knew nothing of Israel or the Middle East, so this was very different especially as part of a Jewish family with connections to Jewish charities in Israel. I remember us sitting down and watching each evening.

Also that summer, one of the girls from my graduating class in the Central Valley announced that she was hosting a little gathering of some of the kids from our class. This would be a mini-reunion two years after graduating. I do not remember everyone in attendance. What I do remember is that I felt better about myself, maybe even a little bit proud. The year before, I had felt so uncomfortable when invited to join my co-worker and two young women at the county fair. Now, I was part of something that was happening; others were not; this was new. I had experimented with drugs; others had not. I had gone away as someone who spoke to few and never to girls; yet, I was returning with a girlfriend. My sense of self was almost entirely based on comparisons—to others but also to my former self. Some of the smarter and prettier girls in the class were at the gathering; I felt better that they could see that I was something more than I might have seemed before. Really, it meant nothing; they probably always saw me differently than I saw myself, and more positively. Nonetheless, I felt better anyway, silly pride. Many years later, one of those girls, who was already married by the time of the gathering, would comment, in an admiring way, that she had been surprised that I had come with a girlfriend who wore a shawl. Daphne dressed differently than the girls in the Valley did at the time wearing no bra, very short skirts with full tights for stockings and colors that were vibrant. Although young women did not ordinarily wear shawls, shawls as an icon of uniqueness must have been particular to that young woman.

That summer was a summer of love for us, even though it started in the spring.

3 .

HAPPY DAYS

Alcatraz, 9/67-9/68

Telegraph, 9/68-9/69

Fall and New Quarters

As that wonderful summer came to an end and the time arrived for classes to begin again, Peter, his friend, Chuck, and I looked for a place to live together. None of us had much money, although I believe Chuck's parents would have paid for him to live in a better place than Peter and I had in mind. We found a studio apartment in a two-story building in North Oakland on Alcatraz, a street named for its direct view down the hill towards the Bay and island prison. The studio was just below Shattuck in a stable, mostly black neighborhood. The stucco, Spanish style building had eight units. Our total rent was $81 per month. We were the only white people in our building and maybe our block. The place was about a mile and a half from campus, a little farther than I had been; however, I would be living with friends for the first time.

Peter and Chuck were not part of the counterculture. They were transferring to Cal to continue their education. They were much straighter. Nonetheless, we got along because we were all responsible, and Peter and I had been friends for two years by then.

They built a bunk bed out of wood and ropes on which they laid their mattresses; while I had borrowed an older single mattress from my grandmother, which I laid in a corner of the one room we all shared. The studio was in good shape. It had an entry area with a decent bathroom to one side, a large closet, and a separate kitchen with space for a small table and chairs. Because Chuck was under 21 and his father was still in the service, he could shop at the commissary on the military base in Alameda, so we saved some money on food. We saved the rest of the money because we were all frugal and planned meals that cost very little. We ate a lot of dried noodles, or ramen, with which I was not familiar at the time but has since become part of the universal diet of college students. We had no TV, but we had a radio, and Chuck had a stereo system that played records. We fell into a comfortable tempo of life at the studio. Our classes ended up being mostly different, but we were usually home for dinner together.

I was faced with returning to my primary course of study after two quarters of experimenting with the other classes of interest as I did not have any other direction to pursue. Since Peter and Chuck were continuing with their program, I felt compelled by default to do so myself and comforted myself with the knowledge that my two quarters of educational experimenting had not cost me any time towards a degree. I do not know whether it was the school or whether I had changed, but the major courses were more interesting. I know it was a little of both. I had broadened my outlook by taking other classes, and the courses in my major were taught in a manner that was more conducive to my temperament. They were also more theory-focused, as opposed to the technical focus at Cal Poly. Living with others at about the same point helped me get involved with my courses. I could be critical and cynical analyzing work that seemed silly or a teacher who seemed odd. Peter and I had a lot of those conversations. Nonetheless, school continued to be fun. I no longer worried, and, as I worried less, I did better.

However, I continued to focus just as much or more on what I was doing out of school. In fact, I would often say that to others. School was only part of my life. Daphne and I were together often. We would spend a lot of time at her parent's house on weekends. She would send me wonderful love letters during days when we did not see one another; I believe I did the same although mine were probably not nearly as good. I would go meet her at her job at Macy's; we would walk in the downtown area, grab some cheap food at a delicatessen, and just hang out and talk and walk. I did not have much money. And of course, we still went to concerts at the Avalon on the weekend.

Being around Peter again, who was very serious and well read, I started reading again. I jumped from reading those early 20th century postmodernists to Proust, an early 20th century modernist, so different from what I had read before. Peter promised I would be taken by it, and I was. From the very start, I was drawn into the tone, senses, and images of the writing. Somehow, I was not put off by the dauntingly long sentences, the drawn out descriptions, and the sheer size of the book. I would carry small volumes of the individual parts with me, reading when I had a moment. It became a regular habit. I read other suggestions of Peter's along the way. I was drawn to the intricate analysis of subtle emotions over the need for a dramatic plot. Nonetheless, Dostoevsky was harder to relate to than Proust because I found it harder to relate to the characters and their names; I found the books oppressively gray at the time; whereas Proust, which I could think might be just as oppressive, was not for me at that time.

Sometime that fall or spring, Daphne decided to try LSD with me. We planned to go to a concert at the Avalon. We parked in an alley along Polk Street. We were feeling the effects of the drug as we entered. To me it was like my first experience: the light show, music, and overall impact was pleasurable although different. The sights and sounds were more intense. The space, an older ballroom with an upper balcony, had a more sophisticated character than the Pauley. Part way into the first set, Daphne was having serious problems. Whatever she was seeing or imagining was scary to her, freaking her out—so scary that I finally suggested we take a break, get our hands stamped, and go sit in the car for a while. As we left, I noticed that even I was now seeing things a little darker; instead of a quality of light, darkness pervaded. The black security guards who spoke with a ghetto accent were now barely comprehensible. We made it out into the cool, foggy air and to the car. I can picture it as if there now calmly trying to reassure Daphne while I was very high myself. After a long break, she seemed to be feeling better so we went back around the corner to the ballroom. On entering, I noticed the lights had changed dramatically. They were light and sparkling again. The guards were friendly and understandable. Of course, nothing had really changed. While I knew her, Daphne never took acid again.

In addition to the Avalon, a lot of our connection to the music scene was through FM radio. Life was simpler then. We had record players and albums; however, mostly in the car and at home we were connected by FM radio. The impact of popular AM stations had shifted with the counterculture to FM stations; in the City, that meant KMPX. Some of the AM DJs made the transition to the more open play lists of the FM stations focusing on our counterculture music. In the spring of '68, trouble erupted between the management of the station and the ownership. We were not very political but we were very attached to our music. For a number of weeks it seemed, we attended strike events in the City and attended free concerts in support. We were not active but rather fellow travelers. Ultimately, a new station, KSAN, with the same people took dominance, and KMPX took a back seat.

The national news was busy and troubling that winter and spring of 1968. The Vietnam War continued unabated with what seemed like high loss of young American lives. The Tet offensive took place in late January, which some now say was overrated as a defeat, fed a surge in opposition to the war. On campus, opposition to the war seemed to be a constant topic and cause for commotion. In April, Martin Luther King was assassinated. Most paid attention to the news at that time. In addition, Eugene McCarthy and Robert F. Kennedy were running for the Democratic presidential nomination. The end of May found LBJ declining to run for re-election mostly because of anti-war sentiment. RFK won the June primary in California but was assassinated. Again, most focused on the news. Locally, a strong anti-war movement dominated the campus community. Later that summer, the Democratic convention provided fodder for the news with riotous protests. This time many of the figures were Bay Area locals brought to the national stage. Even while I was not political, knowing the actual people from a local context gave me a sense of a front row seat to the action. While I remember this as a pretty daunting national context, we were busy with our daily lives and largely unaffected by it.

That year for me was one of peace and comfort. I was comfortable with my school program, even if not enamored; I had a comfortable living situation with compatible friends, even if it was not fancy; I got by financially, which was okay by my expectations; and, I had a stable relationship with Daphne, which was more important to me than I may have realized at the time and protected me, both of us, from some of the more destructive aspects of the counterculture. In that context, we were able to embrace the ethos of the counterculture and be involved without being thrown off by it, or so we thought. We were into the music and its scene without being immersed in that part of the culture, into the drug culture without being consumed by it, and into the anti-establishment progressive politics without being part of its more radical manifestations. We were like those intrepid surfers on Ocean Beach in San Francisco where the water is so incredibly cold but they survive and thrive because of their wetsuits protecting them from the cold. We had our wetsuits of school, work, stable living situations, and a good relationship within which we could enjoy and experience the culture with a safety buffer. In addition, although I was not to realize it until much later, the regular contact and involvement with her parents at her home was a grounding point that protected us, certainly me.

I still saw LK. Often, Daphne and I got together with friends of his, and they became friends of ours as well. One of those times, I realized everyone was Jewish except me. I noticed as an aside; my world had become more diverse. I was a part of the group but tended to see many of them as smarter than me. At one evening get together, one of the smartest and bluntest of LK's friends, a history graduate student, after a discussion in which I did not have much of an opinion pointedly asked, "Don't you know what you think?" The truth was in the specific instance I did not and in general I was not opinionated especially with regards to politics. I was not self-assured and preferred to listen and learn from those who I assumed were smarter or knew more than me. Nonetheless, I remembered his rebuke and years later came to a point where I usually knew what I thought. He probably would not agree with what that became.

A few incidents from that year on Alcatraz had convinced us that maybe, even though we never felt unsafe, we should think about moving when our lease came up at the end of the summer. Chuck had a very nice car his parents gave him to use and one morning found the windows smashed. I do not recall if anything was stolen but the thought that damage was done was enough. Up until that time, bus drivers made change on the local transit buses, which I think was standard practice around the country, until a bus driver was shot and seriously injured just around the corner from our apartment. After that, the transit district only accepted exact change. And still further, one evening some girls from down the hall came to the door and asked to use our phone. We had never had much contact with other tenants in the building. Within less than a week, we arrived home to find all the stereo equipment stolen from our apartment. We quickly figured out who had been the thieves, but the police could or would do nothing. Our lease was up. Moving seemed like a good idea.

Deeper into Oakland

Thus, as the summer was coming to an end, we found a one bedroom apartment deeper into Oakland but in a somewhat safer location. The second story unit was in a four unit building. The owner was a widow who also ran a beauty shop on the first floor and lived in the building herself. The building was near Macarthur Boulevard right on Telegraph Avenue. We were about halfway between the campus and downtown Oakland and about a mile and a half farther away from the university. With a little painting and other touch ups, the unit was very livable for easily satisfied people like us. It had wood floors and some old paneling, a living room in which Chuck lived, a dining room which we used as a living room, a kitchen, a bathroom, and a back bedroom, which Peter and I shared. The apartment was much larger and was a better space compared to our tiny studio.

That fall a hometown friend, Eddie, got married and moved to the City to continue school at San Francisco State. He and his wife found an apartment on Edinburgh in the Excelsior District, which was a bit tough and had no touch of City charm. We often visited there and saw others from my hometown, as Eddie was more connected to them. Without much effort, we got very comfortable with the Excelsior. I had lived on Alcatraz below Shattuck and now Telegraph near MacArthur—not exactly prestigious locations—and got very comfortable with tougher neighborhoods.

Our life continued much like it had been the year before. My classes became more involved in the time they required. Daphne and I were together often. We still went to concerts, although not as often. Daphne had made friends with gay guys who worked at an upscale fashion store in the Cannery at Fisherman's Wharf. That shop became one of our regular stops hanging out in the city. Because of that, we were invited one evening to a party on Church Street near the Castro. On arriving, we found we were the only straight couple in attendance. The party was all gay guys. It seemed to be a normal party except periodically a couple of guys would disappear into a back room. We were offered brownies, which we knew had marijuana added. I had never really been high on grass before. I was in for a surprise. As we left and made our way to the car, I noticed that I was almost as high as on an acid trip. While I did ultimately learn to sort of experience a little high from marijuana, it was never again like that evening.

At some point that fall or perhaps a little later, I decided to drop acid on an outing to the City with Daphne. We were planning to spend the day in Golden Gate Park beginning with a free concert in the panhandle. It was a sunny, warm day without the fog that can be as gray and cold as any winter day. The panhandle, a narrow grassy area of park stretching far into the city, was only thinly populated with people. I removed a string of bells from my car and attached them to my belt which bothered Daphne, probably because she was more self-conscious than I was and because she could hear the bells more than my deafness allowed. I liked the bells in my car and the soft ring which was consistent with other odd hippie emblems of the time, but the soft ring I heard was probably not the din others heard. I was not as self-conscious as I used to be. I accepted that the new rules were that I could be however I wanted to be.

As we sat down on the grass to enjoy the music, the effects of the drug were just starting to pulsate through my body. The opening group, AAA, a group I was only to see listed on play bills a few other times, was nonetheless very accomplished, at least to my drug attuned eyes and ears. Really, that included as far as I could see it, a sophisticated joke played on that part of the audience not in an altered state of consciousness. The group of three guitar players and a drummer fiddled with playing forever supposedly tuning their instruments. This went on and on and on. Finally, they played one recognizable tune, "Silver Surfer," thanked everyone and made way for the next group. Many seemed miffed by the performance, but to my eyes and ears, the tuning times were a series of tunes in themselves structured to seem otherwise by the performers. I do not know if I ever saw again a feigned performance pulled off with a straight face and no acknowledgement that it ever occurred. Of course, maybe it did not occur, and I only thought it did. By the time that group was packing up, the effect of the drug was such that the guitar notes and runs were moving through my whole body allowing each note to be felt.

The main group, Quicksilver, was one of the original San Francisco psychedelic groups, known best for their guitar instrumentals and solos. This was to be the last performance of the group with their current members. Whether because of their talent, skill, the effects of the drug, or all combined, I was drawn into their musical performance and rode the waves of each note. The main lead guitar player— they had two—a very thin young man with long dark hair seemed to be one with his guitar and would with almost every tune venture off on a solo run, always musically pleasing and ultimately leading right back to the original piece of music but letting the continuity get stretched very thin without ever losing contact before softly returning. The performance left an imprint dramatic enough to establish that lead guitar player, John Cippolina, as someone I would listen for in later versions of the group. The performance ended too soon for me.

Daphne and I walked farther into the park proper until we found ourselves near the children's playground by the carousel. Here we, or I, just sat and watched and listened to all that was happening around. Silly actions, like sitting in a broad walkway and watching people, seemed totally logical and inspired. Inhibitions were dropped. Surprises had to be dealt with as well. While sitting in the path and still significantly under the influence of the drug, an odd group of people started to approach me. I could tell by the way they walked, sort of irregular, awkward, and disorganized that something was amiss. When they were upon me, I realized, well I did not really realize, I experienced, that they were simply a group of Down syndrome adults on an exercise walk from their home somewhere in the neighborhood. My initial apprehension dissipated as I found myself making direct eye and verbal contact with each of them at a level I could not have accomplished normally even in the most focused circumstances. The drug, as in previous experiences, allowed a greater range of choice in actions and lack of self-consciousness in taking those actions, and none in my experience that were unreasonable or silly.

I was suitably impressed with myself for a deeply grasped insight, already known, that they were real people with real lives and real relationships. I next encountered a more disturbing vision. A man approaching me, wearing an unusual hat, seemed to have indistinguishable facial features. The closer he got, the more his attire, physique, gait, and other physical features became clear, but his face was still a blur. I was not sure what the drug was doing, but I was disturbed and apprehensive. I was worried about having a bad trip. As he came close enough to exchange a greeting, apprehension and fear met and turned in an instant to understanding and a profound sense of amazement. I hoped the man had not noticed my first impulse. I sat in wonder how fear can be misapplied. The man was physically frightening, and had I not been in the state I was, I would have looked the other way, but he was only another human being, probably getting his early evening exercise. His facial features were hard to make out because they did not exist. Severe burns scarred his face; he had only a misshapen opening for a mouth, oddly stretched skin around the eyes, no nose except for two holes essentially flat with his face, and no ears. I wish I could carry that ability to connect that existed that day into every personal encounter, to draw on that purer impulse to extend myself to others. Shortly thereafter, the effects of the drug began dissipating, and I was thankful that I did not have any more challenges, no matter how valuable, to meet on this trip.

That fall I voted for the first time in a presidential election. I voted for Humphrey over Nixon. I remember listening to the results on the radio in my car on Telegraph. But to me, the election was just background. I was not political, even though I was definitely affected by the culture in which I lived.

Big Changes

The popular FM radio station continued to be our main connection with the music scene. Daphne developed contacts with the new station, KSAN and some of the disk jockeys. She finally ended up going in most evenings and volunteering with the evening disk jockey during his program. He had been a prominent AM disk jockey until FM took over. The station was the most listened to by people like us, and his evening time slot was the most popular. Daphne enjoyed the work and the environment but was hopeful for a real job. She still was working at the department store during the day.

During this time, perhaps in the winter, Daphne found a room in a house near campus and moved from her parent's house. We still went to see them but not as often. Daphne's life was changing.

One weekend we joined some of her administrative friends from the station at a strange get together down the California coast on the way to Big Sur. These friends were joining others who lived in an ancient redwood cabin in Palo Colorado Canyon. The road was like many at the time, a side road off Highway 1 that quickly became very narrow and winding, dodging massive redwood trees and seemingly frozen in time. The cabin was an abandoned relic; I do not believe the residents even had permission to live there. It was dark and rustic nestled in the redwood forest along a creek. This was real hippie living. We were not real hippies. It was fine for a weekend but too loose for me.

People's Park

At about the same time, I got involved with an odd class at the university. Since my first two quarters at Cal in early '67, I had settled into more directed classes aimed toward a degree. However, I still sought out and was blessed with some interesting classes. That spring quarter of '69 I noticed one called "Ecology of the University." It was to be taught by a professor in sociology and one in architecture/planning. I could not tell what it was exactly from the description, but it had something to do with the sociological and physical structure of the university, not whether the creek was contaminated, or the birds were doing fine. This was an odd class, ahead of its time. It fit for me as someone interested with the edges. The class was a mixed group of about 15 young men and women from different programs, perhaps attracted in the same way I was. The class had more than one well-known guest speaker as well as the professors leading discussions that were somewhat abstract. I could not tell you exactly what the class was about even today. However, our main assignment for the class was to write a paper on whatever that was.

Not unlike my experience with sociology of religion, I was saved by a little ad hoc community project. The university had a need for more student housing and had assembled a site on the south side between Dwight and Haste behind the coffee shops on Telegraph. The houses, which provided housing but not as much as a multi-story dormitory, had been demolished. The university did not have the additional funding so the site sat temporarily as a no man's land.

A small group, mostly lead as far as I could tell by a tall, long haired owner of an alternative clothing store adjacent to the park, was discussing the idea of a park for the people on the site—a people's park. The park became the subject for my paper. The work started as a real rag tag effort with apparently no real planning and poor execution. I would go by at least once a day. At that time, I was simply an observer. No direction was apparent. A little work might be happening here or there but it had a character similar to kids building a fort on a vacant lot. I remember watching a couple of guys digging a well. The ground was hard. They dug down about a foot before giving up. A lot of street people (now called homeless people) were sleeping on the site. The nightly fire pit might have even predated the idea for the park.

Word spread, and more people became involved, many with more skills and access to resources. The park got a little more order. As some landscape architects or students took it seriously, some new trees and sod showed up. It did not have a watering system, and it does not rain in the Bay Area in the summer, so I am not sure how it was meant to survive, but it looked a lot better. A sculpture of giant letters, KNOW, was moved onto the southeast corner. Ironically, this makeshift people's project was directly across from Bernard Maybeck's Christian Science Church, one of the nicest historical structures in all Berkeley. While the park was much more orderly, at night it was still mostly a place for street people to hang out. One night, I remember standing near the organizer as he lay on a bench in front of KNOW surveying his creation. I was simply background, even though I was quite close to him and no one else was around. I had mixed feelings about the park. I thought it was a neat idea. I was enough a part of the culture to appreciate questioning the authority structure, but I had real misgivings about how badly it was being developed. I could not see how it was going to work given what I was observing.

In the background, the university leadership was grappling with how to deal with this. Because one of our class teachers became involved, we heard updates on that muddled process in our class. Then, suddenly, Reagan, who was governor at the time, got involved in the decision to erect a fence around the site. The next day, May 15, while I was working an odd job, a rally at Sproul Plaza got out of hand and protestors moved on the park, now called People's Park, to tear the fence down and take it back. Things got ugly, the sheriff was called in for support, tear gas and shotguns were fired, and one person was killed and several injured. That led to a greater crackdown as Reagan called out the National Guard to occupy the park and secure the area. Everything was in turmoil. More people were involved in the protest than I ever saw using or working on the park. Scattered protests happened and tear gas often filled the air. I was never part of a protest, but in recording the activities for my class paper, I experienced tear gas from a short distance and numerous instances of odd behavior from participants and protestors. Even I was caught up some as the protest got out of hand.

Activity and reaction ramped up immediately. The administration was still meeting; the faculty was getting involved; the organizers were meeting. On Monday, May 19, the organizers met in the morning. In the afternoon, our seminar was included in a law school visit and conversation with two congressmen—ostensibly regarding education. However, People's Park came up, and in fact, a whiff of tear gas drifted through as we sat on the lawn at Boalt Hall. We walked with them on a tour, coming close to the site, which was only a couple of blocks away. The Michigan congressman wanted to hang back; the California congressmen wanted to assert his authority and try to talk to someone in the National Guard. However, Michigan won; we held back. At our next class meeting, one of the young women disclosed that she had been surprised that the married Michigan congressman had pressed her quite aggressively for a date the evening of the tour. Some discussion ensued that did not have much to do with ecology of the university or the park.

Two days later, the protests were still going on, and tear gas was in the air. Even non-political professors were expressing displeasure with the situation. That evening, the popular evening radio show that Daphne helped with was broadcast on loudspeakers toward the National Guard encampment with a little more political flare than usual. Later that evening, Daphne and I went to a large meeting of organizers at the Diggers' house above College Avenue. The Diggers were a commune-like social advocacy group that did things such as feed street people. While there was more talk at the meeting about what to do, especially the next day, I was drawn to the wild New York kid who was constantly around at this time. His focus that evening was Daphne; he even had the audacity to ask to sleep with her right in front of me. I was bothered, but I was also naïve and settled in my confidence that it meant nothing. Additionally, we were treated to stories about how the younger kids—and I mean young—living in the house with their "families" had sex together. I knew things were supposed to be free, but when did boundaries kick in?

Wednesday, May 28, there was a teach-in with lots of well-known speakers. Later in the evening, at Newman Hall there was a moderated community meeting. I found the meeting poorly organized and facilitated. People could not get to the microphone. Now it seemed that peace activists wanted to change the message. When the Diggers' leader finally got to speak, the pacifists were not happy with his loose, hippie ways. I sensed a real divide. For the first time in my university experience, things seemed to fall apart; classes met off campus if at all. We met at both teachers' homes on separate occasions, which was an intimate touch. I guess it really had become "ecology of the university." My selection of topic, the park, had been on target without any real foresight.

A huge peaceful parade/rally was held on May 30. I went to the park at the start and saw many of the leaders. I noticed the person I identified as the leader responding in a rather too familiar manner with an attractive young woman I had noticed around since the protests started. Yet, she seemed to be there with her boyfriend, and I thought the organizer had a girlfriend himself. I just filed it away as part of the 60s or a misread on my part. (In verifying a date while editing, I ran across an article suggesting the whole park impetus was to mask their affair. Too simple, I think.) The march was quite controlled and went well despite some skirmishes on the edges.

While at the time I did not question motives much, I am not sure whether the original goal of the park was part park and part provocation. Those who thought the communists had ordered this action and the march were off base. However, the organizers were not totally innocent. The park needed better planning and implementation. Even I could see that. However, the protest against fencing the park off was a flashpoint. All hell broke loose. While it was national news at the time and a significant campus protest related to a local event, I am not sure it is remembered by many today. However, the silly "ecology of the university" class ended up being real. At the time, one of the professors mentioned that he used my unfinished paper (because classes ended abruptly) for articles he wrote on People's Park at the time. When I ran in to him just three years later, however, he had no clue who I was. He was better known by then, and I was "just" background.

II.

DISORIENTED

One Year

1 .

DARKNESS
6/69-10/69

Shattered

I had no time to embrace the experience of my People's Park involvement because in the midst I was engulfed in the hardest personal experience I had yet endured. I was still living in a naïve and happy world. I had everything I thought I wanted: a girlfriend, friends, basic financial stability, engaging university classes, a nice apartment, and a fulfilling social life. I would not have changed much. I also enjoyed the proximity to the music scene through Daphne's volunteer work at the radio station. While I had periodic concerns about some guys there, I was unconcerned because I was committed to our relationship. In the over two years since we had first met, we had been together as a couple with a good match of likes, dislikes, and temperament. I cannot remember us having a serious disagreement. We always seemed to resolve things.

A couple days after the park march, out of the blue, Daphne raised the subject of us seeing other people. An incredible dread came over me—a dread pervading my mind, tightening my stomach and breathing. I felt frozen, not cold but like I could not think or move, all the while trying to act calm. The conversation was horrible. I wondered who I was supposed to be seeing or who she had in mind and why. Though of course I was guilty of looking at other girls from time to time, I had never actually thought of having a relationship with anyone else. I had been with one woman for over two years and had been with no one before that. While I had experienced many things in the intervening years, experimenting with other intimate relationships was not one of them. Not only was that a dark road ahead, but my current reality was suddenly dark. None of what I just described as my happy existence seemed to exist anymore. I asked questions trying to find out what or who this was about. I had no idea what I was doing. I did not know what the right emotion was. I did not know what to say. I tried to act calm when I was anything but. I sought out the pain by asking questions instead of relieving the pain by objecting to the proposition. I was afraid and thrown into doubts about myself. I sensed, correctly, that I was dealing with a forgone conclusion, and we were just having the conversation to legitimize an action, but I preferred the talking because my mind was obsessively spinning without resolving anything. I thought in talk resolution might come. It did not.

Daphne was convinced we should have other experiences. As far as I knew, she had been faithful to me. I knew the evening DJ at the alternate station who was being mentored by "her" DJ had taken an interest in her. Grasping at straws, I asked her how the current DJ was going to react to her being with someone he was mentoring. These DJs were very focused on their sexual conquests, so I thought even though it did not matter; she might reflect. Nothing mattered. I walked Daphne to the bus, saw her off to the City, and a part of my life would never be the same. Only an instant passed from the start of her false proposal and getting on the bus, yet two years seemed to vanish. She would do her radio time with the current DJ then leave to meet the other, and I could do nothing. I did not sleep that night. I was a pathetic, obsessive zombie. This was not clean. While the topic was raised, it was like nothing was changing, as if this was as simple as going shopping.

Broken relationships are as old human civilization. But I felt like I was the first to ever feel this heartache so intensely because I had no preparation for it. No one warned me to expect this; no one helped me understand how to deal with it; no one helped me understand what might have been done to improve our existing relationship to avoid this. I was plunged into darkness. I had so immersed myself in the counterculture as a way of life—like a religion but with nothing more to draw on. I was too despondent and too isolated to draw on a sidelined faith. I thought I had no one I could turn to. My life was wrapped up in my relationship. One of the premises of the counterculture had been free love. Daphne and I participated to the extent we had a relationship without marriage, but in all other respects, at least as far as I knew, we were a monogamous couple enjoying the other aspects of the culture without being sexually promiscuous. I suppose her raising the issue before leaving on the bus was her way of honoring our relationship by trying to be honest. Within the culture, I was incredibly naïve and foolish to believe that we could live as a monogamous couple within a world that espoused something radically different. Had someone prepared me, had someone been there to take my side, I might have made it through easier. Even though I intellectually knew that I was not the only person to experience this, I felt like I was. I felt incredibly inadequate; yet, I did not know how I was inadequate. I knew it must be sexually, but I did not know what to do about it. Even though it had been her choice, I felt responsible for not seeing the signs, not being more attractive or appealing, not being adequate. I was smart enough but not experienced enough to know this was as much or more about her issues as mine. These were clear signs of a fear-based co-dependency of which I was unaware. How was I supposed to face other people? We were not breaking up; we were, or rather she was, "seeing" other people.

My mind was in a hopeless place, unable to escape with no apparent help. Unlike the dark psalmist, I was in a place of darkness where I was all alone with not even God to complain to. I had set my Christianity aside and embraced the culture such that it did not even occur to me that I had someone who might listen to my pain. Yet, in previous times, I had a general faith and hope that could only come from that same tradition. My thinking was so fogged in that I could not see that inconsistency any more than I could consider help was available.

I was supposed to be studying for final exams. Forget that. I briefly thought about how to buy a gun. Could I shoot myself? Could I shoot him or her? Obviously, I felt some anger but more than anything, I felt humiliated and fearful. I found the other guy's phone number and address in my own address book, cryptically entered on the back cover by Daphne. As my day went by in slow motion, and I wondered where Daphne was now, I got sicker and sicker. I drove over to the address but did nothing. I went home. No one else was home. I wept. I had not cried like that for a very long time. Now I had to leave a part of my dream of these special and happy days. Finally, I either called Eddie and his wife or they happened by, and I can still see the look in their eyes as I fell apart in front of them. I explained to them through the tears what had happened. They comforted me as best they could, and I went back to my obsessive mind spinning and my stomach churning. I took one of my finals, but my mind was not there. I never picked up my grades from that quarter.

After that I decided to leave town and visit friends, really of Daphne's, in Santa Cruz down the coast. I hitched a ride down and showed up on their doorstep. They were laid back enough to let me stay as we had for them. They were carpenters who remodeled stores and had met Daphne at a record store. They were more experienced in the culture than I was, and while they understood my pain, they could not appreciate its depth. They told me that they had been attracted to Daphne but dropped the thought of anything happening once they met me. They tried to encourage me to go out on my own—basically start a new relationship to cure the old. They invited me to go to a dance with them and some girlfriends, but I could not. I once again felt I did not fit in, defective. I stayed at their house, sat at the typewriter and wrote some of the most depressing, gray, and unresolved thoughts imaginable. Very little could take my mind off my problem for anything but a short time.

The next day we went on an outing into the Santa Cruz Mountains looking for old barn wood. They essentially took wood siding from barns owned by other people for their carpentry materials. We stopped to see friends of theirs, walked up a nearby stream, and on the way back happened upon a beautiful young woman sunbathing in the nude along the path. Although I think she was surprised, she did not react, and we acted like this was a normal walk on the path because those were the times in which we lived.

The next morning, a very gray morning as often happens on the coast in June, I walked out to catch a ride home. My first ride only took me a short way up the coast. In addition to being foggy, overcast, and gray, that morning was damp and cold, and the people I ended up with were as depressing as my mood. I characterized it at the time as a death ride. The next ride was even worse. The car, the people, the conversation, and the weather were all embodiments of my mental and physical state: a heavy, dark fog. Somehow, I got to San Francisco, across the Bay, and back home with time passed but nothing resolved. The fog and overcast did not clear that day, and neither did my mind.

One Way Reconciliation

Daphne had been back briefly before I left and back again. She understood somewhat the condition I was in but now her concerns had changed some. Either because she changed her mind or he changed his, or maybe it was only ever meant to be a one-night stand, she was back. And to no one's surprise but hers, she no longer had her job assisting the evening DJ.

I was a little better but not much. The trust was broken; my eyes were open, even if that vision was totally foggy. I still felt confused. I painfully listened to the sensitive, intimate details about her DJ. While despising myself, a part of me wondered why if it was so good, it ended so abruptly for them. I had no one to tell me how to keep a relationship growing, how to make changes when nothing was ever said. I was too fearful to push back because I thought whatever was wrong was my fault.

Even though neither of us knew exactly what it meant, we were back together. I wanted to be different. I wanted to make up for whatever was wrong, but I did not know exactly what it was; yet, I was sure it was me, so my carefree days were over. The culture was one of free love, but for me, moving on was not easy. I had to get past the feeling of inadequacy, betrayal, loss of trust, and the sense that the same thing was going to happen again. I had to get comfortable with maybe developing another relationship.

Five Days on the Road

While still deep in this foggy and confused mood, Eddie suggested that we take a hitchhiking trip while his wife and Daphne spent some time together to maybe clear my mind. Thus, began an adventure, which while it did not remove the emotional wound I was carrying, was an exciting trip. I had always envied Eddie his trip to Europe after high school. This was not Europe, but it was more of an adventure than I had ever taken. We thought we would head east, maybe as far as Utah or Colorado, then go north into southern Canada, across to Vancouver, and finally, back to the Bay Area. Our time was flexible, and we only packed a few essentials and a sleeping bag each.

Day 1: Mandy

I was still very depressed. The day was gray and fogged in again, and I was not sure where Daphne and I stood; yet with only a sleeping bag, rolled and tied with a rope so it hung over my shoulder, Eddie and I stood at the Ashby Avenue freeway on-ramp hitching a ride north. We seemed to wait forever; then, a guy pulling a trailer said he could give us a ride to Woodland in the Central Valley near Sacramento. As beggars cannot be choosers and in going with the flow, we took the ride. As it turns out, we ended up driving north down a two lane connector to the highway to Oregon now a freeway. He needed us to help him push his stalled car onto the trailer for him. After that he took us to Woodland, which was not on the main route east, but we had no choice. Woodland was a quiet town that he apparently knew well. He pointed out an old Victorian where the Hershey sisters of chocolate fame had lived. He left us on a quiet road to continue our trek.

A very shabby large, older sedan stopped to pick us up. The car was driven by a rather tough talking young woman who had already picked up a couple of young men and a couple. However, the car was big enough, and seat belts were not yet a fashion or requirement, so room was made for us. Mandy, the young woman, was clearly in control and very independent. It was her car, and she was on her way back to her husband or boyfriend in Indiana. She had left in a huff and gone to San Diego. I think he had been in the Navy. Anyway, she had left and was going back. She had picked up the others along the way. The two young men were from San Jose, very regular guys, and I do not recall where they were going. The couple was odd. They were hippies. She was blond with long hair, a little spacey in her temperament, and wore colorful baggy clothes. He wore a multi-colored, knit beret and used a crutch, as he had a bad leg from polio. I might have been considered a hippie, although I was really a student hippie and did not really talk like those deep in the mindset. This couple did and looked the part as well.

Our progress through the foothills and over the Sierra Nevada Mountains was uneventful. On the eastern side of the mountains, in a small Nevada town, maybe Fernley, we stopped for gas. This was in the days when people did use credit cards but the ability to check them for accuracy was limited to regularly published "do not accept" lists. Mandy had a large stack of what I assume were stolen credit cards and went into the cashier. She looked on as the young man thumbed through the book. I am sure she had a ready answer for the next card if the first did not work.

Night was falling as we headed out on Highway 50 across central Nevada. The night was moonlit and fairly light as we approached Austin in the middle of the state. The old mining town is tucked into a draw of one of many little mountain ranges rising out of the desert. To the south, a single solitary and forlorn little tower rose as a sentinel. The town was basically one main road with a couple offshoots to the south and north. Mandy wanted to stop. I was apprehensive as we walked from the covered boardwalk into a classic, old-west-style bar with high ceilings, an open area with tables and chairs, and a pool table. My impression was that all twelve or fourteen men stopped and turned toward us as we walked in. At that time in the middle of Nevada, a cowboy would have had short hair and a bad opinion of hippies. Now, Mandy and the other two young men were not hippies, but the couple definitely was, and with our long hair and dress, Eddie and I would have passed as hippies. We were an odd, little group. However, Mandy did not lack for confidence, and her outsized personality took over. She approached a cowboy with his feet up on the edge of the pool table, knocked them off, and said, "Hey cowboy, play pool with me." All went well. I like to think cowboys still get together in lonely places like that bar in Austin.

We headed on up the road through the mountains and nearly to the border of Utah before Mandy got tired near midnight. We stopped by the side of the highway east of Ely near what looked like an old, abandoned roadhouse. Eddie and I got out our sleeping bags, as did the rest of the passengers, and made ready to sleep on the ground. The desert air was clear and cold even in June. Mandy only had clothes to cover herself with and asked if someone else wanted to sleep in the car so she could stay warm. Even though she might have been trouble, I would have liked to have been gutsy enough to take her up on her offer. I was, as would happen often on the trip, thrown back to thoughts of Daphne. I thought I should be more independent but was immobilized by fear of action and fear of losing something, even though that something was already lost. Here was an odd chance, for maybe just warmth and ease with a woman, but I was powerless. We all had trouble staying warm that night.

Day 2: East of Ely, Stumpy, and Vegas

I woke up the next cold, clear morning to the sound of metal clanging. Coming out of the back of the roadhouse was an old man hunched over a cane and holding a metal pot. At a snail's pace, he made his way down the stairs and across the yard to some sheds where apparently he kept chickens. The pot clanged as it bumped his cane. After a long time in the shed, he made his way slowly back to the building and up the stairs. This was a major outing. While observing this drama, I noticed our surroundings. We had stopped on our way up a long slope. Like so many scenes in Nevada, looking to the west the vista went on forever across a landscape with few trees, mountain ranges in the distance, and a singular, lonely road, stark but stunningly beautiful. By then, everyone was getting up and shaking off the cold. Our only problem was that the car would not start. We got it turned around and pushed it down the road to get it going.

After stopping for some breakfast at a diner near the turnoff for Lehman Caves, we drove into Southern Utah. Midmorning we stopped to see some red rock formations off the side of the road. Or rather I should say, Mandy decided we should stop while most of us wanted to keep the car running, as we were not in a very populated area, and the car might have trouble starting. Mandy was in charge; she did not need the women's liberation movement, which was just then in its infancy, for her empowerment or entitlement. Besides the dramatic rocks, the stop stood out because the hippie guy suggested to Eddie and me that we should "sandwich" Mandy. I guess he was expressing his sexual attraction for her, which I found odd as his girlfriend was right there, he was not the least bit attractive, and she could have beaten him to a pulp if she wanted to. Maybe he was just trying to seem macho. After our brief visit to the rocks, we walked back with only one thought. The car started.

A little farther down the road, we stopped, made a small fire, cooked some hot dogs, and wandered in the desert a bit. While walking, Mandy asked me, "Have you ever had sex with a girl?" I defensively answered, "Yes, I had a girlfriend," but said nothing of the turmoil I was going through. That ended the conversation, but I wondered where it came from and sensed I was missing something. I thought the worst about myself as the problem with Daphne was just never very far away.

Eddie and I decided as we were not heading to Indiana we would step off into the unknown near Provo where we bid goodbye to our fellow travelers.

We made our way up to Salt Lake City. We either got a ride from Stumpy or met him in Salt Lake. He was short, had a pug nose, laughed regularly, and talked a mile a minute. He was fascinated that Eddie and I were hitchhiking and insisted on taking us to a local place in Salt Lake City that was known for the best milkshakes and malts. While enjoying a malt with him, he talked about Northern California, about going to Stanford, but spending most of his time playing cards in San Bruno, how he now sold used cars for a living, but had worked for a lumber mill in the foothills near where we were from.. Then, I am not sure why, he began telling us about his sexual exploits, how he would sometimes hire two prostitutes, even though he had a wife and children. I was way too naïve to grasp all of this except to be a little amazed. I do not know how he did it all. As the day was waning, Stumpy took us to what he thought was a good on-ramp for our next ride.

Where did these people come from? Eddie and I were picked up by a couple driving a Cadillac convertible. They had left that morning from their home in Las Vegas. She was black, tall, slender, attractive, and dressed like a performer. He was white, thin, and rather short, especially compared to the woman, with a pasty complexion and slicked back, dark hair. They had a kind of confidence that did not question itself. Acceptance of interracial couples was years in the future, particularly in Utah. But they did not notice or care. The guy was popping pills, perhaps to stay awake as we drove north into Montana and into the night.

Somewhere in the middle of nowhere in the Montana night, we stopped at a bar that stood by itself just off the highway. After the Austin experience, I wondered how this couple would be accepted. The place was dark and quiet, decorated with deer and elk heads on the walls. The patrons must have noticed our little group. The couple was so self-assured they were unaffected, and no one was offering to cause a scene. We were just like anyone else coming in from their ranch to have a drink with friends. We continued into the night until we came into a small town with what I remember thinking was a large Catholic Church all lit up, but I was tired and dozing off. Our hosts dropped us off as they checked in to a local motel. Eddie and I walked a little farther down the main street and found a comfortable ditch by the side of the road north of town and went to sleep.

Day 3: The Heist and No Canada

The next morning broke clear and crisp, no colder than the desert even though we were farther north. Eddie and I stopped for some breakfast. I tried turning coffee into a food by adding lots of cream and sugar since we did not have much money for real food. After that great breakfast, we started hitching our next ride. We waited for the longest time with no ride. Finally, we learned the "church" was really the Montana State Prison at Deer Lodge. Our couple was likely coming to visit a friend. Hitchhikers were not normally picked up around there. We got lucky, and a car finally stopped for us—two guys and a girl all piled into the front seat of an older sedan. We gladly took the ride. They were heading for Idaho, same direction as us. They had a distinctly rough feel about them. The younger man and driver, Billy, was probably in his early twenties, had the letters spelling LOVE tattooed on the fingers of his hand. This was at a time when respectable people did not have tattoos—only sailors, bikers, and prisoners. The older man was probably in his early forties, very scruffy, and went by the name Cool Breeze. He kept saying he was like "a cool breeze that just slips in under the door." His speech was liberally laced with profanity. Both Billy and Cool Breeze had just gotten out of prison on parole the day before. Rose, the girl, was a friend of Billy's and was only seventeen. They were already breaking parole and would make matters worse when they crossed the state line with an underage girl. What were we getting in to?

We slowly made our way north and west with our unusual hosts. Billy was fairly quiet; Cool Breeze, on the other hand, talked a lot with a generous sprinkling of anger and profanity. As we approached Missoula, he started talking about robbing a gas station and seemed quite serious. I started to wonder what I was doing here. As we pulled into a filling station to get gas, he angrily muttered something about dealing with the young attendant that seemed to imply bodily harm. Cool Breeze got out of the car and went into the restroom, perhaps as a ruse while Billy dealt with the gas. I was immobilized by fear. Not long afterwards, Cool Breeze came out of the restroom, and instead of going toward the office to assault the attendant and steal the money, he came back over to the car and got in quickly. What would be next?

He threw down a roll of toilet paper and a bar of soap, and we headed on down the road. The great Missoula gas station heist was over. While breathing a sigh of relief, I kept thinking this was a little more exciting than necessary. Even though we were in the middle of the forest, as we got closer to the Idaho border, we decided it was time say goodbye to Billy, Rose, and Cool Breeze. We had them let us off along the highway.

Our next rides were thankfully less eventful, although one careless driver burned a hole in my jacket with cigarette ash. Other than that, we had a pleasant drive through the forests, Wallace with its old buildings, up the panhandle, and past the Boy Scout Jamboree happening near Sandpoint. The countryside was very green, heavily forested, and sparsely populated.

We passed through Bonners Ferry, the farthest north town in the panhandle, and our ride took the road less traveled to the border through dense forests and steep hills. When we got to the border, we were let off to make our own way through the crossing. We were upbeat and excited about crossing into Canada and seeing a country neither of us had been to. The Canadian border guards, however, refused to let us in. Their decision seemed capricious. I went to school at Cal and Eddie at San Francisco State. That seemed to be the reason. We were stuck literally in the middle of nowhere, evening fast approaching, and the nearest town was 26 miles away. We started walking.

My mood sank so deep. Whatever distraction the trip had to lift my spirits now only compounded in reverse. As we walked, the light faded, and the air thickened with mosquitoes. Even this many years past, I can put myself in that place and the sense of hopelessness. Darkness fell and the mosquitoes kept swarming and biting, and we kept walking. No cars were going our direction; there was no traffic.

At long last, we saw headlights on the highway behind us. The vehicle stopped, probably surprised to see anyone walking along that lonesome road at night. It was a logging truck driven by a short guy with a pug nose and one of those hats with a narrow brim all around, turned up just a little in the front. He had been waiting for the scales to close and was going to Bonners Ferry. I did not focus on God much at that time of my life but this was a religious experience of some kind. We climbed in and were joyful beyond measure.

The little cab jerked about as our host shifted up through the gears, then, down, then up again as we made our way on the mountain road. To me, a limousine ride to a fancy hotel in New York City could not have rivaled our trucker's chariot. Unfortunately for our host, as we approached the outskirts of Bonners Ferry, the truck scales were still open. We got out, thanked him, and walked the short distance into the small town.

We found an older, two-story hotel in the downtown, which seemed like it would have inexpensive rooms and inquired. The young woman at the desk explained that she only had one room with a double bed. After two nights sleeping by the side of the road and our recent experience with the mosquitoes of northern Idaho, we thought that would be fine. She looked at us rather oddly, two guys with long hair sharing a double bed, (remember this was only 1969) but rented us the room. The room was like you might expect—not large, not well appointed, creaky bed; however, compared to the ground and mosquitos, it was just fine.

Day 4: Bonner's Ferry and
Eastern Washington

I awoke the next morning refreshed, rejuvenated, and upbeat. I went out on the front porch and, while taking in the beautiful sunny day, said, "good morning" to an Indian guy on the porch. He looked at me without any change of expression and said nothing. *Okay*, I thought. This was the environs where, years later, anti-government survivalists had trouble with the feds. They were fiercely independent and suspicious of outsiders. It is the country of Randy

Weaver, whose wife and son were killed by federal agents, and an agent was killed.

Eddie and I had our usual breakfast of coffee with cream and sugar—"breakfast soup" we called it—and started looking for rides south. A few mostly normal rides got us back down to the region of Coeur d'Alene then west into eastern Washington without much trouble. One of the problems with hitchhiking is that you have to take what you can get, but sometimes that means getting rides that take you off course or leave you in locations where it's hard to get another ride onward.

Eastern Washington is primarily flat, dry agricultural land, very unlike the coastal areas most associated with the state. I do not recall why, but we ended up on one of those sparsely traveled roads with just flatness forever and not much traffic. Perhaps because the driver was intrigued to see someone hitching in this unlikely place, we got a ride from there all the way to Seattle. The driver was a radio DJ and was happy to have someone to talk to as he drove back to civilization from the boonies. He thought we would do best looking for a place to stay around the university and left us nearby. He also let us know it was technically illegal to hitch in Washington, so we now knew to watch out.

Day 5: Home Stretch

The next day we made our way to the railroad yards. We knew we could not hitchhike, so we decided we would try to ride a freight train. We got down to the yards and cautiously made our way out to the freight cars. However, trains and tracks were every where and we did not know what we were doing. We found ourselves on freight cars that moved a little this way and then a little that way but went nowhere. In addition, we had to watch to not be seen. After a while, we decided to forget the romance of riding a freight train out of Washington State.

I do not recall whether we bought a train ticket, bus ticket, or risked hitchhiking. Once in Oregon, we got a ride from a soldier returning to the Bay Area. Our ride was very calm through the greenery of central Oregon. In the mountainous area midway down the state, we suddenly lost a wheel from the car. The lug bolts sheared off, and, of course, we seemed to be in the middle of nowhere again. We may not have had much money, and neither did our host, but Eddie had a life saver AAA card. We got towed into Canyonville, a very tiny place, but fortunately that had what we needed. The tow truck driver who ran the towing and repair shop got busy and welded on new lug bolts—no need to pay for parts or find a new wheel. The repair may not have been to manufacturer's specifications but it wasn't far off. We were on our way again without even losing that much time.

Our host, thankful for Eddie's AAA card, dropped us off in Berkeley. Our lives went back to normal, which for me was not very normal or pleasant, but those few days have stayed fresh forever.

Reconciliation Part Two

I had lived in a happy state in the counterculture for two and a half years. All that was different now. Even though Daphne and I were back together, it did not feel anywhere near the same. We were together, yes, but, whereas, I remember the other times fondly, I remember the times following our "reconciliation" as flat and gray.

Only a month or so after returning from the trip with Eddie, as part of our reconciliation, Daphne and I planned a trip to the East Coast. I had always loved the adventure of new places, and the trip with Eddie had increased my confidence. This was a chance for adventure and to figure out how our relationship should work. Ironically, the now iconic Woodstock Festival was scheduled to happen at this time, and we were heading across country to New York. We could have easily gone, but Woodstock was not on our radar. Much like the Monterey Jazz Festival in 1967, it was too mainstream and commercial for us. We had heard many of the groups and the music in smaller venues, which we felt was a better experience. For some, those two events would be the iconic events defining the music of the time in '67 and '69; yet, we intentionally skipped them both.

We followed some of the same paths Eddie and I did at the start, going through Austin, Nevada, and on to Salt Lake City. We stopped to see Stumpy. I got a spare tire from his used car lot as I was travelling without one. We visited my relatives in southern Colorado. While I thought we were pretty cool and cutting edge, I was surprised to find that my country cousins had a Dr. John album in their collection. We quickly travelled across the flat center of the country to visit friends in New York City. I had never been there and was excited about the experience. We took a swing up through New England, which was more like my young days in Wisconsin than anything else I had experienced, and then headed down south through Virginia on our way to North Carolina.

In Virginia, we came to a halt—or at least I did. The vibes toward us in our VW and my long hair combined with the racial tension between blacks and whites was scary. By this time, a lot of southern rock groups were popular, but maybe they lived in a different environment than these small towns we were hitting near the Shenandoah Mountains. We changed course and headed back through West Virginia, straight onto northern Colorado, and home. In Colorado, we picked up a hitchhiker returning from Woodstock. We did not feel we had missed anything. The trip was wonderful, and I saw country I had never seen before. But even so, a dark cloud still hung over our relationship. There was still no peace—not for me.

2.

UNSETTLED TRANSITION
9/69-12/69

Finally Living Together

Our return was met with the approach of autumn, and we needed to find a new place to live. Peter had been invited by a wealthy, young divorcee to move into a large house she rented on Northside where she lived with her three young children. Chuck was also looking for a new place. So, Daphne and I, for the first time, began looking for a place together. We found a rather dumpy place on Northside below Grove Street in the flats. We had one room in a two-bedroom unit carved out of the back of a house. We had our own street entrance—which strangely led through the other roommate's room—while the main part of the house entered on the other street. The unit was a mess. I had to repaint our room before we could even think of living in it. The living space, eating area, and kitchen were farther in with little natural light. The person from whom we rented seemed like a lost, young man. He was a child of privilege from Mill Valley, a wealthy enclave in wealthy Marin County. He played electric guitar in the middle of the night, only slept during the day, and studied at the art school in Oakland. He had grown up knowing well-known people, but I am not sure his upbringing or lifestyle would be enough to help him survive if he ever finished school or stopped being supported by his family.

The place was a mirror of our relationship. It was so different from our life together up to this point, so unto-gether. We had been protected in the 60s by the fact that Daphne lived with her parents and that they included me as part of the family. We were fully part of everything that was going on in the culture but also grounded by that other world. Daphne had her job, I had school, and we had a close relationship with her parents then. Ironically, the first time we lived together was in this pitiful place trying to get back to what we had before.

The only redeeming feature of that residence was that while reading Tom Wolfe's *Electric Kool Aid Acid Test*, on the genesis of the psychedelic culture, I realized that we lived near a prominent, early LSD factory. Going out to find the address, I was stunned to see that it was this same awful house we lived in. The original address was on the front of the house on the other street. The place was his-torical in the counterculture—nothing more.

This time for me continued to be difficult. It was not gut wrenching, but there was a dullness and sense of trou-ble just around the corner. I went to school without much spirit or enthusiasm. Daphne and I spent time together, but the worry continued. Daphne was very approachable and charming. The hug of the cute, young man while we were in the record store was just too obvious. I still did not know how to respond. I stood there outwardly passive and inter-nally riled. The pain remained.

A Step Up

After a couple of months living in our shabby apartment, Peter's friend invited us to come live in her house. I thought this might be better, as the place where we were living was nothing, and Peter was a good friend. I might find more support with others around as my relationship with Daphne was confusing. So, in late fall, as the weather was changing, Daphne and I moved from our room in the flats to the rented house on Euclid. We were invited to live in one of the upstairs bedrooms of the house rent free. We, or rather I, accepted because it was free, and it was aesthetically a nicer place to live—by far the best place I had lived—and I would be with friends.

The house was on the north side of campus in the hills. The area was less urban and less dense. The main street, Euclid Avenue, rose steeply from the north entrance of the campus with a small, intimate shopping block. It had a few general shops, an ice cream shop, a couple of restaurants, and a small movie theater. Farther up the hill, theological seminaries and apartments surrounded Euclid. Past that were single family homes tucked into hillside sites. The hillsides cascading down into the campus from the north and east have always helped keep this area buffered from the denser city environment.

The house on Euclid sat on the downslope corner of Cedar at the edge of the denser development and the area of individual homes. Cedar and Euclid were busier streets at the end of the regular grid pattern of streets. One could almost sense that the house was on the edge of the physical sphere of influence of the university and something just beyond. Many houses are no more than structures in which to live, some better suited to that purpose than others but otherwise unremarkable. This house was different. It had incredible character because of its Spanish Eclectic style— timelessly romantic. Houses gain character from additions, architectural style, landscape features, interior decor, the character of the residents, and other ways. This house had it all. Without being overdone or trite, it had a solid, comfortable, and complete feel even when empty. It felt good to live there. This was the first time in Berkeley that I had felt quite that way about my living situation.

Euclid rose steeply along the front of the house so that the living room was slightly higher than the street, but the den and its patio, which were on the other end of the house, were well below the street. More like the urban, though intimate, scale of development towards campus and less like the residential area farther up the hill, the house had only a few feet between the public sidewalk and its front door, yet that short distance was a privacy barrier. The landscape obscured the private areas of the house and yard. The windows to the street were small, and the plaster walls had a 1930's look, slightly rough, with a deep, somewhat uneven hue. I now realize that the time difference from the 1930's to the late 60's was less than from the late 60's to this writing, which is hard to picture, those times being so clear and the 30's seeming so ancient and clothed in mystery. The classic curved tiles of the roof seemed like they might have been there when the missions, that used those same tiles, were first built almost two hundred years before. The door was a large, dark-stained single leaf of vertical boards at least two inches thick. There were no glass panes and no view to the entry, so you never knew who or what was on the other side; yet it led to a whole other world.

The large entry hall boasted a stone floor and dark, wooden paneling on the walls and ceiling. The doorway to the left opened to an expansive living room with a fireplace at the far end and an open ceiling with beams that followed the pitch of the roof. The doorway opposite the entry opened to the dining room. A spacious greenhouse of metal and glass had been added on to the dining room. From the outside, it was covered with mature wisteria vines. Both the living room and dining room accessed the level lawn beyond which, over the tops of houses below, laid the distant view of the bay, the City, and the Golden Gate Bridge. To the right was a small hallway that led to the den with its small, private patio. That hall turned left to the kitchen, which also had room for casual dining. Off the back of the kitchen were a small servant's room and bathroom and the garage. The second floor had three or four bedrooms and two or three bathrooms, all unique spaces. Below the living room, because of the slope of the property, was a large basement that only had windows on the lowest end. I had never lived in a house this nice with this much character.

The house and grounds looked and felt like substantial people must have lived there in the past. This was a site as good as any in the neighborhood and had been so since the day it was built. A trust of some kind owned the house. Its history surely existed somewhere, full of stories.

My time living in the Euclid house was not one of rare and transformational experiences; yet, this was the first time I had lived in a house with a lot of people. The people living in the house were a mix of students and others. None were hippies; Daphne and I were the closest to that. Peter's friend, a recently divorced woman, lived there with her three younger children. Her father had been an official of some kind in the Eisenhower administration and was a developer in the D.C. area. She could afford a house like this because she had a trust fund of some substance. The children were a boy of about six, a girl of about four, and another boy of about two. One of her friends stayed there, as did Peter, of course.

For me that was particularly important because my relationship with Daphne was still causing me emotional stress and being with friends made me feel better. So much of the supposedly new lifestyle innovations coming out of Berkeley were really an attempt to fill a void caused by the modern disconnection from traditional family support. The arrogance of youth was running rampant. We thought the old supports were not needed. Life could be easier. The truth is that everything was different, but, at the same time, it was all the same, only most people were not making the connection—including me. Although I did not realize it at the time, moving to the house with that support of friendship was an island of safety in a stormy sea. My friends may not have been as wise as they thought they were, but they were thoughtful and serious. They could be a support; they were what now passed for family.

The problems with Daphne, while universal and timeless, particularly reflected the foolishness of the time. Daphne's unfaithfulness still bothered me. Her other relationship had lasted but a moment—so typical of the times—and in the spirit of the times we supposedly reconciled as if nothing had happened. Even after the initial emotional turmoil subsided for me, I was left confused and muddled. The fog was thick and not dissipating. I was trying to be modern and deny that my heart was scarred. Unsettled, uncomfortable and unacceptable as that situation was,

I was only surviving. When Daphne again suggested, at about the time we moved into the Euclid house, that we should see others while maintaining our relationship, the partially healed wound was opened again. That horrible feeling in my stomach returned.

My mind reeled. This is what the sexual revolution was about? This was what the late 60's were about? This is what the psychedelic revolution was about? The music, the free-flowing art and color, the concern for disadvantaged people, the carefree university life drifted to the background. I had enjoyed the last three years in that environment in a predominantly traditional way. I was responsible; I worked to pay my expenses with odd jobs; and I completed my coursework adequately. Much as I tried to get my thinking outside the box of the usual solution sets, I kept coming back to feelings as old as human relationships. Something was wrong. I knew it was me, but I also knew it was not me. I could not see the picture clearly because I was in that fog. The joy was gone; anxiety and fear had taken over. Those bright, sunny December days when I first came to Berkeley were gone.

I had a chance for developing another relationship myself. A young woman who lived in the house introduced me to her sister who was visiting from Sonoma. The sister was friendly, and I could converse with her. In fact, I spent the day running errands with her, but I had no confidence to take it further. I knew my relationship with Daphne was a mess. I knew from conversation her marriage was not in good shape, and she was looking for a friend herself. I had no clue what to do. Much like with the young woman on the excursion to the satanic church almost three years earlier, that was it. I had failed with an intimate relationship, was sure I was inadequate, and had too much fear and pride to fail again. I did nothing, and the sister went home to Sonoma County. Somehow, I felt good about the day and bad about my passivity.

That December a draft lottery was being held to decide who would be called to serve as Vietnam continued very real. Many of us students were coming close to the end of our programs. I got a very high number. I think my poor hearing would have caused me to be rejected, but I felt a sense of relief in knowing I did not even have to think about it. Peter, on the other hand, got a low number. He was much more conflicted about serving and started thinking about whether to move to Canada, as many were doing at that time.

On one weekend about that time, Peter and I decided to hitchhike to Altamont for the infamous concert. It was not a big deal to us, just something to do. We found a spot on a hill farther back from the stage. We could hear the music well and had a good time. I say that because the conventional wisdom is that the concert was a disaster. We would not have known that without reading the news and much later seeing the movie. To us, it was amazing that a concert of that magnitude with great bands could be pulled together in such a short time and be offered for free.

Canada, Finally

Christmas was coming, and I would not be going home for the first time in my life. For me, although my family would never have helped with this kind of personal issue, the safe, intimate structure that provides comfort without words that family can supply was unavailable. This was a time during which I could not go home because of things my father had said while drunk, which he regretted the next day but because of pride could not retract.

Of course, I never thought about the fact that this was advent or what Christmas was truly about and that Jesus provides a support system—ultimately the only support system. As a part of the new generation, I thought I had left my religious faith and Christianity aside. My religion at the time, although I never thought about it that way, was secular humanism. I was rational. My idol was a relationship with a woman.

That Christmas was spent in Canada. Peter's friend and her kids, Daphne, and I drove up in her station wagon listening to the current tapes of English rock groups. She was one of the few people I knew who had a tape player in her car. The first mass market personal music system for cars, it played 8-track tapes the size of a book. We crossed the border at midnight on Christmas Eve—much different from my experience just six months earlier, no questions, just waved through. My hair was just as long and I still went to Cal! We spent a little time in Vancouver and Victoria as she looked for potential places to live. I loved both places, particularly the English feel of Victoria. Peter really was worried that as his college career ended, he might be drafted. He was seriously considering Canada.

Shortly after our return, the emotional pressure I felt increased. One day, while walking up Euclid with Daphne, we stopped at a tiny shop near the end of the block. This hippie shop sold a variety of items typical of the culture of the times including candles, incense, tie-dyed clothing items, eastern religious and cultural items, and the like. The shop was owned and run by what would have been described as a typical hippie. He was of medium build and height, had long blond hair worn in a ponytail, and a full beard. His clothing was baggy, multi-colored, and more typical of an eastern European gypsy than an American in his late 20's. He was a man in tune with his times. He felt no discomfort being openly flirtatious with Daphne, although observing the loose code of etiquette and culture given my presence.

On another occasion at a record store, we talked with the same long-haired musician who had flirted with Daphne months earlier. The situation was the same: obvious flirtation to a point of questionable etiquette even for the time. For me, it caused anxiety, a churning in the stomach, and an impotent inkling of righteous anger. I was too afraid to object. It seemed I did not have the skills to start a relationship or even keep one.

Daphne informed me a few days later that the young man from the hippie shop had asked her on a date. At least she raised the subject this time instead of just acting. I at least objected, but I was lost. Emotionally, the scar tissue on my heart had separated me from her even while I was still attached to her. This new way of life was not something I could deal with. I had been through a break-up, but at least I knew that was something that happened to people everywhere.

Nonetheless, with the unsubtle pressure from Daphne and the kind help and attentions of Peter's friend, I worked up the courage to make a break—more to escape impending embarrassment than from any boldness of action. I could see the relationship was not going to be resolved, and I did not want to suffer another DJ experience. Because my friendship with Peter was the real reason his friend had invited us to live in her house, she and he wanted me to stay, but because of my pride and my sense of failure, I could only think about escaping exposure by being the one who left. I did not know what to expect next. I felt a sense of loss and dread.

Daphne and I had rarely argued. We were compatible in most ways. Both of us were moderate in our drinking and experimentation with drugs. We were both upbeat, optimistic, and enjoyed doing things together. Our involvement in the music scene of the time had become more real for her with her work at the radio station. We did not really talk or understand how to talk about our relationship on a more personal level. I did not know to think of that, even though we were both good listeners. The culture taught us that we were who we were, and if we just were cool, things would work. I naively believed that.

Given the times and our age, we had been together for a long time—over two and a half years. We were passionately in love when we had first gotten together and had lots of common interests. Being first lovers, we also offered one another a path into young adulthood. We were both responsible and from stable middle class homes. As time went on, the things we did and the experiences we had within in the culture changed from music, concerts, hanging out in the City and the park, and drives down the coast. I thought I knew who I was and who she was, but I was too naïve. I do not know that talking would have helped us at that time. I think Daphne would have been reluctant because she was less introspective and more attracted to what was going on in the counterculture than I was. At least, that is how I perceived it. It really did not occur to us to look for other ways for our relationship to grow. We were too young, too inexperienced, and too distracted. As we fell apart, I was still stuck on the idea that our problem was sexual and that I was at fault. Boy, did I have a lot to learn, and I did not learn it easily. My passivity and fear in even approaching a relationship was a real block; my reticence to say what I thought was a real block; and my ability to think about next steps but not actually pursue them was a block. Years later, understanding the concept of co-dependence from recovery terminology, I could see that even then I was a passive and co-dependent person, even though alcohol was not involved. I was not a controlling co-dependent trying to keep everything together. I was a passive co-dependent always carrying the emotional weight of keeping things together, often withholding what should have been said. I did not even think of spiritual help, nor did I focus on my faith and hope in this dark time. My thinking was so foggy.

For the first time in almost three years, I was back to consulting the bulletin board at the university and found a room available in a house. The people living there actually interviewed me. I thought that was odd given the times. The people seemed very businesslike. They wanted to make sure whoever they let in was compatible, and I was in fairness a total stranger to them. I was accepted and had a new place to live.

I was surprised when Daphne appeared shocked at the news; yet, she had been the instigator for more freedom all along. I was simply accepting reality and getting out of her way. Perhaps some part of her still held something of our relationship. Maybe she really thought seeing other people could work. Or, maybe my taking the initiative and moving out was totally unexpected. It took a few days, maybe a week, before I actually left—left the girl who was my first love, left any hope of a traditional boy meets girl story of getting married and having a family, left the connection with her family, and left even my surrogate family at the house on Euclid. Peter's friend, more intimately than our feelings perhaps dictated, helped me bridge the gap. She later periodically brought me admittedly painful updates as Daphne moved on quickly and then some while still living in the house. I think I would have been better in the dark about that. The less I focused on the past, the better. I was wise to make the change and move. I stepped into an almost totally new world, even though I was at the same university and lived in the same city.

If this experience of the Euclid house was the only one I had, I doubt I would bother reflecting on it much. The house was the same house when I returned only a half a year later. Things changed so quickly then. The people were all different, and I was a lot different. Life had taken on a different character for me and was about to change even more. From then on, I moved more often, my intimate relationships changed, and I developed more friendships. I thought I was moving to a new level of learning how to be a part of this late 60's experience. I knew I needed to move on; not like I had in coming to Berkeley, with excitement, but rather with no choice and real trepidation. I would be alone; Daphne would not be. I was holding her back from her desired experience of the late 60's. I was on my own, and I was still a long way from recapturing any spiritual comfort or strength. Deep in the background though, I did have a faith and hope that everything would be okay. I continued failing to connect that faith to something other than my rational, secular humanist vision, which had no room for the kind of faith and hope I continued to carry.

3 .

DANA HOUSE
1/70-6/70

The Anchors Gone, Living in the Culture

The new house was on the busy south side of campus on Dana Street. It was across from the First Presbyterian Church and a few blocks closer to campus from where I first lived with LK. The style of the house was typical in Berkeley at the time, but few remain in that neighborhood. It was a two-story, Craftsman-style, wood-shingled frame house with a space underneath almost six feet high, making the entry door up a flight of steps. Originally a single family house, it had been converted into two units. The lower entry was on the right with a large covered porch and formal door with glass side lights. To the left on entering was a living room, to the right a dining room, and farther back a kitchen. Two bedrooms and a bathroom were to the side and back. The living room functioned as a bedroom with the dining room serving as a living room. The upper unit entered on the south side of the house. The entry was much less formal. Inside, a small foyer led into stairs to the main, second level. At that level, there was access to a small room and stairs to the attic. This unit also had a living room, dining room, and kitchen. The two bedrooms and a bathroom were to the side. The attic had a small room to the front and a larger room to the rear. The living room and dining room both served as bedrooms with the extra space in the kitchen serving as both the dining room and the living room.

The lower unit had four residents: an Oakland city planner in the living room, a bookkeeper in one bedroom, and a park ranger and his wife, a craftsman, in the back bedroom. The upper unit had eight residents: William, either a recent graduate or not quite graduate of the university in the living room; a student in the dining room, a university employee and his girlfriend, a student, in one side bedroom; another student in the back bedroom; a recent graduate in the front attic bedroom; Joelly, a recent graduate of another university, in the large attic room; and now me in the small front room off the landing. All were university educated. Some had temporarily or, as it would turn out, permanently stopped before graduation. The ranger was the only one employed in a full time manner that would indicate commitment to a career. Most had a fair amount of free time. Most were in a transition between the university world and the work world. By sharing the house and food, expenses were not high, and each person could survive working only part time. It was a commune of sorts but not a hippie commune. I may have been the most hippie in appearance and lifestyle, although we were all very similar, responsible members of our culture.

When I first arrived to the house, I was intimidated. Besides recovering from my relationship with Daphne, I was now an individual in a new environment. These people lived differently than I had. I had been insulated from much of the lifestyle innovations of the late 60's having lived with friends. This was a house of 12 individuals, many of whom had not known one another before moving into the house, and yet, they functioned as a family and independently. They were not a commune in the sense that each person shared their personal money, but they were a commune in the general sense in which the term was used at the time. Decisions were made as a group; food was purchased as a group; cooking the evening meal was scheduled in rotation; and everyone shared in the evening meal. Even though the upper and lower units were separate and had separate meals, meetings and food purchases were combined. This level of fellowship built relationships quickly and a sense of a surrogate family. Even friends who would come to visit would become a part of the extended family. Obviously, the house had a history before I became a part of it. Although I do not think any of the current residents had been there more than about a year, one year was a long time with a group like this.

One of the previous residents of the house, Charlie Brown, was a zoned out hippie icon. He used to stand at the entrance to the campus on Sproul Plaza dancing and playing finger cymbals in his multicolored, knit sweater and hat and loose baggy pants. He had lived in a tent in the backyard and had run for mayor of Berkeley. I do not think he got many votes. At the time of his "campaign," the counterculture was still testing its power out on the university, had not even gotten to People's Park, and had not graduated to the city administration, as it did only a year after I moved into the house.

While many types of "families" or communes existed, all were different based on the individuals and their focus, although a few broad categories could be discerned. Dana Street was one of responsible, well-educated, well-meaning, if somewhat naive, young men and women, all near an important transition in their lives because they had completed their education, or were about to, or had dropped it near the finish.

Food Conspiracy

My new housemates, before I moved in, had been a key part of the inception of the Food Conspiracy, a loosely organized food cooperative. Food orders were taken early in the week, assembled into a bulk purchase, purchased at the various wholesale outlets, then distributed on Saturday. At the time, most normal families would eat a lot of pre-packaged and brand name foods from a supermarket. As a part of the counterculture, a much greater focus on and market for natural foods developed. The food conspiracy purchases were almost all generic grains, fruits, vegetables, and dairy products.

The people in this house were not particularly political. They had political views and were far more liberal than the mainstream population, but they were not radical in their politics and did not live for political revolution. They were not particularly musical. They were into the music of the times and went to concerts, but none were band members themselves; they did not live for concerts nor the latest recordings. The people in this house were not particularly drug oriented. They almost certainly had all experimented with a variety of drugs, and certainly smoked marijuana if offered it at parties, but no one lived for drugs or their drug experiences. The sexual revolution was not an organizing principle for the people in this house, either. They were living in a group situation with men and women, and most were sexually experienced, but the relations between the men and women were traditional. None of the residents were sexually loose in the context of the culture. Some were in relationships with a member of the opposite sex and some were in between relationships.

While I had not been in a living situation like this before, I had certainly had many opportunities to interact with people who embodied various extremes of the counterculture, whether it be politics, drugs, sex, back to nature, eastern religions, or something similar. Yet, being a part of this house by chance of timing, I am struck by the solid nature, if naiveté and idealism, of everyone in this house. Perhaps the extremes, as is the case in all times, were not as common as their reported prominence made them seem.

The intimidation for me was getting used to having to play an active role in this new family. I was shy, so having eleven new people, already a group themselves, to get to know was daunting, not to mention having to cook when I did not really cook. I solved one of my problems by negotiating out of cooking by being the designated shopper. I was responsible for doing the weekly supermarket trip and for picking up our items at the Food Conspiracy distribution. Others in the house were active in the operation of the Food Conspiracy itself, but this must have gone beyond their household chore responsibilities.

I started out seeing the group as if looking from the outside in but barely distinguishing the individuals from the group. Quickly, the individuals came into focus, and I saw the individuals primarily and the group secondarily. In some situations, I am sure, the group identity would not end up even existing as it was only an organizing tool for understanding a new situation, but in this situation, that group identity never vanished; it only if ever receded to the background. The interactions between people in the house and the common activities were a part of each individual. A true surrogate family existed.

Consistent with being shy, I was passive and went along, within reason, with whatever was happening at the time. I also believed that this meant I was in tune with what was going on, not uptight or rigid, but flexible and open minded. Any consideration on my part that I was overly passive or co-dependent was still far in the future. Later, knowledge of the people and my personal observations would cause me to question internally, but my fear rarely allowed any of that to be expressed. Internally a part of me was and had been ready to stand out and lead more, but I did not know how to do that. I was clueless, afraid, or both and in a fog.

Right from the start, I got involved with house activities and my new housemates. Dinner time was a great time for exchange and connection. There were so many people, and I did not know any of them. Conversation was the primary activity as a group. We did not have a television. Most of us looked down on watching TV. The conversation happened around dinner, or after dinner, or during a party, or on the front steps, or just any occasion, as most of us had extra time for talk. I also learned to eat different foods. When Peter, Chuck, and I lived together, we ate in manner much like we had in the families we came from, no not exactly like we would have at home. That would not have been fair to our mothers. However, we did eat in a manner that frugal students with not much culinary skill might eat. The same was true for the short while that Daphne and I lived on our own. I knew nothing of fresh salads with different kinds of greens—not just iceberg lettuce—mixed with sliced mushrooms, scallions, bell peppers and with different oil and vinegar dressings made from scratch. Obviously, all of this was not new to everyone. Many of them could cook all kinds of exotic dishes.

What really stood out were the omelets. I usually had eggs over easy. I had never had exotic egg dishes with scallions and mushrooms or bell peppers and onions. I was open because I liked the people, and I was excited by the new living situation, so I learned more new ways to eat.

The spirit of the kitchen and eating area was for me—someone not set on any goals, naively open to all paths, and recovering from my relationship with Daphne—magical. People who may have individually been ordinary in the unordinary way of Berkeley became a family for a time at the Dana house.

William and Joelly

Of that family, William and Joelly stand out the most largely because of their temperaments and mine. We were similar and interacted more closely. Their personalities defined the Dana house experience for me.

William was the putative leader of the upper floor. That really did not mean much except that his name was on the lease, and he had to pay the rent. At that time, and given the inhabitants of the house, to have expressed leadership in any more formal way would have been heresy. William and everyone believed that within the house we shared everything: leadership, work, and expenses. Beyond that we were individuals.

William was one of those many talented residents of Berkeley who had recently almost, but not quite, completed his course of studies for a degree. All standard measures of completion or success were suspect, so reason would have it that the value of a degree was in question. William was in that state of limbo. He was not sure what he wanted to do. He had artistic talents; photography was the primary focus of his attention at the time. I believe he made some money doing odd jobs and may have even gotten some money from home. Most importantly, William was a true believer in the alternative lifestyle as practiced at the Dana house.

He was about six feet tall and normally wore his thick, brown hair just above his shoulders. While straight, his hair tended to wave a little under at the ends. William generally wore, as it was still winter, heavy, woolen sweaters, dark denim jeans, and heavy hiking boots. I do not remember him ever going hiking, but lots of people wore them as a fashion statement. Describing one set of clothing for William is not far off describing his whole wardrobe. While the mainstream wore different clothes for different situations, the counterculture usually wore one style of clothing for all occasions. William had a way of walking that was true to his investment in the lifestyle. He ambled. He did not hurry. He walked as if consistency to his form of movement was more important than whatever was going on around him or wherever he was headed. Or, rather, just like with dress, one way of walking applied to all situations. He was a good-looking guy with thin lips, which he used to his advantage when making a point in a discussion. You could read his mood in the shape of his mouth.

Although William enjoyed fun and frivolity, I always got a sense of a little depression or moodiness in the background. His commitment to the house was serious; his commitment to the lifestyle as he lived it was serious, his commitment to his art was serious; and he was serious. This is as it should be, but it can be too much. William's sister, who lived in the lower unit with her husband, was also quite serious. Maybe it was genetic, or maybe it had to do with their parents with whom they did not have much contact.

Joelly was like William's female counterpart on our floor, something of an unspoken leader. She was a bit domestic and brought a spirit to the group that no one else could. She was relatively tall with very long, straight, dark hair, dark eyes, and fair skin. Her mouth would break into a wonderful smile at the slightest provocation, exposing her perfect, white teeth. She would dress, almost exclusively, in clothes she had made of light, East Indian cotton print fabric. The different versions of this outfit were of the same pattern: a loosely fitted blouse and loose pants that could read as a skirt without careful notice. This loose, eastern, yet feminine outfit was completed by heavy boot socks and leather hiking boots, which were both popular and practical.

Joelly was very loquacious and generally upbeat; so, her spirit more than any other acted as a catalyst for conversation, even if that conversation might sometimes be lightly at her expense. Because she was the verbal leader but not actually seen as a leader, as we did not have leaders, she got more than her share of verbal retorts from the well-educated but still immature, undiscerning, and semi-lost young men of the floor. All of us appreciated her, but few, no, none could openly acknowledge that fact. Joelly was committed to her ideals. She had graduated from college and had taken a quasi-charitable job helping people. She found the living environment of the Dana house consistent with those ideals in that the work was shared, food was shared, the house was part of the Food Conspiracy, and the ideals of the residents were essentially the same as hers.

While a very attractive young woman, she was not, as far as I know, generally seen as a potential girlfriend by the young men of the house because of her familiarity and unrepressed, spontaneous readiness to engage in conversation. She was more mature in many ways than most of us and less reserved and aware in others. Therefore, she was somewhat threatening and safer as another friend than a romantic interest. She did have a boyfriend: a nice, quiet, slender, pony-tailed graduate student. However, he was at Stanford, across the bay, and they did not seem to see one another that often. He did not play a role in the dynamics of the house, although he provided a further reservation of intimate involvement.

Mendocino Hippies and Santa Cruz Mountains Again

In addition to having our day to day life at the house, we also went on excursions out of our Berkeley environment, often in smaller groups or with friends from outside the house. We took one trip to a commune in the country in Mendocino County where house members had friends. This was getting closer to a core, countercultural experience than I usually had. The commune was situated on acreage a few miles outside Philo, a small town on the way to the coast. The small group—while it varied in size depending on who happened to be there at the time, who was having a relationship with whom, and other similar factors—consisted of six to eight young men and women. The property had one or two crudely constructed, small buildings that passed for living accommodations. These accommodations had no running water, toilet facilities, electricity, or natural gas. One of the buildings had a small wood stove. The people slept together in whatever space or alcove they could find with intimate relationships happening in the same room and presumably changes in partners from time to time without undue concern. In the afternoon, a couple of the resident women were comfortable removing their blouses and laying bare breasted in the sun. Thank goodness not everyone took off their clothes, which was also a custom of the times. I was not experienced in that custom, nor did I want to be. My fitting in with the culture had limits. The time in Mendocino was sunny, quiet, and ill defined. The residents did not work or go to school. I am not actually sure how they managed to survive or how long their commune lasted. I enjoyed getting a flavor for what their life was and what a slice of Mendocino was like.

On another occasion, we traveled as a group to the Santa Cruz Mountains between San Jose and Santa Cruz. Except for the brief visit with my carpenter friends when I was in that dark, emotional pit, I had not been for a visit to this beautiful area since my childhood. It seemed an area lost in time—and still does—with its rustic cabins and barns, narrow, winding roads, roving creeks, and lots of fragrant bay and eucalyptus trees. The smell of bay, even today, immediately evokes the Santa Cruz Mountains to me. In the summer, the hills are dry, and the creeks slow. In the winter and spring, the creeks are full, and the undergrowth is lush often with lots of ferns.

We were visiting a cabin the park ranger's family owned. It was very rustic and only had the barest of essentials. A couple of extra people came along, as well. One was a very thin and somewhat somber but, to me, very appealing young woman. I had seen her around at least once before the trip, and I had found myself very nervous around her because of my attraction. Since leaving Euclid, I had not approached a girl with any thought of romantic involvement. I was lucky, given my low self-esteem, that the Dana house was so active with interesting and intelligent young men and women that I did not feel pressured to seek anything more. Thus, while I could talk to Joelly or the park ranger's wife, I could not even say a word to this young woman. She was quite shy, too, so she said very little, which left even less opportunity for conversation. I had been in a relationship for longer than most of those around me; yet, I had not grown in my ability to approach and converse with attractive women. I was more confident in most social situations and no longer thought I was uncool with the exception of romantic situations. The damage from my relationship with Daphne had set me back. I once again knew, as I had known in high school, that others knew things that I did not know. I did not want to look foolish, so I did nothing. At one point, the young woman and I were the only ones down by the creek, both aware of the other, and yet not a word was spoken. I liked her but was immobilized. Again, I liked the adventure and experiencing a place with others, but my hesitancy to even hold a conversation weighed on me.

Culture Shock

This seemed to be a time for adventures. A friend from school was going to Mexico during Easter break with his girlfriend and her friend, and he invited me to join them. I jumped at the chance. He was a very friendly young man. We had always gotten along well. I knew we would have a good time. His girlfriend was sociable, but her friend was a little distant. We traveled in his VW van and packed all our own food as we were worried about getting sick. None of us had been to Mexico before. We drove all night to camp in the Saguaro Cactus Monument near the border in Arizona. We spent the next morning foolishly looking for peyote in the desert. A popular book at the time, *The Teachings of Don Juan*, had a lot to do with peyote and the area. One of Joelly's former roommates had dated the author, so we thought we were connected in a real way. After a little of that silliness, we moved on to the border where my friend was forced to cut his hair as the price of admission. At least they let us in, unlike Canada the previous year. My hair was a lot longer than my friend's, hanging past my shoulders, but I had tied it up and kept it in my cap. I was very apprehensive that I would be discovered but luckily avoided detection. I would have probably felt worse than my friend if I had to cut my hair because it was one of the defining elements of who I was. So much for not worrying about status and appearances. I remember the dread clearly.

The culture shock the minute we crossed the border was powerfully dramatic. This was definitely not Canada, and it was completely different even though we had only crossed a border. Things were obviously in worse condition and everything seemed poorer; nonetheless, it was utterly appealing and beguiling—the language, the different construction, the dress, and the bright colors. We traveled through the dry inland area to Guaymas on the coast and saw people living in houses made of scrap metal and cardboard. After camping for the night, we went farther down the coast to Mazatlán, then drove at night alongside outrageous truck drivers who used whatever part of the road they needed. We listened to music on tapes that framed our trip—Starship, Gabor Szabo, and others—while drinking Mexican beer and Coke and snacking on granola.

We had heard legends of San Blas and headed there. We swam in the warm ocean; it was crowded and had bird droppings floating on the water—not very impressive, but who was going to know? We had been to San Blas! We found ourselves late in the evening in Tequila, the town, where we met some young locals, had a beer in a café, heard a mariachi band, and finally were experiencing a little of Mexico instead of just driving by, looking out the windows, eating our foreign food.

The next day we found ourselves as far south as we could get, Guadalajara, slept by the side of the road, and headed north up the center of the country through the dry, inland regions. Near one town, we happened upon a festival maybe related to Easter, found a camp with lots of Mexicans in it where my friend and I made friends with a young Mexican drinking tequila straight out of a large bottle. He offered to share with us, and we accepted graciously. It turned into a great evening. The towns up the center were even more unique than what we had experienced on the coast. I thought we were back in some old western movie. The towns were adobe stucco around a central square with a church, rows of trees, and a mercado, or market, that sold essentials from small vendor stalls. My friend and I finally ate some real food at one of the stalls. Finally, even though we had only been gone a few days, we found ourselves in Juarez. For me it was a little connection to that long ago visit with my family while in El Paso. We got lost in Juarez and it was Easter time too. It actually rained a little, which we thought was cool because that was a line from a Dylan song. Back in the states, we grabbed dinner at a restaurant instead of eating our granola and headed home. It was another strange trip, not long, but full of experiences I can remember as if it was yesterday.

Surrogate Family

The Dana house had provided me in just a few months with more intense living in the Berkeley culture than I had experienced previously. Dana house was a surrogate family. The house regularly had parties, and we often went to parties at similar houses. Even on a day to day basis, because so many young people lived in the house who knew others, people were always dropping by. Some of the people in our house changed a little. The bookkeeper moved upstairs into the dining room along with a musician and photographer such that we had more people. The guy in the back room had his girlfriend from Chicago move in.

Someone had the idea to build a bed on the ridge of the roof, which provided a flat spot to sit. This was quite high as the main level was well off the ground and had high ceilings, as did the second floor, and the roof was very steep to allow for the attic rooms. I do not recall any other house having a similar feature. It was noticeable from the street. We had our first roof party to celebrate the completion of the bed. All the parties usually included inexpensive port wine, music, maybe some marijuana, maybe some dancing, but mostly socializing. The inaugural roof party just featured some wine and socializing, no dancing. Miraculously, no one fell off the roof.

Not all the time was spent in parties, house activities, and trips. Normal days involved classes and extra class work at the university for me. In addition, I still supported myself with the odd jobs, most of which were painting jobs at this time, still coming from my initial contacts through Daphne's mother. I was passed from nice Jewish family to nice Jewish family, painting inside or outside at private homes in the Oakland hills mostly, sometimes in San Francisco. It was mutually beneficial: I made a living, and they got decent painting done very inexpensively.

One day while walking down Telegraph from classes, I was stopped to be interviewed by some student filmmakers.

I forget the exact questions, something like, "Do we have too much academic freedom?" to which I answered, "No." They paused. I think I was supposed to say more. They prompted me with another question, like, "Do we have too little academic freedom?" to which I answered, "Yes". Again, they paused; I was answering the questions too simply. I even believed what I said at the time. They thanked me and I happily continued my walk back to the house feeling good at having participated in one more unexpectedly odd adventure. Several weeks later, William and another friend of his came up to me laughing and saying they had been to the screening of a student film by a friend of theirs, and I was in the film. I did not ask more to find out how the clip was used nor did I ever see the film. My simple answers made the cut even if I might have been the comedic foil.

On evenings when I did not have other things to do I would walk. Berkeley was always a wonderful city to walk around and continued to interest me even though by this time I had lived there for over three years. During this time, I would primarily walk on south side as I was not looking forward to running into Daphne on north side. South side had more activity with coffee shops, bookstores, and other shops. I was always too shy and intimidated to frequent the coffee shops even though they were popular. Somehow I felt it was another culture I did not understand and to which I did not belong, which was odd because it was mostly students and intellectuals; whereas, the San Francisco community I hung around more was not associated with the university or student life. People's Park was still there, fenced in and inaccessible right behind the coffee shops. I would generally just walk and look and feel relatively comfortable in my loneliness. If shops were open,

I would browse. The best for that were the bookstores. Cody's, the large bookstore on the corner of Telegraph and Haste, was the best for that because of its size and selection. I would look in different sections dependent on what was on my mind at the time or would just look for things of interest, not unlike the way I used to "read" the encyclopedia when I was younger—not looking for anything in particular but enjoying the journey and occasionally taking a detailed side trip into something I could not have thought I was interested in at the moment.

On one of those evenings, while browsing the psychology section, I happened on a book called *Function of the Orgasm* by Wilhelm Reich. The title embarrassed me but intrigued me. I thought maybe this book might have some answer as to why I had been unsuccessful with Daphne. I looked over my shoulder to make sure no one was watching then began to scan through the book. Normally, I am a very slow reader but can under certain circumstances read or skim fast. Using the contents and key passages, I found myself intrigued by the thesis of the book: that the body and mind are tied, and simply working therapeutically on the mind when past training and experience has already structurally affected the body's response will not work; both mind and body need to be worked on at the same time. This is what I had been thinking in my own amateur way. Emotional, psychological, and sexual fulfillment needed openness of body and mind. I needed to read this book. Now the only problem was that my mind and body were not so perfectly open and free such that I could even conceive of going to the counter and purchasing a book called *Function of the Orgasm*. I found two others, which I am sure were good but cannot remember, to camouflage my purchase. I went home and read the entire, long, and not simply written book in just a few days in between classes and work. The actual reading only deepened my sense that I had found something brilliant that spoke to so much I had been thinking and feeling.

The ideas made sense to me like a religious conversion, and Berkeley was a haven for all sorts of diverse religious and psychological/human potential options at the time. Thus, I was emboldened to start talking about what I had read, trying to see if others had heard of this guy or knew anyone who did this kind of therapy. Reich had been a student of Freud, took his ideas in this mind/body therapeutic direction, and actually ended his life treated as a nut himself. I had hope that maybe I could find out what was not right with me or could be corrected so that I could have a more fulfilled life, which I think to me meant having a woman who loved me and I loved, too. Even though I found no more concrete connection, I was encouraged by what I read.

Cambodia Protest and Freckles

Once again, as with People's Park the previous year, toward the end of the school year, the university was disrupted by protests, this time because of the invasion of Cambodia, a part of the Vietnam War. I was still not political, but classes essentially stopped. This seemed to be a new pattern that had started the previous year. At the design school, posters were being printed for protests or whatever related event. I thought it would be neat to know how to make posters, so I spent the whole time working there. Another student whom I only knew a little was quite talented at silk screen poster design, and I found it fun to work with him. I only did minor support work and printing while he designed the posters, many of which showed up in a *Newsweek* article on the protest. He was a unique character, very talented. One night, he snuck us both into a classical violin concert featuring Josef Suk in the music school next to where we made the posters. I do not believe I had ever gone to a classical concert before. I did not have a clue who Josef Suk was. While I did not forsake my preference for psychedelic rock bands, I was surprised by the powerful impact and the juxtaposition of this calm, inspiring concert taking place in a beautiful, older venue right next to the bare concrete, disordered poster studio cranking out anti-war posters to the din of rock music on the radio.

One weekend as a part of the protest, a free concert was held in Tilden Park high in the hills above Berkeley. Although the politics did not really interest me, I think I probably would have said I supported the protest. While I did know the political talking points, I was not convinced that all those espousing them were not actually in it for themselves, just as People's Park ultimately seemed, but I liked the energy. I got a ride with Joelly up to the concert, which showcased a couple of bands and a lot of dancing on the edges of the lawn. I may have danced a little with Joelly or perhaps a bit on my own, as that was acceptable at the time. Then, I found myself realizing that an attractive young woman was sort of dancing with me, then, was most assuredly dancing with me. Her eye contact and warm smile were all I needed. We danced the rest of the time with one another, talked a little, and I had the courage to ask for her phone number. This was a big change for me, but the risk was low given the non-verbal communication we had in dancing and glances. I felt a little better about myself. Joelly, even commented that we seemed to hit it off.

This was exciting as I really still had no clue how to approach a woman. This felt like my original meeting with

Daphne. My new friend was a slender blonde with fair skin, freckles, an engaging wide smile, and bright eyes who responded optimistically when I called. She came to see me at the poster studio; we talked and walked, then made a date to go to a music concert on campus. Even though she was maybe a year or two older than me, had been married, had been a school teacher in New York, and seemed less in the culture than I had been for years, she had been at the free concert, and now as we walked on the campus, suggested taking off our clothes and running naked through the sprinklers. That was still not me; I side stepped that suggestion and wondered a little, but only a little.

Other than that, we conversed easily and had fun together. I am not sure if it was my suggestion or hers but we both dropped acid for the concert date. I remember it being an easy trip of music, dancing, and a peaceful feeling. The drug allowed a greater connection with music, definitely riding with the music, colors, movement, and images of the light show. I could now easily dance the freestyle of the time whether high or not, but I felt and probably was even more in sync on acid. In addition, I was thrilled to be with someone I liked who seemed to like me. I didn't feel the need to hold back much. That has always been a blessing and a curse for me—a blessing because not holding back and being vulnerable allowed my true feelings to be expressed to the extent possible, a curse because I was not acting defensively and that vulnerability left me easily open to hurt. I was mostly all in. I was proud of the Dana house and how we lived, so it seemed natural to make our way there after the concert. After showing her around, I showed her the bed on the ridge of the roof, and we spent the night there. While I thought that was a great spot and a great idea, she may have been afraid of falling. The roof was really quite steep. If she was, she kept it to herself.

We got together again later in the week, and while everything was fine in some ways, I noticed that when I talked with her I learned things I found disturbing. I found that, while I was ready to be close, open, and vulnerable, she kept an emotional distance. I already knew she had a boyfriend in the group that was playing when we met in the park. I knew that they did not live together and somehow thought maybe I would be her new boyfriend. But, I was apparently just something extra. Either because her boyfriend lived the unattached life of free love, she had to as well, or because she also bought into it, she saw her relationship with him as sort of steady and anything else as fine, as well. I tried to understand and hang in there but did not want to run naked through the sprinklers on campus or hear about what she thought about sleeping with some other guy near her apartment. She really seemed committed to her life style. I was attracted to her and liked her but was totally confused. I cannot remember how we came to stop seeing one another. I probably stopped calling as I knew I could not share her, and she was not interested in a relationship with me alone.

I did not fit her lifestyle because I obviously wanted some other kind of relationship. I did not fully recognize what was going on as I still had doubts about myself. I knew I did not feel right, but as with Daphne did not know if the problem was mine. I thought maybe I had found someone new to replace that empty space, but not so. Although I did not think of it then, the easy contact with a guy of some interest at the concert for her was fine. I thought it was something else. It had been with Daphne, but our initial attraction turned into something because we were looking for essentially the same thing at the start. I did not know my new friend and I were looking for different things when we met. I did not realize how much I was really looking for a relationship. Yes, sex was good, but even with my doubts, I was rediscovering the free love counterculture of sex and no relationship did not work for me.

Ironically, one of the books in her bookcase at her apartment was Wilhelm Reich's *Function of the Orgasm*. I do not know that she ever read it, as a brief attempt to have a conversation related to it did not go anywhere. It was like a door was closed. As open as she seemed to be, she was not at all. Intimacy was not intimacy as I understood it. Even though I sensed that, I did not know what to do with it. I really liked her, and I was disappointed. I sure did not get how this was supposed to work.

Rent Strike

During this time, concurrent with the Cambodian protests was a rent strike between student tenants and landlords who owned a number of apartments. Berkeley again may have been the first for this kind of student protest but I am not sure. Our landlord was one of those targeted. While the instigation did not come from anyone in our house, once the issue took life, the consensus seemed to be that we should support the effort and withhold our rent. I remember clearly not understanding and not having the courage to argue to the contrary. As with People's Park and the Cambodia protest, the purity of the execution could not withstand close scrutiny. Motivations were varied. With the rent strike, some in other houses were clearly only looking for free rent for a while. Those in our house were principled. The landlord's representative set up a house meeting with the landlord that everyone attended. However, the meeting quickly dissolved into an ultimatum being delivered to the landlord that halted conversation and the meeting. The ultimatum had been discussed before the meeting, but no one thought through the consequences. I sat quietly wondering why we were doing this. The landlord did not seem to be a villain, and his representative, who showed up a little late with a cake to share, was a nice lady. They were willing to work with us, but that would have been seen as a cop out. While we thought we were leading and standing up to injustice, we were following the script of our local culture. We were conformists where real leadership—resolution—was not really an option. I said nothing but knew I did not agree.

Ironically, while some of the less principled houses got their free rent and did not have to move, our principled house stuck to its position and was evicted. That wonderful surrogate family of young people was broken up and scattered about town due to its own myopic principles. I had lived in the Dana house for less than six months. I came to the house as unanchored as I had ever been; yet, that community relationship anchored me with a spirit that is hard to describe. The house and the people modeled that new culture we were all trying to be a part of as well as I have ever seen. Although the individuals were very diverse, the attitude of integrity and respect that subtly infused the inter-relationships was consistent, not divisive and self-centered.

Dana house had been a step into a different experience in the same Berkeley I had lived in for three years. In a way, that surrogate family provided a safe haven for me, a place where I was protected even though I was unanchored from my previous connections. Not a place where everything was great and I had no worries, but where I had a sense of rest and relationship of a different type. I did not think of it that way then but when coming to Dana house I was stepping away from the close relations with a friend from my old school, a relationship of two and a half years with Daphne, and, I really would not have thought of this at the time, the relationship with her parents. All those regular mooring points of relationship were gone or changed. I was still very disoriented by the break up with Daphne and did not have a clear sense of moving forward. I did not have anyone to turn to, or rather I did not know to whom to turn. I could discuss it but felt I needed to deal with it on my own. I still did not have any sense of a spiritual comfort. I had put God on a shelf. I thought my life was filled with just what was before it. I was not seriously considering ultimate reality or what my worldview might be, but I realize now that I had a faith that was not connected with how I was conducting my life. Way deep inside, hidden by the fog, I could not see the inconsistency. I could not see that at the time. In my reality, with the loss of the Dana house and that sur-rogate family, I would not have even that anchoring. And, one serious attempt (on my part) at a relationship with my freckled friend from the concert went nowhere.

All of a sudden, we all had to find new places to live.

III.

REFLECTING IN A FOG

One Year

1.

BRIEF INTERLUDE

6/70 TO 9/70

Forced to Move

On Etna farther up the hill, William had a good friend whose house had space opening up, and he suggested we both move in there. The space was not yet available, but the house would let us live in a basement they controlled under the neighboring house. The older house on Etna had been designed by Bernard Maybeck, the famous turn of the century architect who had designed the historic church across from People's Park. Our house was on a small lot with huge redwood trees. The house itself had an all red-wood, original interior, which made it quite dark particularly as the wood had darkened with age. Paint and posters, the primary decorative arts of the culture, were deemed inappropriate. Attached to the house was an old carriage house with a high, open beamed ceiling that was used as a bedroom. The house was not large, so the group was much smaller than our Dana group. William's friend, a Japanese American, was the only one I got to know well. He was quiet, I think shy except in our group, and a great cook from whom I learned to love tempura. He was to become well known much later in southern California as a supplier of fine produce to restaurants. The others were fine, but unlike at Dana, they were really people living in their own rooms sharing a house. They were individuals; the house was not like family at all.

Even though I was to live there only a very short time, my life changed dramatically. I had completed school at the same time we were evicted and had started a very basic part-time job. I cannot remember how but I made contact with the Sonoma sister associated with the Euclid house—the girl I was afraid to approach the previous fall when Daphne and I were going nowhere. I had some hope of becoming closer with her, but the relationship really did not develop.

Joelly came to visit us periodically. I can remember returning from Mexican food with her and another girl, walking through the streets around Telegraph that were all torn up for improvements and new paving. We were like happy-go lucky-refugees in a bombed out city shambling home from dinner and having had a little too much alcohol. Compared to the stability of our life just weeks before that comparison was valid. Compared to someone really suffering physical distress, it was not close. Our physical lives were fine, even if our emotional lives were confused.

Shortly after moving into my room in the house, I got to know the Chicago girlfriend of the Dana tenant a lot better. She was a really nice, young woman. I came close to starting a more serious relationship with her but backed away. She told me things about other relationships that she probably should have kept to herself. She told me that she had cheated on her boyfriend with William, my friend. I guess it was just sex as William was a part of the house, and they had no apparent relationship. She also told me a young Middle Eastern man she dated had treated her badly sexually, though she did not express any anger or disappointment at it. She was passive, almost certainly did not have a very high opinion of herself, and was not getting what she deserved. I had a very low opinion of myself as well, but I knew she would have been willing to be my girlfriend. Nonetheless, I had the courage to tell her I did not think it would work. She took it in the same way, I was learning and would continue to learn to take the same message from other women: with graciousness even if she was disappointed inside. She was actually a treasure who needed to stand up for herself more. I am sure she was, like many young women, dealing with the female version of this culture and foggy thinking, just as I was on the male side.

Big Change

From William, I learned that one of the women living in the house actually knew of a Reichian therapist and was seeing him. I would never have known how to find one; I would have just kept talking about the therapy without ever pursuing it. She said her therapist was very busy but gave me a number to call, which I did knowing I would have to wait months before a space opened up, so I would not really have to do anything. He was busy but gave me the name of his associate. He called back saying he had one open spot in just a few days. Before I could back out, I was scheduled. I was excited and nervous, talking and acting were different; yet, I was eager enough that I kept moving forward.

While I had read the book, I really had absolutely no idea what any kind of therapy was, let alone Reichian therapy. If I knew people who saw therapists, I was not aware of it. Outside of movie representations, I had no clue. The human potential movement/personal growth was such a big tent in the counterculture at the time with Esalen Institute, Gestalt psychology and therapy, encounter groups, scream therapy, EST seminars and training, and of course traditional therapy. This was mixed with the quasi-human potential/self-exploratory Eastern religions and meditation, Zen Buddhism, Transcendental Meditation, teachers like Krishnamurti, Gurdjieff, and assorted gurus who focused on personal growth through spiritual effort. I did not find the spiritual path meaningful but found the therapeutic path meaningful. In my worldview, if I could understand myself better, I could be a better, more successful person. Nonetheless, while I was generally informed on the topic and had been totally taken by reading *Function of the Orgasm*, I moved forward with a confidence based on something like blind faith and no experience.

On the appointed day and with major trepidation, I drove across the Bay Bridge to San Francisco and out on Geary to a very ordinary, modern duplex on a side street near Mel's Diner in the inner Richmond. I waited out front as instructed and as one person left, was greeted by an imposing man with a neatly kept beard and long blond hair. While he was tall, he carried himself in a way that made him seem even taller, something in his stance and his shoulders. While he was quite heavy, he came across as big, not fat. He wore his white dress shirt loose with light-weight trousers and simple, slip-on canvas tennis shoes with no socks. Everything about him exuded confidence. He greeted me with warmth that was gentler than I expected from my physical perception of him. I instantly knew I had never met anyone like him—nor have I since.

Dr. Terence Bold escorted me into a back apartment behind the garage on the ground floor. The main room had a double bed and a comfortable chair in the middle. I knew and was attracted to Reich's ideas because of the connection between the mind and the body but did not recall reading specific accounts of how the therapy was accomplished. Without much wasted time, I learned that I was expected to remove my clothes, lie on the bed, and breathe. Threatened as I was, I kept moving forward. At least I was not being asked to remove my clothes and run naked on the university campus nor lay naked on a hillside in Mendocino with a group of people. I was not comfortable being naked in front of a man, but it was private. In my nervousness and enthusiasm, I talked too much. I explained to him my sense that I was inadequate, probably sexually and other ways. I explained the pain of the experience with Daphne which while a year earlier was still huge to me. Of course, nothing was resolved, but I left with a sense of having entered into a challenging journey. I did not know where it was going or how challenging it would be, but I would go along for now and return once a week.

The first few weeks I had very little idea what I was getting into. Dr. Bold held a license as a chiropractic rather than in medicine, psychiatry, or psychology. He listened a lot and said very little. Despite his long hair, he did not seem to be a part of the counterculture. He lived in LA and commuted to San Francisco; his background was acting, big time wrestling, and sales. I remember being dropped off by a large group of my friends after adventures along the beach in Marin County to the north of San Francisco. We were giggling and silly. As Dr. Bold watched us from the doorway, he just took it in without being dragged in. He did not convey judgment, but rather a sense of, "Okay you're having fun, so? You think that's an accomplishment?" Often, we tried hard to show how un-hard we were trying, how laid back we were; yet, we were actually trying hard.

My limited understanding of what I had read was that the connection of mind and experiences caused armoring in the body and dysfunction. From my reading, the focus seemed to be on sexual dysfunction. The "session" was mostly spent breathing with some time spent talking. From the early conversations, I got the sense that maybe the point was something bigger than being better sexually whatever that might be or just having some tricks to deal better with life. I did not know what I was getting into, but this felt like a big change in a positive direction.

I did not think of it at the time, but this felt like a spiritual awakening again, like stepping onto the Berkeley campus three and a half years earlier. I was definitely stepping out in faith. But, faith and things spiritual did not really have a place in my supposed worldview. I, with little awareness, conveniently avoided examining how my worldview did not really fit with how I actually lived. However, the pattern of discovering the book and then the therapy that went with it was not unlike reading about and listening to the music of the counterculture and then coming to Berkeley.

About this time and continuing forward, I spent more time reflecting on my background and how that might have affected who I was. I was trying to take maximum advantage of the time with Dr. Bold, sometimes more casually known as Terry, to solicit his thoughts on what might have had an effect on me and maybe understand better why I was in therapy. I did not have any serious dysfunction I needed a cure for. Therefore, while I had often thought of my past and had many fond memories and some not so fond, I now intentionally started to think about them more and ask questions. For the first time, I looked more seriously for some order in who I was or the meaning of life.

Patterns Changing

Patterns in my life were changing even if I was only just beginning to notice. When I came to Berkeley and the Bay Area in late 1966, I was a student, not working, not very connected socially with interest in folk music, the downtrodden (even if I did not know what that was), 20th century existential and other modern writing, and the counterculture I was reading about. On coming to Berkeley, I was still a student; at first, I did not need to work, but most other things were different. I did not live in a dormitory; I did not live near campus; I was not in a fraternity; what was going on in the community, especially the counterculture and music scene became very important; I was excited rather than bored. I moved to Berkeley. I added in experimentation with drugs to the music. Then, in meeting and becoming involved with Daphne everything was different and the same at once. We were both into the counterculture, but we were different in many ways. She did not choose to go to college and lived at home. My life became different as I was part of a Jewish family for the first time. They were not religious Jews, but rather cultural Jews, as were most of the Jews I knew. By that I mean they did not go to temple regularly and did not observe the Sabbath ; however, they were different from my cultural experience. They celebrated Jewish holy days and periodically had Jewish meals. All of this meant and was embraced as expanding horizons.

It seemed like I coasted along until slammed by the realization that Daphne was embracing the culture to the extent that she had another relationship while I was happy with the pattern we had. That dark, startling shock upset my sense of balance. Nothing else mattered. I never picked up my grades from that quarter; I do not know how I took my finals; I think I walked in my sleep, a bad sleep, for the next six months even though we were together again and took a significant trip cross country.

Making a decision to leave Daphne and the safety of a free place to live connected to old friends was huge step for me. Dana house was a completely new experience even in the context of Berkeley 1966 to 1973 for me. The people of the house were not hippies nor serious political activists, but they were living out a part of the counterculture dream with communal meals, communal responsibilities, involvement in the Food Conspiracy, and finally involvement in the Rent Strike. Dana house was a safe harbor. I was not comfortable starting intimate relationships. I had lucked out or been blessed by one that lasted a long time and allowed me to skip for a long time that part of the counterculture. Unfortunately, the false start of a relationship with my carefree freckled friend made me unsure how to find another relationship. I was uncomfortable and lonely, but I had a surrogate family, Dana house, which helped buoy me in that dark time. With that ending and being at Etna, I was not in a surrogate family but rather a group of interesting people who shared a house. The experience was new to me, but I had lost the comfort of the Dana house family. I had a little distance from my relationship with Daphne, which gave me some comfort, but I was lost in a fog. Of course, it was the same when I was with her; I just did not know it.

Starting therapy completely changed my focus. I went inward and outward at the same time. I would not have said it at the time, but I was searching for meaning, just as I had when I first came to Berkeley. Dr. Bold was encouraging me to challenge myself with all kinds of things, including initiating relationships and action in general. I do not remember Dr. Bold explicitly encouraging the inward journey—I initiated that, but he never was critical of it. I wanted to understand myself better and to immerse myself in the process. I saw this as a huge door opening for me.

Why was I so painfully shy especially in a group setting? Why was I unable to speak up when my viewpoint might actually have been good for the situation? Why was I so reticent to initiate conversation with young women, especially those I found attractive? Why was I full of ideas but unable to act on them? I was not idle or hidden in a closet; however, I was limiting myself all the time out of a fear that was often irrational. On a personal, private level, I was trying to confront this fear and understand myself better.

Back to Euclid House

Starting therapy with Dr. Bold cost money, and my part-time job provided little income. While I could have gotten a full-time job, I was still into my alternative lifestyle and also did not have the confidence to apply for a real job. Peter and our hostess, who were now a couple, at that very time asked me to move back to the Euclid house. I needed to consider the offer because my rent would be free. Thus, in July 1970, only six months after leaving the Euclid house, only about a month from having to leave Dana house, and after just moving from the basement into my room in the Etna house, I was considering moving back to the Euclid house. More changes happened in this period than had happened in the previous two years.

Peter and our hostess had a whole different house full of people from when I lived there before. She still had time on her lease, but she and Peter were planning a lengthy trip across country in a bus like the early Kesey group had done. While they liked the people in their house, they did not trust any of their new guests to be responsible for it. I needed to consider moving in with yet another completely new group of people. None of my friends would be there, although I knew some of the people from visits to the house. Moreover, I would be responsible for the house until the lease was up and turning it back over to management.

Daphne no longer lived there with her new boyfriend from the record shop. By that time, they had their own place, and she was already, from her perspective, living the free life she desired. Yet, her boyfriend probably never remembered how he openly flirted with her when I was in the position in which he now found himself, and he was reaping the unintended consequences of loosely structured relationships. While the culture was supposed to be different, the real way individuals responded to classic relationship situations was in classic ways. Nothing had truly changed. Cultural patterning, which supposedly led to uptight prudishness, did not determine this, but rather timeless relations between men and women, which are not easily or ever changed. Unfortunately, I did not understand this nor did I understand relationships very well. I was hoping therapy would help me with that. Notice, I said hoped. Hope like I had does not come as a part of secular humanism. I was not thinking about spirituality or God. I was immersed in the effort of doing better.

Although moving meant leaving new friends at Etna house, I made the decision to do so. I had no intimate relationship at the time that might have affected my decision. In fact, although I was generally happy—out of school, working, earning my own keep—but among all my friends and acquaintances, I still felt alone. I would rather have been in a steady relationship with a young woman. Being free of that to be independent did not appeal to me, as I did not feel tied down in a relationship; I actually felt freer. I could never understand the kind of independence that allowed for multiple partners of the opposite sex. I was traditional enough to want a committed relationship, even if marriage was not required, and while attracted to the concept of a different girl every night, could not see how that was possible. While sex was appealing, I guess it was never so appealing that it ruled out some sense of honor that went both ways in a relationship. My freckled friend lived that other way; Daphne wanted freedom like that; for many others, that defined the "free love" of the time. I knew I could not be on the receiving end of that kind of relationship based on my previous experiences.

My possessions over the time I had lived in Berkeley had remained fairly constant. I did not own much. Everything could fit in my '63 Volkswagen including my bed, which was really just a mattress that could be rolled up and tied with a rope for moving. I once again bundled everything up and moved to the Euclid house.

Peter's former room in the Euclid house had been the maid's room off the garage, and it was to be my room. This was like a separate apartment in the house because it was not near any of the other bedrooms and had a private bathroom. This suited me so I could be a part of the house and yet separate at the same time.

The other rooms were filled with a diverse group of artists, hippies from Mendocino, and others, many of whom I can only slightly recall because my time at the house included work, therapy, and a lot of visiting and going to parties. The house was more of an odd collection of people Peter's girlfriend had allowed to move in rather than a cohesive surrogate family.

The Dana house people had all moved to new places, which in turn expanded the new people who joined the group of friends I would visit or see at parties. William and I had moved to the dark house. I think Joelly may have taken my place later. Others moved to a house at the top of Grizzly Peak on north side. Some moved into houses near the boundary of Oakland in the Claremont area. Only a few people of this group actually lived in their own apartments by themselves. Most situations were group living arrangements where much was shared.

One of the remarkable people at the Euclid house at the time was a young man from L.A. who seemed to have a very charmed way with young women, which I would have loved to have understood. He amazed me. I knew almost nothing of his background even though we conversed a lot. He was not very open about it. He had grown up in Los Angeles but had almost no contact with his family. His appeal to me was that he seemed to have a comfortable grasp on life. He was tall, good looking, and wore his blond hair long. A small, blond mustache, soft, gray-green eyes, and a soft, measured voice completed his demeanor. His dress was casual, consistent with our peers. Although apparently untrained, he had a talent for photography, but the only money I ever saw him make was from selling drugs. He was a study in potential—potential in spite of no nurture, potential in talent, charm, and lost relationships.

His photographs were mesmerizing. He developed them primarily as slides that could then be presented in a show. His subjects were often beautiful young women or other portraits, or close-ups of flowers and plants. The photos were always well composed and lighted in the context of the overall image, but that was not the only power of his work. The power was in the contribution of the background. They did not overwhelm the prime object in a trick juxtaposition, nor did they simply support the prime object as in a traditional composition. The color, composition, and emotive strength of the background were key parts of the effectiveness of each image. That sense was not something that came out of deep critical analysis of his work that might come from a technical study of art but rather a very simple realization from an untrained eye, nor was it some psychedelic drug-skewed sense of importance that only exists in an altered state of consciousness. His images were more physically and emotionally pleasing than many I saw at the same time exhibited in the modern art museum in San Francisco. Ironically, those photos to me seemed like cold lifeless compositions by someone who had very little connection with life. This photographer had some disconnection from life, as well, but his art was directly connected. It said what he could not say, expressed relationships he did not have, and exuded hope that I am not sure he had. Cody's bookstore on the south side of campus offered authors, artists, and others opportunities to present readings, talks, and showings, which he took advantage of to publicly show his work. He also gave us the opportunity on a couple of occasions to host shows at the house.

For someone like me who was not confident in my approach to women, he was appealing to focus on, to study. He could meet women who were interested in having a relationship with him anywhere, anytime. He did not seem to form any lasting attachment and even introduced women who were interested in him to other friends of his. He seemed to live the sexual revolution and fit the Don Juan or Casanova type. While I was envious of his easy way, I never put two and two together and realized that he was a loner. None of his relationships could have been much more than sex because they never included any other connection. My relationships, clumsy as they may have been, were always intended to be relationships; I am not sure his ever were. He was not really a very good model; I just was not experienced enough to realize that.

While he stood out, I am not sure why some of the people were even allowed to live in the house. One odd, seemingly straight, normal person would engage in conversations about how adults could have intimate sexual relations with children. Being a child of my generation, I accepted his right to hold this belief while thinking he was quite creepy; yet, I was not mature or confident enough in my own worldview to tell him so and get him out of the house. The culture was like that. It was not just me. Another fellow resident was a talented but very shy artist I had met previously at the university. A lot of people were invited to stay temporarily on their way through the area. Some of them were from the commune I had visited in Mendocino because they had made friends with Peter and his girlfriend, maybe even through me. Our house was not a drug house, so it was not a crash pad or house where uncontrolled movement, activities, and people led to chaos. Yet, it was also not a house where each person had a full-time job, a steady relationship with a member of the opposite sex, and regular contact with their nuclear family. Although I did not think so at the time, it was a very unsettled environment.

I continued to go to my part-time job and therapy with Terry, which was now a little more affordable since I did not have to pay for my lodging. I continued to visit my friends from Dana house at their various new homes. One regular stop was on Grizzly Peak where they had regular parties, and I enjoyed visiting with them on other occasions. I would also fairly regularly travel to visit my grandmother or go for "coffee time" and see other relatives.

I met a young woman who was a friend of the Reichian therapy woman. We started seeing one another and began a relationship. We made friends and spent good times together. She was a talented artist and had a bright sense of humor. Nonetheless, I continued to be clueless. Out of nowhere it seemed she would say things intended to irritate me. I am not sure whether she was playing or whether she, like me, was having an equally hard time evaluating potential relationships. She too freely exposed relationships she had entered into with other friends, and I found my sensitivity to her verbal barbs put me even more on edge. Although I did not evaluate it at the time, my ability to go with the flow of the times was disturbed by a sense of betrayal where none had occurred; I was insecure in my relationships. In going with the flow, I had no sense that I could have said something to try to set things right. For all the talking about all kinds of things that went on, I did not have skills to have that kind of conversation, and I do not remember a single young woman trying to do the same with me. Maybe it was not just me who was clueless. I do not recall Dr. Bold encouraging me to try to talk about it in our time together. In fact, maybe I misunderstood, or I was so passive that he thought it was not time to talk. Instead, he seemed to encourage me trying my best and moving on. I have since learned that relationships require communication. Skipping from attraction to conversation to sexual intimacy was the pattern; intimate communication was assumed but not practiced. On the other hand, I was so passive and insecure that maybe at least trying had to come first.

Perhaps, as a result, our relationship did not last very long. I snapped in a very uncharacteristic way. As she was driving us down the hill toward the university, the end of an offending group of sentences, said in a tone of disdain and aimed at getting a rise out of me, coincided with us pulling up to a stop sign. Not knowing what to say or how to respond, I simply got out, slammed the door, and walked away. I felt justified in my anger. I did not try to evaluate why it felt so intense for what seemed provocation that was consistent with what I had previously absorbed. I could not stand it this time. However, I could not start a calm conversation or even an angry conversation; I could only make the statement I did. Why was I so cold to someone who, I think at worst, may have erred in sensitivity? Perhaps her comments served to test my dedication to the relationship. If so, she got an answer and was saved from further pain. Perhaps, I was protecting myself from the kind of hurt I had suffered the year before given her exposure of successive relationships. I did not call her; I did not move on to someone else; I just moved on to nothing.

Several weeks later, I ran into her while walking across the campus. I said a polite hello, and she did likewise and no more. While I thought of myself as a pretty nice person, and I think others generally did as well, I felt I was right in this situation. In retrospect, I am just as clear that in addition to being clueless as to the basis of relationships between men and women, I was getting farther from understanding what was right and honorable, even though those were supposedly the ultimate pillars of faith in the love generation. I was truly and deeply lost in a fog. The scar tissue from my hurt was distorting feelings; my therapy was exploring new territory in a way I did not understand yet, and the culture did not help at all. I went back to my work, the general flow of life in the house, and my loneliness. Looking back, I can say that I was coming out of total passivity to a kind of assertiveness but did not have the experience or maturity to soften the edges and blew right past to anger.

Even as I was only just beginning in my therapy with Dr. Bold, I was sure I was doing the right thing to invest in this inner exploration. Sure, I was making progress, although I was not sure what that progress was. I shared with him my experiences and thoughts. He mostly listened and occasionally offered words of advice that I sometimes could not quite comprehend. His advice was very direct and not at all a part of the culture I was immersed in. In some ways, it was more like what might have come from my parents. He was very practical, and he did not make excuses, like so many at the time, for defining a situation. I was trying to take action as he suggested without fully understanding the results I might get, how to deal with the results or if they were consistent with what I wanted or expected, or how to deal with the results if I did not get what I wanted or expected. I had a blind faith, a strong sense of hope, and moved forward in the confusion and discomfort. While I would never have said it at the time, I can look back and realize that faith and hope were continuing to quietly run in the background and had nothing to do with my worldview and how I thought therapy would help me with my life.

Terry often shared more about himself than I have come to believe therapists normally do. However, at the time, I had no other experience of therapy or therapists. As I said, he had been an actor, a professional wrestler, and a salesman before becoming a therapist. He was truly bold in the way he handled himself and perhaps always had been. He had gone through therapy himself with the person to whom I was originally referred. Yet, unlike me who was meek, had never been in a fight, was afraid of speaking in public, and was very shy speaking to women, he in grade school had gone to other schools purposely to pick fights just to beat someone up. Confidence was never an issue for him. Obviously, he had dealt with something else in his therapy than I was dealing with. He was just so completely different from me; yet, I connected with him, and he genuinely seemed to connect with me. At this time, I was only a few months into therapy, so even though I was looking for easy results, I could tell change would take some time.

A Walk in the Park

As the summer and my time at the Euclid house was coming to an end, one of the residents passing through came to interest me. The young English woman from Canada may have been invited to stay there by one of the photographer's friends. She lived in Canada because of a government job her father had gotten her. To me she looked how I imagined English people would, despite never having met any. She had a very pale complexion with just a tinge of that pink cast that I associated with freezing weather. She had a medium build with medium length, blondish-brown, wavy hair. Her most distinguishing characteristic was that she dressed and looked like she wanted to disappear into the background. She made no effort to make herself look in any way feminine. Her clothing was baggy and masculine. It did not fit any of the current styles except anonymous. That and her accent intrigued me.

While I knew she would not be there long, I found a chance to talk to her more than once. I learned that she had only come from England a year previously after finishing her degree. In eastern Canada, she lived in a house like those in Berkeley with a collection of people. She was in our house because she was on a tour, totally on her own, and had hitchhiked across Canada down to Berkeley. Even though I had hitchhiked myself, I was surprised that she had done it alone as a young woman. I had been comfortable talking with her—I thought we were similar—but had a feeling of dread when I heard this, that she was actually more experienced and bold than I was and would not be interested in me.

About this time, the photographer/drug dealer let it be known that he had some mescaline, the psychedelic of motion. I had not dropped acid since my concert date at Dana house in late spring. Before that it had been well over a year. I had never, however, tried mescaline. It was one of those drugs with a great mystique. Part of it was the mushrooms from which the psychedelic affect came, and part was the apparent dominance of motion in the altered state. In my earlier experiences, I had been somewhat careful about who provided the drug. Even in those loose times, I had gotten conservative in just a little time, but I trusted my photographer friend. Whatever the English girl's experience with drugs had been, she was interested enough that we decided to see what mescaline was about together. I was attracted to her even though I expected I was inadequate, and I was pleased that I was an acceptable companion for this adventure.

We bought two tabs and early the next day after taking them, hitched up to Tilden Park, the large regional park behind the Berkeley/Kensington area. We figured that for a drug known for nature's rhythms it would be a good place to be. The sunny August day was warm, not hot. The park was mostly undeveloped forest rather than a formal planned and planted park. The hills rose steeply from a small lake and picnic area and were heavily wooded, particularly with eucalyptus that had been imported early in the century. Hiking trails led off in many directions. We followed a trail up into the eucalyptus wood and paused in a quiet area to just look and listen. By that time the drug was having some affect, and we both noticed the motion of the wind and the rhythmic undulation and individual play of each leaf. The experience was profound and moving, not strange or weird. At the same time, we found ourselves more aware of one another and a sense of unity that in the most natural of ways led us to look into each other's eyes, embrace, and kiss.

We did not notice as a hiker came along; after apologizing for the intrusion, he asked for directions. We were not bothered by the intrusion because we were stoned; we gave him his directions and continued to explore the hill. We found an area not far removed from general trail activity but screened a little by brush. The spot was not intrinsically beautiful; it was spare and foreboding with thorny brush closing in from the sides, yet on the other hand, it was an organic gazebo glowing in the sunlight with stalks and twigs forming a tracery structure. That was the reality—the reality that the drug catapulted into focus. We spent some time there, talking more and then moved on. We spent the rest of the day talking and walking hand in hand sensing the world around us. The images were not peculiar, drug-induced sensations rendered silly in normal circumstances. The drug simply slowed us down and focused our attention on elements already there. The incredible sense of nature blended with our conversation. Looking toward the lowering sun over the hills across an open vale imparted a sense of unity with the elements, and our unity let my verbal expressions of joy and relationship flow unfettered. As we stood on that knoll gazing out, I commented on how two people like us could find some happiness in this world, feeling a sense of closeness with the English girl that was effortless. She did not say anything, but that was okay. A sense of quiet, colorful moving peace defined the rest of our walk in the park.

Because evening was approaching, we made our way to the park entrance down the hill to look for a ride to the Euclid house. In one of those serendipitous moments that too often seem to be tied in with a drug experience or an extraordinary situation, we were picked up by a couple in a white Corvette. The car only had two seats, and in addition to the couple there was their huge St. Bernard dog. I have never understood why they decided they should pick us up. We squeezed in with my friend on my lap and thanked them in our spacey, at peace with everything way. They were a working-class couple; the dog and the car were obvious status symbols. Many might have found ways to mock or roll their eyes. All I could see was nice people, enjoying themselves driving around on a beautiful August evening with their dog, and taking the trouble to give us a ride.

On returning to the Euclid house, we continued talking in my room, or rather I continued talking because the comfort of the day, our relationship, and communication made it easy when normally I was so tentative. I was in a very open and vulnerable state and had been all day. She changed that in a way I did not see coming and in a way that caused that old familiar dread, anxiety, and confusion to descend on me as if it had never been far away. As day turned to night, the light of the potential relationship turned to darkness, and I wondered if the whole feeling of the day had been a figment of my imagination.

She told me that the next morning she had an appointment to meet up with her boyfriend. Being still quite passive, I concealed my emotional shock. The drug by this time was mostly, if not totally, worn off, so I was able to call on whatever faculties allowed me to carry on a conversation as if this was normal, almost expected information, when in fact I was reeling in confusion and stunned into emotional immobility. It would be years before I would understand how co-dependent I was, how afraid I was to state the obvious, and what great expense emotionally I continued to pay for pretending everything was okay. I learned for the first time that she had traveled from Canada specifically to meet her boyfriend. He either lived in Southern California near his mother and stepfather or he had been down visiting them and was just returning to Berkeley, perhaps on his way back to Canada. We continued to spend some time together, conversing in a manner not unlike we had all day, although I was somewhat disconnected. I assume she was even more so though she did not show it. Then, she took the lead, said good night, and went to where she had been staying in the house. Up until her earlier announcement, I had hoped she would be staying with me that night, and I thought we might stay together much longer than that.

I just did not have correct information on which to base my hopes and thoughts. I acted in accordance with what I was experiencing and the feedback I got, which was incomplete or not even real. I sat up most of the night confused, feeling sorry for myself, and wondering why I was such a fool. I assumed she had wanted to be with me but maybe she was naïve about what that might mean. Even though I saw myself as fairly passive, I may have been imagining responses and reactions that were not real. Was all the sense of communication and relationship totally in my mind? Was she just tolerating this ridiculous, silly guy with this sense of peace, nature, and relationship until she could get back to reality? If so, the drug was more powerful, effective, and deceptive than I believe possible. If anything, the drug should have made disguising emotions harder even though we had taken a relatively a mild dose; in fact, it may not have actually been mescaline but really acid. Nonetheless, I was facing a disappointing reality and total confusion as to what I had just experienced. The feeling of connection seemed so good and so much like things were supposed to be. A romance with a happy ending could be written around it. Was it possible she forgot about her boundaries, actually feeling what I felt until reality took over again? I had too many questions that I could never answer. Even though we had only spent the day together, because of the intensity of the experience, my heart was wounded. I really did not fit into this world of easy love. I wanted to be with someone who wanted to be with me.

One of the wonderful conversations I had with her that day concerned how she dressed and presented herself. She purposely disguised her femininity. She would not have been considered stunningly beautiful; however, like most, attractive is the norm and is adequate depending on how a person feels about themselves or their ability to express their attributes. If this were not the case, the world would not have known billions of men and women attracted to one another. The stunners are a small fraction. She was an attractive woman in disguise. Perhaps too frankly but meaning to compliment, I asked her why she did not let her femininity show more. Why did she not dress and present herself in a way that allowed her beauty to show? I did not get an answer, but I did not get a retort either.

The next morning while grabbing some breakfast on my way to work and still confused and disappointed, I saw her in the kitchen. She looked lovely. She was different. She had on jeans that fit and a simple white blouse with a pink sweater over it—a pink sweater! Her hair was neatly combed, and she may have even had on some make-up. We were not alone in the room, but I felt comfortable telling her she looked nice. With a direct, appreciative look, she thanked me. Was her changed appearance because of my conversation with her? Or just for her boyfriend and her previous lack of care purposeful in order to be less attractive to young men? I hoped it was, at least partially, the former.

That was the last I saw her. A couple of days later, one of the residents told me a young woman came by looking for me. I was not expecting anyone, so it might have been her, but I had no way to know or follow-up. I thought about the experience after that without ever a clear understanding of what actually happened. At the time, I just bucked up and accepted it as part of the culture and saw the day with her as cheerfully as possible. The wound to my heart healed, as a relationship never really started. Looking back, at one point in the gazebo of thorns, she paused in a way that might have had meaning, but she said nothing. She also said nothing when I made serious, but perhaps silly, comments about happiness looking toward the sunset. I guess she spoke up when she felt she could and had to. Drugs certainly are selective about the senses they magnify; truths are not necessarily the result.

I was too easily caught up in first impressions and going with the flow. That had been pretty successful with Daphne given the times. However, I was not learning that things did not always work out that way, and I was not ready to accept that. Despite all the popular songs and movies depicting relationships in dysfunction, I naively believed this could work. Daphne and I, being young, got to know one another well before becoming intimate. Things had changed though. Given the circumstances and the times, expecting a relationship to blossom with my English friend seemed reasonable. Nonetheless, as I reflected afterwards, I realized many of her connections mentioned in our day of conversation were quite well-known, political radicals. We might have found ourselves less compatible in real life. Who knows? And, of course, she lived in Canada, a minor detail! Long years would pass before I realized my priorities and expectations were muddled and how blindly I was wandering around in a fog.

While I am sure of my being lost in a fog, clueless and rudderless, I now realize most of my friends were dealing with similar issues. A relationship was my idol. Having set my spiritual side and Christian faith aside, and having replaced it with the religion of the counterculture, I was now replacing or augmenting that with therapy, the human potential movement, and self-improvement through self-awareness. At this early stage, that growth was not working any better in relationships. Something was wrong, but I was in such a fog that I could not see any governing order. Therapy and Dr. Bold gave me a mooring point, and I had hope but I could not see where I was going.

Only a short time later, the Euclid house needed to be turned back over to its owners. The managers must have been panicked about the condition of the house. From an outsider's perspective, meaning outside the culture, houses with a lot of different young people moving in and out must have all looked the same. They were not. Some were treated really badly, not so with any I lived in. I was not mature or confident enough to be the kind of manager I could have been; nonetheless, when the time came to relinquish the house, my sense of responsibility in showing the owners that they did not have a bunch of loonies on their hands destroying their property kicked in. The house had been cared for fairly well, but there were a lot of things to remove and a lot of cleaning to do. Somehow I made sure we did it all. The only mess was that all the keys for the house were in a mug in an undifferentiated mass because we never used them. I think the property manager was truly shocked when I walked her through the now empty house and showed her rooms that were clean and needed almost no work. It had been one year since Peter's girlfriend and her kids moved in. I walked out the door for the last time only seven weeks after having moved back in.

MORE NORTHSIDE
9/70 TO 11/70

Crashing at Grizzly Peak

With the need to leave the Euclid house in the fall of 1970, I had nowhere to go. A room was supposed to be available for me nearby in a house on Milvia near Cedar where my friend from the Mexico trip lived. However, it was not available yet. Some friends from the Dana house now lived up the hill on Grizzly Peak Road and offered to let me stay for a while. Grizzly Peak does not have any grizzlies, but it does sit near the top of the hill looking west toward San Francisco. Euclid curves up from the north side of campus until it meets Grizzly Peak near the top—near Tilden Park where my English friend and I spent the day and where I had gone to the concert during the Cambodian protests. The house was very ordinary. It had three bedrooms on one level above a lower garage. The house sat on an upslope with the street below and a private yard behind. One of the guys from the Dana house was my main contact. Even though we were not close, we had talked often.

While there, my car developed serious engine trouble again. I had little money so was not sure what to do. At the time, John Muir's rather informally published repair manual was very popular and suggested that just about anyone could repair and maintain a Volkswagen. The book consisted of loose pages bound with a plastic spiral and a definite counterculture feel to it. My friend was not too busy at the time and offered to help if I wanted to try to rebuild my engine. I had no experience at all with auto mechanics. I had always been interested in learning new things, especially practical things like this, but had no obvious mechanical gifts or the confidence to try something so unfamiliar. However, he gave me confidence; I would not be alone. Together we got the car into the garage and managed to follow the directions to remove the engine.

I was still working at my part time job in Oakland, so I did not have much time. During a couple of those days, my friend followed the directions to take the engine apart. I then took the heads down to a repair facility to have the machine work done on them. When they were ready, I discovered that my friend had either gotten busier or had lost interest in the project, but I was left with a car taken apart, no experience, and no talent. I did not even have the knowledge, from having taken it apart, what had come from where.

Fortunately, my friend was very methodical—if absent. I seem to remember he was an accountant or bookkeeper. He had marked each item just as suggested in the book. Somehow, over the course of several days, I managed to follow the instructions and get the engine back together. At the very end, my friend jumped in again to help put the engine back in the car. Miraculously, the engine ran, and the car worked. The book may have been informal, but it was effective.

During this short time of living on Grizzly Peak while my car was out of commission, I was forced to walk, hitch, and ride the bus to get to work. The journey was not easy with those combinations of transit. On a clear, warm, sunny day, while walking by the grassy area near the County Courthouse in Oakland, I happened upon an older white man and a younger black man conversing alone. As I approached, I realized that the older man was a well-known lawyer, a defender of various political radicals and the younger man was a noted leader of a black radical group who was accused of murdering a police officer. Their conversation was calm and seemingly ordinary. They made no note of me, even though I was quite close to them and could have heard anything. I was part of the background of grass, trees, and clear skies. Well-known people have ordinary conversations and interactions most of the time. They are only "on stage" for a short time in their day. I was background for their day, but they were also background for mine.

While I wanted to be where things were happening when I came to the Bay Area and even defined myself by being a part of it, I was happy being an anonymous part. Even with the exposure to well-known rock groups of the period, I had never gotten closer, in fact had somewhat purposely avoided getting closer, not wanting to be a "groupie." I did not have a clear sense of myself independent of being part of the culture, yet somehow the next step of actually being a participant rather than an observer was not something I was motivated to pursue.

Because one of my younger brothers had started working up in the High Sierra, I was attracted to exploration. My first effort was typically insane. I hitchhiked into the remote mountains with just a cheap sleeping bag carried over my shoulder with a piece of rope and arrived at the base station late in the day. I bought some individually wrapped American cheese slices and a package of fig Newtons, and I headed out on the trail. The first logical place to stop was a reservoir 2000 feet up a steady ascent. I took no water. Do not try this. Ever. The climb was steep, and the summer weather was hot. A little way up the hill, I met a young man coming down on a horse. We talked, and he loaded me on the back of his rented horse and took me to the top, which was totally against the rules. Only thanks to him did I make it. I walked around the edge of the reservoir and happened on a family from San Jose. They invited me to join them. They were an interesting family of three young girls, a dad who made his living playing music on cruise lines, and a mom who made her living at an adult bar in the San Jose area. They shared their food and water with me and made me part of their family. I think I was partially entertainment for them as San Jose was definitely more Middle America and I looked like a hippie and was from Berkeley. After breakfast the next day, we hiked out together. We passed many serious backpackers with all the proper equipment, some even critical of my friends and their informality—yes, even back in 1970, wilderness snobs existed. I made a mental note and kept hiking. The family gave me a ride back to Livermore where they turned off toward San Jose. They may have forgotten me, but I never forgot them. Perhaps the young girls remembered me because I was their first experience with a "hippie."

That experience hooked me on the High Sierra, and I have been captivated ever since. They are a range with big impact. Climbing slowly out of the central valley, the majesty is mostly unnoticed, simply row upon row of conifers as the foothill oaks give way to the higher elevations. Then majestic granite outcroppings rise amongst the trees. There are many old reservoirs dotted around the landscape. It's a beautiful setting with mountain peaks, streams, rivers, and granite boulders. I often thought of myself as a passive, nerdy kid. In the mountains, I knew I was not. I had no clue in my foggy thinking that I was connecting with something I was seeking.

I talked a lot about my experience, and one of the guys at the Grizzly Peak house wanted to go on a backpacking trip. I arranged it—only this time I drove and had gone to the co-op to purchase a Camptrails backpack, the standard at the time. No snobs were going to look down on me. Otherwise, my gear was somewhat makeshift. We took off with adequate provisions and climbed that horrible hill to the reservoir and beyond. However, the mosquitos were quite bad at the time. My friend could not stand it. I cannot remember if we stayed one night or turned around right then, but we definitely went back. I was very disappointed. I had gotten farther, but I had not reached the backcountry, at least as I defined it.

Another House

I was at the Grizzly Peak house less than a month before the space I was waiting for at a house on Milvia on the north side of campus opened up. Even though I would no longer be crashing there, important connections with the Grizzly Peak house were still in the future. As always, I loaded all my possessions into my VW bug and in one trip moved everything to my new lodgings. The neighborhood, to the west and downhill from the Shattuck Avenue business area, was primarily residential and part of the same north side neighborhood where Daphne and I had lived together for a short time. The house was a small, two-story, older, wooden structure of a style we would have called Victorian, although it probably was not technically so. The entry opened into a living room, the dining room *cum* bedroom, a small kitchen, and informal eating area. Upstairs were two larger bedrooms, a very small bedroom, and the only bathroom for the house. A small cottage with its own bathroom was located in the backyard, which served as the fifth bedroom. My connection with the house was the friend with whom I had gone to Mexico earlier in the year. We had always been casual school friends, but from the trip on, we had become better friends and spent time on several occasions talking about relationships and other such topics. He had the back cottage; a thin, intense, young woman who was an art student had the dining room; a friend of my friend had the front bedroom; a blonde, somewhat spacey, young woman had the other large bedroom; and I had the small upstairs bedroom.

The house had its own character right from the start. It was much smaller than the Dana house and, in fact, smaller than the other houses I had lived in. The group of people was also small since there were only five rooms. We interacted some but were functionally separate residents in the same house. I cannot recall this house ever having a party, for instance.

Shortly after I moved in, the blonde's boyfriend came to visit. Once again, if it was still possible, he was a unique character. He was not a university guy. He had a customized, older pickup truck, wore shiny, dark, leather pants, and carried himself in a confident manner that was compelling, yet not arrogant or cocky. At a time when tattoos were definitely the emblem of working class men or sailors and not, as later, trendy for lots of men and women, he had tattoos.

He was gregarious, the opposite of his quiet girlfriend, and despite our different backgrounds, I enjoyed talking with him, maybe more than some of the esoteric, philosophical conversations with others. This was an ongoing issue: often the "important" conversations did not seem as important as the casual conversations with regular people.

On the morning after his second visit, I was awakened by a great noise of many people in the house. The next thing I knew, the door to my small room was thrown open by a uniformed police SWAT team member demanding to know if I knew our guest and where he was. My heart was racing. We were in the middle of a police raid. They eventually found our guest naked in the attic. They helped him slip on his leather pants and took him away in cuffs. He probably should not have parked his very distinctive pickup truck on the street across from the house. I do not recall knowing what they wanted him for. Needless to say, it was a rude awakening.

A Visual History of Myself

During this time of continued disconnectedness and stumbling around in an emotional fog, I was regularly going to therapy with Dr. Bold. It provided a real anchor of connection because it was consistent, and we were working on me. Otherwise, I was pretty adrift. I did not fully understand what was going on with therapy; yet, I sensed that I needed to keep on, as I would be less afraid and could handle more even if I was unsure what I was doing.

At the time, I had real faith and hope that things would be better and that the fog would clear. But I did not connect that my secular worldview even with self-help did not allow for real faith and hope; it was a dead end on its own, as it did not allow for the metaphysical and something other than the seen reality. This was it and nothing more. I truly thought from reading Reich that I needed to learn to be healthier including sexually or more confident. I could not see that more as a function of my extreme shyness. Dr. Bold was so different from anyone I had ever known. I did not fully understand the process even as I experienced it. However, I knew I needed to keep going; I needed to step out in faith. I sometimes had the courage to disagree with him, having trouble confusing some countercultural nonsense with reality. Sometimes, he would simply, calmly respond, "Oh, really," which I would mentally record only to realize much later that he was right.

As I bounced from Etna, to a free place at Euclid, to crashing at Grizzly, to my own room again at Milvia, therapy was continuing to draw me into reflection. I was starting to grapple with what made me me—what was I born with, what was environmental, and what I could change. Now, I was able to move into the larger front bedroom. I had room to set up a little table and worked on many ideas, trying to think forward and "do" rather than just think, as Terry seemed to suggest. I made the little makeshift table myself with a salvaged piece of thick, clear sheet plastic and some wooden sawhorses I built. I would sit on my bed, as I did not even have a chair. I had "inherited" a regular bed! This was only a step beyond processing ideas in my mind but an important step.

One of my ideas was to take my personal reflections and put them in a visual form. I did have little notebooks where I recorded random thoughts. I had started that with People's Park as part of that "ecology" class when I wanted to keep the chronology straight. I continued that discipline somewhat intermittently after that. However,

I had a vision of an outline that I could see at once that was manifested as key words on a timeline. I wanted to order some of my memories and other factors because I wanted to get maximum benefit of Dr. Bold's insight by providing him with thorough details of my past and what might make me tick. I took a fairly large piece of paper and laid out a chronological timeline horizontally. Vertically, I put in factors such as location, family, memories, and other environmental factors, then placed applicable items in each along the timeline. It was like a matrix with different variables along each axis. In one glance, I had an outline of my life and what I thought had affected me at the time.

Dr. Bold could probably see a lot of my issues and the work necessary without my effort, but this was valuable for me nonetheless. He may also have seen this as more inward focus on my part; whereas, he may have thought I needed to be more outwardly intrepid. Nonetheless, he expressed honest amazement when I showed him the timeline. He said he had never seen anyone create that complete a picture. I did not need encouragement more than that because reflecting on how situations had affected me, even if I could not discern a pattern, was part of the journey for me. I found it immensely useful to more clearly understanding the context of what influenced me and to think about context going forward. I had not been in therapy a year yet, but I had accepted the odd structure of naked breathing, that I was starting to access deeper feelings of sadness and anger, and because of the influence of Dr. Bold, had a mooring point while I drifted through the fog.

While I am struck by the detail I included, I am also struck by how clearly that graph shows my limited and foggy thinking and my subtle but total immersion in my worldview—subtle in the fact that I did not notice it. The chronology and factors were not limited, in fact they were quite complete, except the metaphysical or spiritual was completely missing. Since moving to Berkeley and away from my faith tradition, I had by default accepted the secular humanist "religion" of my environment. I did not think much about the metaphysical. It was not a topic of conversation among my friends. Then, being stunned and lost after my failed relationship with Daphne, I later discovered new hope in the human potential denomination of that religion. I thought I was on a path to finding myself and meaning. Instead I became more lost in the fog. I did not understand that the metaphysical or the spiritual that I had set aside had anything to do with that search for real meaning or ultimate reality.

This narrative has fleshed out a portion of that timeline. While I have, over the years, reflected on what has made me "me," the period while I was in therapy and created the timeline was when I genuinely started a more structured reflection into the context of me, which was really not me but, ultimately, true meaning.

3.

PAST REFLECTIONS

Greater Internal Awareness

The timeline was a tool to clarify the personal reflection and exploration that started running in the background for me. I was trying to discern patterns to better understand who I was. I clearly still believed if I knew myself better and mixed that with understanding how to function better in the world, my life would be more cohesive, and I would be happy. Reich's ideas of how the mind and body were linked still made sense to me—the idea of how the mind through patterning affected the body and in turn that body pattern or armor limited the openness of the mind. I was looking for how I could control things better without noticing that ultimate control was simply not in my power. Nonetheless, I found the exploration very meaningful and still do. I was trying to see more clearly even though I did not know I was in a fog. I have always liked maps and could immerse myself in places near and far by studying a map. This exploration was like an internal mapping, the visual timeline the resulting map. In this case, I had been there, but my perception of "there" was not as clear as I thought it was.

Much later when I set to flesh out details of the timeline, it gave me a sense of order. Most of that is a narrative for another time; however, a brief summary of that narrative timeline is important context for why I was so naively drawn into a fog, took so long to see more clearly what may seem so obvious, yet, had the capacity to do so, and how even with that capacity had to face the humbling reality that foggy thinking was just a step away if I thought I was in control.

Beginning Awareness

My earliest memory is from the trip back from Japan on a converted troop carrier. We had lived in Japan a little over a year while my father was stationed there with the military. I was young enough, only two and half on that trip. I can remember wanting to leave our ship cabin one morning and being told I could not; we could not until the orderly came through the hallway ringing a xylophone-like chime. My father even had the young man come in and show me the instrument when he came past. I can say with only slight hyperbole that one way to describe me from then on was that I waited for the chime to ring before taking action.

When we were back in the states and living in Oklahoma, I have a clear memory of a time when my grandmother from the Bay Area was visiting and we needed to have the water heater replaced. I had somehow conjured up a reality in which an infinitely deep hole existed right below the water heater. I could not be cajoled in any way to come see that it was not true. I was terrified. I can picture it as though I was there at this moment. I have no idea where that fear came from. If you have an idea, please let me know.

Greater Awareness

When we moved back to the Bay Area to San Bruno on the Upper Peninsula south of San Francisco, I was almost four. I was to live there in one house a longer time than anywhere until I was an adult. I lived in Berkeley/Oakland longer, but I lived in fourteen different places.

While the memories from before I moved to California are infrequent snapshots, they changed with that move. Those memories cover a time from the age three and a half to eight such that snapshots changed to scenes. Then, recollection gained meaning and internal questions would be recorded, even if the seamless flow of events and understanding was incomplete. Is it ever? Perhaps because the event of moving is such a striking new experience, I remember clearly approaching our new house as a number of neighborhood children about my age were standing at our driveway. I was intensely shy and would not leave my father's side, but he gave me a pack of chewing gum and told me to offer a piece to each of the children. This I could do; it took the focus off me and onto the gum, so we could all engage through that medium. As I recollect, simple relationships with the children started that day.

My father was stationed at the Presidio in San Francisco. However, housing on post was not available, so my parents had settled on our house. San Bruno was much like the other small towns lined up on the peninsula south of the City. It had grown from the flat area closer to the Bay and along El Camino Real, the road that ran from San Jose in the South Bay along the west shore of the Bay to San Francisco, slowly up the hill to Skyline Boulevard, which ran along the top of the hill. Eventually, it grew beyond that boundary, as well. The businesses and retail stores, at least at that time, were clustered along El Camino Real, and the areas on the slopes, in addition to much of the flat area, were primarily residential.

Our simple home with a Spanish-style character had a stucco exterior and curved terra cotta roofing tiles at the parapet and at small projecting elements. The house sat on the upslope side of the street with a garage underneath and the living areas above with an exterior covered stairway leading to the front door. The back yard was slightly higher than the street, so stairs from the living area led back down to grade from the kitchen area. The house faced across the street and over an empty lot to a view of the Bay and part of the San Francisco Airport, which has never been in San Francisco except through mapping magic. Our house was on a street parallel to the Bay and part way up the slope from the flats and El Camino Real.

My mother soon decided I would benefit from nursery school as an antidote to my shyness. I hated it and cried when she left me. It was called Happy Hall, though it did not seem that way to me. Kindergarten was only slightly better. I walked to school: down a hill, across a busy street, then a park, and up a hill to the school. Where I live today, no one would let that happen because of safety worries. However, the times were different. I got by well enough in school. Answering roll was another matter. I was the only child who never had to answer roll or raise my hand. I only made eye contact with the teacher. I could not do more; I would have fallen totally apart; the teacher understood and made adjustments. I have never known anyone else quite so scared.

First grade was a bigger challenge. Because of the shortage of schools at the time, I had to be bused to a school a long way from home. The school was in a neighborhood close to the Bayshore highway, now the 101 Freeway, close to the airport. Getting there was easy; I caught a bus just down the block. However, no one told me how to catch the bus home. I guess my mother assumed the school would take care of it, and the school assumed I knew. I did not. I was only at that school a short while and must have miraculously taken the right bus most of the time. However, one day I got on the wrong bus. The bus delivered kids way above Skyline Boulevard, now about I-280, and near where the disastrous PG&E gas line fire happened years later. I did not live anywhere near there. Finally, the bus driver got back to the El Camino with only me on board. He asked where I lived. Even though it was not exactly true, I pointed and said, "just over there" in the general direction of where I lived. He let me out and I made my way home. I knew the way. Years later, I suspect a bus driver would be reprimanded or possibly fired for what that driver did. I actually enjoyed it, but I knew well enough not to tell anyone. Often the bus would be late for school because it would have to stop at the tracks for the train to pass. No big deal for some, but I would fall apart on entering the already started class as I took it as a personal failure.

Nonetheless, I liked living in San Bruno. My awareness was expanding. I liked going the Crystal Springs Park and exploring. I remember the occasional trips to the City with my father to tag along to work on a Saturday. I was not aware of world events at this time. I only later knew my father had gone to Korea twice: once when the U.S. was not technically even there and much later when he should have been killed. That incident was the catalyst for my mother's adult spiritual awakening. She had gotten an inconclusive telegram about my father being seriously injured, immediately called a priest who had visited once, and recommitted to her dormant faith. She never wavered from that commitment for the rest of her life. Thus, we began going to church, church school, and church bazaars for the first time in my life. I found it passable; I think I liked the bazaars the most as there were always curious items for sale. Generally, I played by myself and with friends and went to school. We sometimes went to the beach at Pacifica or Half Moon Bay, went on trips to visit friends in King City, and regularly went east across the Bay to visit my grandmother and other relatives. We visited the Santa Cruz Mountains one year, and I particularly recall the scent of the Bay Laurels and the dappled creek water with water skippers. Much like Proust, that smell, not madeleines, immediately transports me back to that place and time. When we finally got a television, later than most, I liked watching old western movies and the Lone Ranger, Cisco Kid, Superman, and Davy Crockett. We took an exhilarating trip to Disneyland not long after it opened. Over time, I was a little less shy and apprehensive because I had come to know and be comfortable in my environment. Getting used to living there took time; however, I developed real roots.

Thus, I was crushed when my mother told me we would be moving to Colorado. I cried. I did not care that I was in my underwear at a family friend's house getting ready for a bath and one of the daughters of the family came in to use the bathroom. Even though that disappointment does not have an active life in me, and I did move on, I can access the incident and the feeling as if it was yesterday.

More Awareness

We did move, and I became slowly anchored to our new life in Colorado Springs. For the first time, I became aware of my Colorado roots through my father and spent time with relatives and my paternal grandmother. I learned the history of the state as part of the fourth grade history curriculum. I loved history. I read lots of simple history books and Landmark biographies on plainsmen and the like. I was enamored of the American Indian culture. I also studied the Civil War. We bought a set of *World Book* encyclopedias when I was in the fifth grade, and I would read them for fun. I also became aware of current events and global players for the first time: Cuba, Russia, nuclear risk, sputnik, Eisenhower, and Khrushchev.

Colorado in general was a dramatic departure from the Bay Area. I really did not know anything else. Initially, coming down off the Wolf Creek Pass near the San Luis Valley of southern Colorado was so dramatic. Leaving California, the Sierra Nevada are almost unnoticeable as the foothills slowly climb and then drop precipitously into Nevada. Then, crossing the large seemingly flat expanse of Nevada and Utah to my young eyes must have been boring. However, my young mind wondered at the experience of climbing the mountains out of Durango and then dropping into the valley surrounded by steep mountains, dark conifer trees, and snowcapped peaks here and there. My dad was now back in his country; he always referred to himself as a Colorado boy. At the time, I did not fully appreciate the San Luis Valley as it was very flat. I would come to appreciate that I could see the mountains all around: the Sangre de Cristo on the east, the La Garita Range to the north, the San Juan's to the west, and to the south, the Valley seemed to pour into northern New Mexico, Taos, and beyond.

Colorado Springs was more dramatic being solidly anchored by Pike's Peak, dead center, just west of town. Most of the city was a relatively flat plain looking right at that peak. I only much later came to see San Francisco and the Bay as the defining physical elements of the Bay Area with the Golden Gate Bridge and the fog being the iconic elements. At that time, my world was San Bruno, the hills, the El Camino, Bayshore Boulevard, and the Bay in the distance. Colorado Springs was different; the iconic Pike's Peak immediately set a sense of place and order. If ever in doubt, just look west; I saw it that way then and still do. For the first time in my awareness, I experienced snow and the thrill of being snowed in for days.

I loved to explore our neighborhood, which was on the outskirts north of town with lots of empty land. I had quite a few friends. We would ride bikes and play together. Even though I was terribly afraid, I asked to take swimming lessons at the YMCA as part of a Saturday activity program. I learned to swim, but diving was not in the cards. I had a better time with the crafts part of the program and later continued in the summer with day camps outside of town that involved hiking and exploring. I learned to dislike church school while living there. I found the teachers uncomfortable with themselves, and that made me uncomfortable. I was a generally compliant child because of my shy, fearful nature; however, I hit a wall with church school. I would refuse to go in and would just sit in the car. One time, I decided to walk home despite living about five miles away. I arrived home at about the same time as my mother. I am not sure how she dealt with it. I was not punished, but the next time I refused to go, I was. Ironically, church was okay. I cannot explain why but it made sense; church school did not.

As I entered sixth grade, I started to become aware of popular music. I was the oldest in our family, and we did not have a record player, so I didn't have a ton of exposure. On visits to the San Luis Valley in the summer, my uncle, who delivered appliances to the small towns around Alamosa, would take me with him. He would play early rock and roll music on the radio. Shortly thereafter, we did get a small portable record player and a few albums, one of which was a compendium of popular songs of the time. Many were iconic and still represent the times such as "In the Still of the Night". I even had a girl I liked in school, nothing more than that. Others knew as well. One of the girls who had parents a little more "advanced" than mine had a party where boys and girls were invited. She asked if I wanted to come and could she invite that girl. Maybe she liked me too; I do not know. It was a good party. I enjoyed myself and even danced. But, that nice girl moved away.

I had done well in school and was set to start advanced classes at the junior high. However, I was once again informed that we would be moving. It was not as heart wrenching for me as before but close; all my roots and connections would be gone. The disappointment of having to leave another home was only slightly dampened by a summer of travel adventures, which fed my yearning to see and experience the world. Because my father was taking training in Texas, we were left with the burden of packing and leaving the house where probably the happiest years of my youth were spent. I remember looking out the front window at the small tree and consciously placing myself years in the future with the same view and seeing the tree grown. By now the tree has probably come down, but the scene lives on in my memory as does that little suburban neighborhood north of town.

First, we took a trip to California on the train to visit my mother's family in the Bay Area. Then, we returned to get our car and went south through Taos, New Mexico, and Indian country to El Paso. Once there, we also got to go to

Juarez for a day, which I found fascinating. The culture was so different and yet just across the river. The whole trip was breathtaking and inspiring. Unfortunately, we had to end it, return to Colorado, and drive to Wisconsin.

Spiritual Awareness with Backward and Forward Internal Growth

The trip to Wisconsin was another adventure to me. This was my first experience with the plains states and the edge of the Midwest. The mountains were gone. Eastern Colorado and Kansas seemed really flat and not that interesting to me except that the towns had a western agricultural feeling I had found appealing in their remoteness and independence, separated by miles and miles of fields. Nebraska was similar except corn forever was the dominant element, and that flowed right into Iowa. From Nebraska on, the countryside was greener than I was used to. Wisconsin was verdant, moist, and of varied terrain with lots of trees and towns situated in natural rather than urban landscapes. The humid weather was new to me. I tolerated it but never got used to it. Air conditioning was not in homes at that time. Our new home was located in Hales Corners, a small, outlying community that had become a suburb to the southwest of Milwaukee.

The year was filled with tumultuous, internal experiences for me. I think I could write a book about that year alone. For the first time in my memory, we did not live in our own house. We lived in one provided for my father, and it was the nicest we had lived in. It was bigger, on a large lot with some woods behind, and in a good neighborhood—maybe one of the nicest houses in that neighborhood. For the first time, I noticed feeling prideful. The kids were way more urban and advanced than in Colorado. They were big, socially advanced, and intimidating. Even so, they were kind, and I made some good friends, even though I knew we would only be there year.

Despite being in a good neighborhood, the school was not close to the quality of my Colorado school. The history program used the exact same book I had studied the year before in sixth grade. The rest was paltry. I could not control myself. I came home crying with frustration looking for my parents to get me out of this mess. They were sympathetic but were not used to making waves. I did get to do a separate history program along with the existing one. The teacher was very accommodating, and the kids took total advantage of him by playing practical jokes. I found a way to cope, and if I could have broken through into the social culture might have liked it more. Once I walked all the way to a dance and turned around, unable to go in. I was more aware of the youth music then. American Bandstand was still broadcast from Philadelphia. I remember the New Year's broadcast of 1959/1960 with Frankie Avalon and Fabian. That was long before Dick Clark moved to L.A. and New Year's became "Rockin' New Year's." The music was a vicarious way for me to participate in the youth culture, as so much of it was focused on boy/girl relationships. My only other participation, also vicarious, was in regular television programs. The early westerns had now been replaced with iconic 50s classics like *Ozzie and Harriet*, *Father Knows Best*, and *Leave it to Beaver*.

I discovered *Mad Magazine*, which had only started publication a short time earlier. I immediately subscribed with my meager funds and was to do so for a long, long time. It was a lifeline; I loved the quirky humor. I was particularly drawn to *Mad*'s depiction of Beatniks, the precursor to my attraction to the counterculture. At that time, I also became familiar with another publication that was very new on the scene, *Playboy* magazine. I had zero knowledge of this aspect of life. We were at dinner with friends. They had no kids, so my siblings and I were on our own. I would often look at books; however, in this home a few copies of *Playboy* were laying on a table. I looked and was intrigued by what I saw—needless to say I liked it. At this time, Playboy was a trailblazer in legitimizing the "girlie magazine." The images were very tame by standards soon to develop, just pretty, young women with bare breasts. However tame, I had taken a step out of my childhood, never realizing that it was not really innocent at all.

My attitude toward church took a dramatic shift immediately on moving. Our church denomination had different styles of worship known as high church and low church. I had only been familiar with low church, which I found pleasant enough (as opposed to church school, which I hated). Our new church was high church. They genuflected and sometimes crossed themselves. I believe they used incense as well. Something more powerful than just the form was transforming my approach to this part of my life called church. The rector was the one who dealt with kids my age—confirmation age, or about 12 years old. The rector was very comfortable with his faith and communicating it. Sunday school was gone. I understood the gospel message that Jesus was God and man and that he came to offer salvation that we could get no other way. I learned the creeds and understood them as well as I could at the time. I was confirmed by the bishop and knew this time as a true spiritual awakening and transformational experience. I never missed youth meetings and church. I was hungry for more.

Back at school, one of the girls in our class died of leukemia. This was a small-town school where many kids had been together their whole lives. A vote was taken on attending the funeral; I knew I did not want to but did not have the courage to stand out. It was an open casket funeral service, and we all filed past. She looked like she was alive. I was internally terrified and conflicted. She was here; she was gone. The experience took on a life within me, and it took me a long time to process. I had terrifying dreams of being buried alive for ages after.

During the summer, I had a great time riding bikes in the large regional park nearby. We would go to the Dutch-land Dairy to get ice cream or French fries and catsup. The most fun was going in the evenings to the car races. Our little community had an iconic small dirt track where modified roadsters raced on the weekends. My friends and I went all the time and got to know the names of certain favorite drivers. At that time, many of the cars were chopped up '32 Fords. When it had rained, we dodged mud clods churned up by the rear tires at the chain link guard fence, which did not serve as an effective barrier.

For the disappointment of school, my social immobilization, and enduring the haunting funeral, that short year was transformational. I mean this particularly in the spiritual sense but also with the awareness of the music of the times, *Mad Magazine*, and through the experience of the racetrack. Music became the common language of the youth culture, most of it focused on unrequited love, which I could relate to. *Mad*, as I said, was a godsend to my isolated, developing self with its sophisticated, quirky humor. The racetrack was something the like of which I never experienced on a regular basis again. As far as I know, they did not exist where I lived before or since.

Regular people attended, and I was very comfortable in the environment.

Some Freedom from the Youth Culture

Alaska was our next stop with a brief stop in route at my grandmother's house in the East Bay where we lived for about 3 months. I enrolled in the local school to start the eighth grade. School presented a new challenge for me this time. The school system was good, and I was placed in an advanced class. I felt some prestige in that. I was more and more aware of status. While I liked the status and the challenge, I found I was actually way behind because of my year in Wisconsin. As an example, our spelling list was 20 words long, all nouns and verbs; in addition to writing them out, we simply had to identify them as nouns or verbs. I did not have a clue how. Saying nouns were words for things and verbs were action words did not help. My mother had to help me each evening with my English homework, learning about punctuation, diagramming sentences, and the like, just so I could keep up.

Our class won a contest, and the prize was an evening party and dance. I do not remember how I mustered the courage to go. The kids were not as threatening as in Wisconsin. It helped that the party was just our class, and the teacher was supervising. For that evening, I recaptured some of the feeling from Colorado: I was comfortable in the group; I was comfortable dancing; and I had fun. In mid-November, I had to leave abruptly. There was a silver lining. One girl who I had danced with actually came up to me and said good-bye—I was easy to please. Years later, while looking at one of my cousins' high school yearbook to see if I remembered anyone, I saw that this girl was the valedictorian. Socially, I actually felt a part of this school because situations were structured to include everyone.

After a brief stop in Washington, we flew to Alaska, arriving at Thanksgiving time. That was my first plane flight. Flying was not as common then as now, but it was a primary way to get to Alaska as only one rugged road existed. I was excited about this move and adventure for a change. At the time, Alaska was more remote and less populated. It had only been a U.S. state for about a year. The pipeline, which was to bring so much work, money, and people to the state, was still many years in the future. The entire state is more than two times larger than Texas; yet, at the time, the population was only 100,000, and Anchorage, the largest city, only had a population of 50,000. The post we lived on was just a few miles out of Anchorage. We were surrounded by nothing but dense forest with the steep, snow-covered Chugach Mountains immediately to the east. Huge moose regularly walked through where we lived. The winter, while not as dark as in Fairbanks, left only a twilight midday. We went to school in the dark and returned in the dark. Anchorage had relatively mild weather for Alaska due to its proximity to the water and position fairly south in the state. Wisconsin actually had more snow our previous winter than that first winter in Alaska. It was colder, but the summers were pleasant.

For the first time in my memory, we were living on an army post rather than in a regular community. Our home in Alaska was on a full remote military installation. I was excited by the adventure of that, as well as the frontier aspects of the state. Everyone on the post was part of the military; all the kids were from military families. The schools up through the ninth grade were on the post. It was a small integrated community. Stores, movies, sports, and entertainment were all there. They needed to be: Alaska was still a modern frontier. Initially, at least, I was drawn to the movies. I had never gone much, but now could because they were only $0.25. Because it was a military post, it was a small integrated community racially as well. I never witnessed any negative issues around integration there. It was seamless. One of my best friends was Filipino.

My spiritual life did not actively grow during the two and a half years we lived there. We sometimes went to the main church in Anchorage. More often we went to an early chapel service on post. I still felt the same about my commitment, but without mentoring, my dedication was mostly legalistic in not ever missing church on Sunday. I did not have the mentoring of my Wisconsin priest; I was not growing spiritually. My social life with young women did not actively grow during this time either. I was still on the edge. I listened to music and went to the post cafeteria for French fries with my friends during regular school times, but social functions were not as big a part of life. Alaska was really remote. Television shows were several weeks behind their normal schedule. While the movies were cheap for the soldiers, most things were quite expensive. A Coke that was $0.10 in the lower forty-eight was $0.25 on post.

I did not sense any of this as being left out or stuck in the "boonies" as I would later when moving back to California and the Central Valley. Alaska was far more remote. For that reason, the youth culture of young love and rigid standards of dress, activity, and status was quite weak. Alaska had elements of this, but perhaps because the state was so separate and the nature of life so different, the reality of the place was stronger than any new culture. No one cared very much. It may be that the youth culture had not yet arrived or that living on the edge of a huge wilderness made that culture seem frivolous. There were not many people, retail amenities, or other distractions of the lower forty-eight. Only as we were leaving did Anchorage get a JC Penney store.

School was my main activity. I was on post for the end of eighth grade and all of ninth grade. Ironically, in this wilderness environment the schools were excellent. Many teachers were there for an adventure themselves. I got to take shop-type classes I took leather work and drafting, both of which I enjoyed. The academic classes were more rigorous than my Wisconsin classes. I took Latin. My home room teacher did a special set of lessons on Vance Packard's *The Status Seekers*. I devoured it. I had a thirst for anything that helped me understand order in life, especially history. Unfortunately, I also was too naïve to see that whatever was called status, while maybe describing order, did not help with ultimate meaning. When I got to high school in Anchorage, the choices in classes expanded. I continued with a solid curriculum that included Latin and Geology, taught by a Ph.D. in geology from Bryn Mawr. I loved that class. Alaska is a terrific place to study geology. Living in the environment made it possible to better understand those USGS maps and forms.

The wilderness was wonderful. During the summer, I worked as a caddy at the golf course just outside of the post about a mile. I would ride my bike hands-free down the gravel road, often seeing a bull moose to the side and sometimes smelling bear in the distance. The mountains rose straight before me. Once we went to see as a herd of caribou spent days crossing the highway in the Matanuska Valley. I do not know how many there were—thousands maybe? On drives to Seward on the weekend, we would drive right past the Portage Glacier. On other trips, we had to camp because no motels existed at that time. In Valdez, long before the infamous oil spill, we saw salmon spawning such that every bit of water was absolutely brimming with fish. Alaska was an incredible place to be at that time and at that time in my life.

We lived through the Cuban missile crisis in a very palpable way. We were on the front lines because of the SAC air base next to us. We were moments from being evacuated to a more remote location when everything settled down. Toward the end of our tour, the uncle I used to tag along with delivering appliances in Colorado passed away. On the way back from his funeral, my father was in a plane crash; miraculously no one was killed.

His plane went down somewhere in the ocean near Sitka. The panhandle of Alaska, which reaches most of the way down to Washington is an area mostly accessible only by boat and plane with thousands of islands and often overcast skies. His plane had four engines and lost one at a time as they kept going. Finally, with only one engine, they ditched in the ocean. Fortunately, it was a clear day, and several fishing boats were able to mobilize, saw where they ditched, and were close enough to come to the rescue. The plane sank in 20 minutes; the frigid water meant certain death in a short period, but they all survived and were taken to Sitka. My father had to leave his post in Alaska early to transfer to Walter Reade as he got a serious ear infection. When he should have died in Korea, his ear drums were blown out. As a result, he no longer swam; however, in the plane crash, sea water found its way in, causing the infection.

Back into the Cauldron

My parents had arranged to purchase a home in California while we were still in Alaska. Our new home was to be in a small town in the Central Valley, the great agricultural area that at the time and maybe today grows most of the food for the nation: more rice than Japan, more cotton than the south, etc. The particular mix of agricultural focus varied: cotton, rice, corn, tomatoes, peaches, apricots, walnuts, almonds, grapes for wine and raisins, dairy ranches, cattle ranches, and more. Industry was usually related to agriculture: canning, eggs, food products, wine and the like. The Central Valley is relatively flat, lying between the Coastal Range on the west and the Sierra Nevada on the east and from Redding in the north and Bakersfield in the south. My parents had picked our town because it was not too far from my mother's home in the East Bay.

My parents met during the war at Camp Roberts near Salinas, which was the huge deployment staging post for the South Pacific campaign. They married at her home in the East Bay, and honeymooned in Carmel on the Monterey Peninsula near where they met. Their adult lives were tied to California. Many of their wartime friends still lived in California. Our house was a nice one in the country, just outside a small town with a population of about 3,750. The whole valley was connected north to south by Highway 99 along which most commerce moved. To the east and west, smaller communities like ours that had a high school, banks, and other businesses served as centers of activity and were fed by even smaller, more limited communities. Our town's downtown was only a few blocks long and a few blocks wide, but it was still lively.

Alaska finished the school year in early May, so we travelled to our new home while school was still in session in California. My mother and I went to the school bringing all my high school records. They accepted them with no notice whatsoever of my top marks, and I was registered for the next year. Even though the high school was in a small agricultural town in the Central Valley, I found it intimidating because I immediately noticed that the kids were different from those I was familiar with in Alaska. They were part of some group or culture I could not identify because I had never seen it before. They looked the same and wore the same clothes. In Alaska, people, even kids, were individuals at that time. I had been separated from the growing element of a youth culture which had its rules and regulations for almost three years. I may have been in the "aggie" Central Valley, not even the sophisticated coastal urban areas, but the kids were sophisticated compared to me, or so I thought. The guys were athletically good looking, and the girls seemed to all be blond, thin, and attractive. Everyone seemed to have tanned skin.

I spent the summer without friends. Reading Herb Caen filled the gaps, and I began to tour and familiarize myself with the City through his writing. I was already connecting my earlier experiences with USGS maps; I could "be there" because of the mixture of place, history, characters, and day to day life in his columns.

Our house had a swimming pool, so I tried to get a tan on my skinny, pale white body to look like the other kids. It was hopeless. I was naturally pale, but, beyond that, I needed time to get used to the change in environment. The Central Valley is incredibly hot in the summer. Air conditioning, if available, was not in common usage. The sun shines brightly every day, and in the summer, it never rains. Some days start so hot in the morning that any thought of coolness or a breeze vanishes from the mind. At least the heat is dry, unlike Wisconsin, but with temperatures often over 100 for days on end, I needed time to adjust.

Along with high, dry heat comes great agriculture where irrigation is present otherwise only dry, yellow grass in the fields and foothills. The dirt was so dry that the slightest breeze could pick up dust. The original Spanish settlers had stayed mostly out of the valley, but they had developed a lifestyle that dealt with the heat. Houses were built with adobe walls, courtyards, and overhangs. The day started early when it was cool, stopped midday for a rest when it was oppressively hot, then continued into the evening when it was cooler. Although most construction now was wooden and uninsulated, most of the older farms and most of the valley had porch overhangs for houses, and there was extensive tree cover for yards both on the farm and in the towns.

That summer moved by swiftly because of the new environment and visits to my grandmother and extended family in the Bay Area. School started again much too quickly. I had become familiar, I thought, with the youth culture and had observed the clothes to wear to fit in. I went out with my mother to our larger city on Highway 99 and purchased the clothes, only to find that students were dressier on the first day of school and then settled into the real uniform. So, I spent the rest of the year wearing clothes I did not like and did not really make me fit in better. Oh, for Alaska.

I also learned quickly that my grades and the classes I had taken in Alaska meant nothing to the administration. The school had advanced classes, but I was not offered them. Most of the better students took a full course load, while mine was one class short with a study hall instead. I tried to take advantage of the time, which almost no one else did. The classes were not as rigorously taught as those

I had taken in Alaska. The contrast was striking. I was left feeling once again that I was missing opportunities and being shortchanged in my education. I was not as unhappy as I had been in Wisconsin, but I was very unhappy and felt powerless to make any changes. My parents knew I was one of the better students, knew I was frustrated, but were still not equipped to do anything about it. It would not have occurred to them to talk to the school or consider an alternate, nor could we afford a private school. I accepted the disappointment and did my work. The teachers were good enough and the students friendly enough, but the discipline and respect afforded the teachers which I had come to expect in Alaska simply did not exist. I was really sad, and the work was just not demanding. I was in the middle of nowhere Central Valley farmland with no friends and with the one challenge I had come to appreciate—school—a step backwards, again. I yearned to be somewhere else, but did my best to adjust to my environment with a positive attitude. How ironic that the wilderness of Alaska had a more rigorous educational environment and more personal freedom to grow; it did not have as much of the conformist youth culture that was to more and more push me to the edge.

One of those teachers ill-treated by the students taught U.S. history. He was an excellent teacher and mixed in current events, which for the times meant the civil rights movement that was in full flower. Martin Luther King's Washington March and "I have a dream" speech had just happened at the end of the summer of '63. The earlier protests were all fresh events. The civil rights legislation was being considered. I had never encountered racism as far I knew. I had mostly lived in white communities. However, that did not mean everyone was white; others were a minority, but I was unaware of any conflict. When I lived in Alaska, I was part of a fully integrated community. Although that does not mean some of the minorities may not have felt fully appreciated or that racist incidents did not occur. My hometown was mostly white, although we had lots of Hispanics in our classes. We did not have any blacks. One of the most popular young men in our class was Mexican-American..

Nonetheless, we had two groups who took the opportunity of our history class and the engaging teacher to introduce racism. I kept up on the news, so I was aware of the civil rights struggles. The anti-black sentiments in the civil rights discussions were mostly voiced by a young man whose family was originally from the South. He was a football player, and other football player friends joined in with his position. Most of the comments were obviously stupid and may have had some real basis for him, but mostly he wanted to push back against the teacher. The other racist sentiment was anti-Semitism. I am not aware that we had any Jewish students in our school. The two students expressing these sentiments were smart and I believe acting a part, again pushing the teacher. I did not really know anything about Jewish people other than that they were part of the Bible. I was not aware of the conspiracy theory that Jews controlled banking and other important institutions. The two faux Nazis talked about the Latin teacher being Jewish, but I knew she went to our church. It made no sense. Again, they got a stage on which to perform in history class, and it made for good, if ugly, theater. Certainly, none of this was what the teacher had in mind when he brought up the power of the civil rights struggle in a modern context.

I was much too shy to try to join in with those who shared my interests, and because my grades could no longer define me, I had to start over. Being on the edge, I befriended edge people. Some were just quiet like me, some waited for the same bus as I did or had a class with me. Most were just regular people who had not mastered the skill set of the youth social system but would probably be fine in real life.

In the time before physical education in the morning, I spent my time visiting with a friend whose background was totally different from mine. He was my age, but to me he looked much older. He lived like no one I had met before. My communities had either been very similar to me or stringently defined, like the military. My new hometown was different. While mostly white, in one place it ran the gamut from rich to poor and traditional to shabby. My friend lived with his father in the poorest part of town where the houses were dilapidated. Although the town was small, we never drove in that part of town, but once with friends, I asked to drive through to understand better where he lived. His house had an unkempt, mostly dirt yard with weeds sprouting all around. The whitish paint was peeling off the exterior walls of the house. Many of the boards had no paint at all. His mother lived in a nearby town. I did not know anyone else whose parents were divorced, partially because of my environment and because divorce was not as common as it came to be only a few years later. I also had never known anyone who lived in town and shot at rabbits out of the kitchen window without even opening the screen. I liked him, and we had many great conversations, but our shared world was those locker room conversations before class. If I felt I was in fairly traditional classes for those advancing toward college. My friend would be lucky if he made it through graduation.

High school football and basketball were big attractions in small valley towns like ours. We had a fairly good football team, so I started learning to daydream about the heroics of those playing. I couldn't help but notice that those players were also the ones who would be noticed by the cheerleaders and other girls in demand. I lacked both the talent and size to play. I could only imagine.

The school had one recent graduate who had gone to the Naval Academy and made the football team. The whole town, or at least it seemed to me, was as proud as if he was their own son or brother—or even themselves. My family did not particularly watch football or any sports on television, but it happened that my haircut appointment downtown coincided with a nationally televised Army/Navy game that was tuned in especially because of this young man while the two barbers cut hair. The shop was typical of many at the time: a small, main street storefront where getting a haircut and connecting with the culture and community were equally important. The conversation ran from politics to hunting to just about anything. I particularly liked the discussions, heard on more than one occasion, about mountain road adventures. I could picture these rugged, primitive roads and wanted to go explore. One in particular, the Tioga Road, wound its way steeply down the backside of the Sierras from Yosemite and was, in the not too distant past, still dirt and known for its steep, narrow curves. However, on this particular fall day, the TV, the attention, and the conversation were all on the game. The team's quarterback was nationally ranked and expected to go on to a professional career, so most of America was focused on him. But I had not experienced anything like the thrill of hometown pride as the native son hero caught a pass, and his name was followed by "from our town, California." I had lived there all of five months, but the sensation was no less for me than if I had lived there my entire life. I had not experienced this kind pride in a person connected to a place and time before.

That fall JFK was assassinated. As with everyone else in the country, I watched the endless coverage on our basic television. I remember clearly first hearing the news while waiting for the bus at school. For me, the coverage of the Free Speech Movement at Berkeley was an event almost as memorable—not that it competed with the assassination, but that it related to a place close by, college life, and an alternative culture that was intriguing to me. This was like the Beats only more political. Not much really changed at high school though.

Cars were a big part of high school life, and lots of the guys had cars. The '54 Chevy was the iconic car to have at the time. It was not even that old, but a lot of kids could afford to have them, or their parents could. In those days, kids came from many miles, maybe as many as 20 or 30, from outlying rural areas to my high school. The bus took forever, and a car served a very practical purpose for many of the kids. I dreamed of having a car. I learned to drive that fall and would drive the extra family car. When we needed a new one, I went shopping with my father. Because of me, we looked at an ad for a '54 Chevy. It was on a used car lot. The price was too good to be true and was simply a teaser to get people onto the lot. It was a piece of junk in the back. I did not understand that people even did things like that. My father did and got quite angry with the salesman; I was quite angry with my father because he was being so rude. It took me awhile to come around to understanding that he was right about what was going on and right to call the salesman on it. He refused to consider anything else they had as he did not trust them anymore. I filed that humbling lesson permanently. No '54 Chevy, but just like the clothes, it was just not me.

That fall, those of us who were college bound took the PSAT. The test was used to prepare for the SAT college entrance exam the following year and was also used for qualifying for National Merit Scholarships. The results came out after the new year. I had no idea how I placed in this school except that I was not even included in the college bound group though I knew I belonged there. A student I knew somewhat and would come to know better had the highest score and qualified for a scholarship. Next came me and then one of the attractive, popular girls in the next category: not qualified for a scholarship but receiving recognition. I was pleased and a little too proud of how I had done; now someone would have to at least include me. I took a different notice of the girl, as well. She was not one of the studious girls I would have expected to have the highest score. She was an enigma to me—attractive, moving in what I thought was the fast crowd, yet the smartest girl by test results. I noticed but only from a distance. All of a sudden I was called into the counselor's office, told I had done well, and that they would like to have me take some other tests as they thought maybe I should be in the college preparatory class. I was pleased and said not a word about my transcript from Alaska that had been ignored by the administration. At least I had gotten to experience study hall, which included guys turning their pencils into darts by pushing a pin up through the eraser and tossing them to stick into the ceiling; to my horror, I was given detention along with them just because I would not squeal.

My senior year was to be different. My parents had decided—with us kids' agreement—that we should offer to host a foreign exchange student for the year. I was excited if for no other reason than that things might be less boring. Our student was a young man about a year older than I was from Italy.

We made the trip up to Mills College in Oakland to pick up our student. I was taken by the feel of that campus. The buildings and the grounds gave me the sense that this was a substantial place at which substantial things happened. The buildings were predominantly Spanish eclectic stucco with arched roof tiles. The grounds had open lawns with majestic trees shading the area. It added to my romance with the Bay Area.

From letters and pictures, we were already prepared for our student to be different but not for how much different. He was not shy. He was physically and verbally expressive, and not reticent about his interest in women. At school he was sometimes made fun of because of how "out there" he was. A part of it was his liveliness, and part of it was an almost manic egocentrism. Considering our differences, we got along fine. Actually, for me it was good to have him forcing me more into the life of the school. Sometimes, I got the real feeling of phoniness though. Our school had a service club; not many existed then even though now almost every school requires service hours. This service club was by invitation only and primarily had the popular boys in it. I had not been invited the year before; appropriately, our exchange student was invited, and by default I was, too. I was probably overly sensitive to that but always felt I was extra baggage.

Our student would have some contact with other exchange students in the area and arranged to go with an Italian girl to a dance in a nearby community. Eddie, a friend of mine, who was friends with our student as well, helped arrange it. For some reason I got wrangled in too because a third girl was involved, as well. I survived. In fact, I actually had a good time. I enjoyed the dance, although I think I was in a constant state of stress. I was certain that everyone would notice that I could not dance, did not understand social rules, and was not cool.

Because of the service club, I was set up to sell tickets at one of our school dances. Usually, the dances were after football and basketball games. I went to most of the games as a lot of people did, but never went to any dances. My social life with young women had not advanced at all because I was so fearful. I was very lucky in that the other student selling tickets with me was very comfortable with people. He could easily make contact just in selling a ticket. He was the student who acted as the MC at school gatherings in the gym whenever something was being presented or announced. I was able to watch him, stand in his shadow, and enjoy what I was doing. I wish I could have done it more. I stayed for the dance, although I only sat in the stands. I could not have risked making a fool of myself or letting others realize that I was an outsider who did not know the rules. I admired the same attractive girls that other guys admired, but I believed that I was not cool like the other guys who were good at sports. I did not understand at the time that they really did not know who they were or what they were doing either, but they could take action, and I could not. I was immobilized.

The extension of cars being a big part of school life was cruising on the weekend. Kids from all the small rural towns would converge on main cities along Highway 99. My friends were no different. The pattern would vary—it could be a loop, or it could be a strip. Where we lived the pattern was up a one-way street several blocks, cut over, and down the reverse one-way street. This allowed for lots of car to car conversation and some fake racing. The real racing took place on very straight country roads. Just past our house was one of those sites with hand painted, white lines neatly done by the county, perhaps not realizing their purpose. The cruising itself sometimes ended in seeing a movie, getting food, and meeting other young people— hopefully of the opposite sex. I was very attracted to this scene but avoided it for obvious reasons. No way would I know how to function in that environment. Eddie and his friends went regularly, and he regularly threatened to take me. I was intrigued but partially thankful each time he did not come through. Finally, he came through. I went along and was thrilled and terrified the entire time. What a frightened, simple person I was. I did not have to talk to any girls other than those Eddie or his friends knew, which did not count. I had to ride with them as they ate condiments in restaurants then placed the unfinished part back in the common server, put pepper in the top of the salt-shaker, and urinated in people's gas tanks. At least, they did not rob anyone. I had fun; for who I was, once was enough.

The history teacher who was teased by some of the kids was one of my favorites and also taught speech, debate, and drama. I could never think of doing speech. I only went along on some of the debates because our exchange student and Eddie did. I was interested in the presentation of ideas but could not think of actually having to say something, be looked at, and perhaps appear foolish. However, for some reason, when the same teacher announced auditions for the senior class play, I went and tried out. I was excited and so anxious that days later after the list had been posted, I was too afraid to look. When the teacher asked if I had looked; I could not even respond. He must have been wondering who he had picked if he could not even look at the list. I was not disappointed. While my part was more solid background than full of chances to be dramatic, it was fourth in number of lines.

Participating in the play was my first and only real extracurricular involvement in all of high school. I found it easy to learn and play my part because it was not me, it was the character. I do not think I was particularly good as I was still very shy, but many were surprised, maybe shocked, that I was even in the play. I enjoyed the interaction with the others, which I had never had before. I got a chance to stand out during one late practice when I changed my lines in mid practice to respond that the protagonist "would not be down because he was on the john." It fit right in; a slow double take was necessary to catch that something was wrong. Everyone enjoyed the joke, perhaps even more wrestling with the idea that it came from me. During one of the practices, one of the girls, an attractive, young woman who was something of a flirt, took my glasses, put them on and was generally playful. I thought she was making fun of me and responded with too much concern for my glasses and no humor. She was just playing and maybe flirting a little, but I did not have a clue. I was at my limit just being in the play. Being a part of the play was the best fun I had in all of high school.

About this time, Eddie introduced me to new music. Like most kids of the time, I followed the top ten-type songs on the radio. The late 50s groups had blended into Motown, surfing sounds, then the English groups. First came the Beatles, who did not really appeal to me but could not be ignored for their impact. The Stones, Kinks, Animals, and Them resonated with me. They were counterculture to me. Into this milieu, Eddie introduced folk music, especially Bob Dylan. I had heard folk music since the late 50s and knew its tie to the Beats, but had not followed it since its earlier popularity. Dylan was different. This was not pretty songs from Peter, Paul and Mary or the Four Freshman; this was a challenging counterculture more than English rock groups. We were not rebels, we were not civil rights activists, we were not anti-war activists, we did not know about drugs, we were just middle-American kids in a small, rural town in the middle of the most productive agricultural valley in the country; still, the music resonated with us.

Eddie had always promised we were going to go out and drink. In fact, he had lost a bet and owed me a bottle of champagne for one of the times he did not show up, but he never paid the debt. Eddie would regularly forget what he told me he was going to do. We still got along even though we were so different. Finally, one evening when my parents were gone, the guys showed up, and Eddie had my bottle of champagne. With them, I was comfortable and took some risks. I did not like the taste of champagne, but it was better than beer. I could at least sip it. I had a good time with the guys that evening. I think my father had a smile on his face in the morning when he asked if I could explain why there was an empty champagne bottle on the bottom of the pool. After graduation I joined the guys again at a beer drinking party in a cow pasture. I failed miserably as I did not like the taste of beer.

I attended church regularly and took my faith very seriously. However, I look back and realize it was a compartment, and I was continuing to live on the embers of my confirmation. I was not being mentored; I was not growing. I was somewhat legalistic in that I thought I needed to try to be as good as I could and go to church. I tried to grasp the sermons, but they were too abstract. I may not have had a deep understanding, but I had a deep acceptance of my faith. I tried a couple of youth meetings, but they were more like church school memories than like my priest in Wisconsin. For the first time, I had friends who were more religious than I was. They were Catholic, and three of them went to mass every morning. As I edit this years later, all three are avowedly anti-Christian. I am still amazed that in doing my timeline I had been so fogged in by the secular and relativistic teachings of my betters that I had totally bought into them and did not even include a spiritual element in that timeline. Unbelievable, but I was that far off by then.

Looking back on the time in my hometown, I realize we lived in a special age, even if not golden of a certain character of small-town Central Valley life that was being permanently eclipsed. After the war, the urban areas of California had grown phenomenally; the rural small towns had changed little. The assassination of President Kennedy, the civil rights movement, and the Vietnam War ushered in a new era. Race relations, which for us did not include blacks but did include Hispanics who were already a part of our community, became more difficult. The assassination tempered the optimism of the post-war era, and the Vietnam War changed everything. Our classmates died, some were wounded, and others served and returned unharmed; everyone worried, young men and young women. The youth culture was strong but nowhere near as strong as it was to become. Drugs were not yet a factor for at least four more years. Sexual promiscuity leapt forward with birth control pills. Truly the times would seem naïve and quaint by comparison. Other aspects of the environment changed as well. In the earlier part of the century, regional and national retail stores had come to small-town America. Just after our time, this progressed dramatically especially for "fast food" restaurants that served a limited menu, cheap and fast. All towns became more and more the same and in most cases bigger. As I write this, my hometown has a population of about 25,000. When I left, it was still under 5,000.

That last summer before college I had some fun with my friends, actually more Eddie's friends, but I was included. I tried water skiing behind a pink Cadillac on the irrigation canals, and we went tubing through rapids on a feeder canal from the river to a reservoir. Otherwise, I just sat in my room and read or daydreamed about being somewhere else. The summer felt like an empty pause with some bright spots leading to I knew not what. I was too afraid to do anything except float along. I hoped college would prove a release and relief.

The timeline I laid out ran through the time to 1970-71 in Berkeley. It included these past reflections which are only summarized and the events and experiences of this narrative. It was my first serious attempt at a deeper understanding of myself (combined with therapy), which was ongoing, and while I did not understand it at the time, I was actually searching for real meaning, ultimate reality, God.

4.

BACK TO THE PRESENT PAST

11/70-3/71

Back to Milvia

While I had Dr. Bold as a mooring point at this time, all through the last three years going back to first living in Berkeley/Oakland, I continued to have another mooring point of sorts with my Grandmother. I periodically drove down to her house and spent an hour or so visiting in the evening. She would often be making a rag rug or some other project, just as she did when I first lived in her attic. I would usually have a toasted sourdough roll and cup of Postum. She would often be watching *Masterpiece Theater*, but when I was there we talked instead. I do not remember the exact topics, but we spoke as peers somehow. Often I think I was quizzing her on family remembrances, how people related, much like I was exploring in my own life— me with my naïve, Berkeley countercultural assurance and her having left her parents at 16 in the Polish part of what was Germany at the time, never to return and to work as a domestic after that. She seemed to me to be very wise in her quiet manner. At Christmas time, I would make the trip to decorate her tree. I am not sure why, but this was my job. I am sure she was very disappointed when I moved to Berkeley from her attic. I know that even if I gained lots of new experiences, I lost others.

My new place at the Milvia house was primarily a place to live rather than a surrogate family. My friends from the Dana house and those connections were the ones I hung out with. I continued to go to parties at Grizzly Peak and other houses where someone had a connection. The parties usually involved a little food, loud music on a stereo system and inexpensive wine. In addition, some marijuana might make the rounds. These parties were the primary social events or times of connection outside your own house. By some point in the evening, there would be lots of dancing, even in the tight spaces of apartments or living rooms.

During one of these parties at a house off Claremont Avenue on the Oakland side of Berkeley, I found myself talking with a couple who were friends with someone from the Dana house. He was a tall, self-assured, young man who was in the insurance business. His wife was a quiet, attractive brunette who stood out even in those open times as she had come to the party wearing fuzzy bedroom slippers on her feet. We talked awhile, and when dancing started, I found myself dancing with them. This was quite normal as couples and singles would come to parties, and people often danced on their own anyway. However, as the music continued, I found that I was very obviously dancing with her and her with me, and my heart beat faster as I realized that we were sharing an awful lot of meaningful eye contact. Her husband seemed to drift to dancing with other women and have no concern whatsoever. Since I had no one, I was thrilled with the attention but apprehensive at the same time. What was going on? As the party ended, the three of us found ourselves under a streetlamp on the street below in the cool dampness of the foggy night air. We exchanged hugs and a few words that seemed to amount to me giving her a call sometime. I went home expectant and perplexed, but the situation seemed to be consistent with the character of the times. Who was I to wonder just because it was not part of my experience? Go with the flow. This was the flip side of "seeing others" but with permission. Was there a relationship in that or just momentary pleasure?

I did call her, and we got together. Even though I was probably supposed to act like this was all so normal, I found a way that I hoped was tactful to ask what kind of a relationship she and her husband had. She indicated that they saw other people. I guess this was the kind of relationship Daphne had suggested. Even though she said "they," I got the distinct impression that the instigation was primarily from her husband. While I thought I was pretty sophisticated to find myself in this situation, I was nonetheless apprehensive. I assumed, as usual, that she must be experienced in a different way than I was, even though she did not seem to be. I was myself and someone I thought I was supposed to be at the same time. I should have just been myself. I did not have a clue how foggy my thinking was. The time I enjoyed most with her was the conversation when we were out to dinner. She had graduated near the top of her class in college; she was very bright and very appealing. She was not a hippie and gave no appearance of being part of the counterculture. Something was very strange about her marriage, even though this was the cutting edge of the culture. At that time, I could not have expressed my sense of her place in it. From a distance of time, she seemed to be a nice girl in a trap and did not have a clue how to get out any more than I had a clue how to function in that odd world. I left at sunrise the next morning feeling a sense of pleasure as I breathed in the cool foggy air. Nothing more happened between us. Although she was the one to demur on further contact, I was confused as to why but was not particularly wounded this time. I, of course, blamed myself, but medicated any pain with the knowledge that the relationship was odd to begin with. I thought that was it. Maybe I was getting better at this no pain relationship thing when forced to confront my real feelings about the relationship.

I had not run into Joelly for a long time, but then she moved into the Milvia house. She took my small room when I moved into the larger front room. I came home from work one day to find Joelly hosting a group of men and women in our living room. I found myself overwhelmed with a sense of having my private space invaded and jealousy because my fuzzy slippers friend was part of the group. I was caught off guard by my feelings. By now I was less reluctant to express my feelings but very clumsy and insecure in doing so. What was going on? The meeting did not concern me. I did not control the house. Where was my laid back attitude? I was clearly bothered, so obviously the break was not painless. I had just hidden it from myself.

After expressing a casual greeting, I went to my room to suffer even though I knew I was not supposed to. I was not supposed to because the new culture of free love had done away with that. I was not supposed to because she was not even available; she was married. Yet, I really felt my private space violated. She and I had a relationship even if it was not much of one; yet, she was free to be with others. But having her in my house, even though others had rights to that house, and even though her purposes may have been benign, made me feel caged and upset. I was not able to act as if nothing had happened between us.

I went downstairs and with a quaver in my voice asked if she would come up for a moment. I do not know what she expected, but certainly not what I had to say. Barely maintaining calmness, I explained to her that I was bothered by her being in the house and that she should not be there. I am sure she thought I was some kind of insane obsessive, certainly not in tune with the times. If she had other thoughts, she did not express them. I am sure I caught her off guard. She left angrily and in a hurry. I am sure my friends downstairs wondered what had happened as well. As it was, our paths did not cross again except once very casually a year or so later, at which time we could greet one another in a cordial manner. She was still a very appealing young woman.

I was trying to understand relationships with young women better but was not having much success. Except for the relative ease of falling into a relationship, the culture did not work for me. After my experience with Daphne, I doubted whether it would ever work for me or whether it ever really worked for anyone. Therapy was allowing me to be bolder in many ways, but it did not seem to be helping much in relationships although I was able to express my sense of personal boundaries at last. While expressing some boundaries, I was blowing right past other more traditional values that might have protected me better in the first place. Dr. Bold did not offer much specific advice. He seemed to believe I needed to act to learn—even if that meant failure or disappointment, rather than analyze too much before acting or never acting. This worked in the culture and secular humanist worldview but might not have been the best. Dr. Bold, while culturally Jewish, was a secular humanist who believed in the work he did to help people deal better with life.

More Grizzly Peak Surprises

In the midst of my relationship with the young woman in slippers during a party at Grizzly Peak, the one young woman who lived in the house and had always been just a good friend all of a sudden approached me. I do not mean subtly. In her room during the party, she directly, vulnerably, and intimately approached me. I was confused. She was available and real; the other woman was married, and while our relationship was not anything yet, I thought it might lead somewhere. I was involved with the slipper-wearing woman and told my friend so. She was shocked: she was married! I guess all of us did not get as confused about relationships during this time as I did. Certainly, my friend had some clarity. I had to shut off a part of me to pull away from her and end the discussion, even though this was the same young woman I had only recently seriously considered a potential girlfriend. I was quite lost in a fog. In less than a week or, at most, two, the woman in slippers and I were no longer an item, if we ever really were, but I did not, could not, or would not go back to my friend and say I made a mistake. Here, I could have had two relationships at once but chose not to, reserving honor for the one that made no sense but sort of existed, instead of one that might have been real. Like I said, my thinking was very foggy.

Prior to that experience, that same Grizzly Peak friend taught me another significant lesson. I did not realize the importance of it at the time but remember because of the quiet power of her emotions. She had broken up with her boyfriend; then, found she had become pregnant. I am not sure how many others knew about her pregnancy; he surely did not. She and I discussed the situation at length and the conflict she felt. Roe v. Wade was still in the future. Abortion had only recently gone from something almost unheard of to something a woman should be able to decide and more readily available than in the past. Our common 60s culture, hippie or not, accepted that and the right to choose without much question. She did have an abortion, and in our conversation afterward, I lightly dismissed it trying to be supportive of her. I quickly learned by her rebuke that this simple decision to choose was, at least for her, much bigger than I understood and not simple at all. She was deeply troubled, did not seem sure she had done the right thing, and definitely did not see this as something that could be lightly dismissed. While I did not fully understand, I filed the thought away because her rebuke was so passionate and her emotional pain so clear. Much later and on more than one occasion, I was to hear similar confessions from other women.

Additionally, I did not connect that she had broken up from a serious relationship and that the pregnancy resulted from an intimate, passionate, and consensual experience. How could I be so traumatized by my intense experience just a year and a half earlier with Daphne, not connect that with my friend, and only just abstractly discuss abortion? I was numbed and scarred; the world does that.

A little later in the spring, another Grizzly Peak party brought more fun and confusion. The extended family from Dana had shown up, among others. The group that evening included a quiet guitar player who had moved into Dana after I had lived there awhile. He was there with his fiancée, Annie. I had not seen him since leaving Dana house and had not met her before. It seemed like a number of the others knew her. While I was generally a part of this social circle, I had my work, therapy, my own shared house, and other interests, so I missed some of the day to day interaction. The all-encompassing Dana house family no longer defined my life, and I was much better with being alone and on a separate, even if ill-defined path. Thus, it stood to reason that the people at these events would change, just as people's lives would change.

Annie was a very thin, petite blonde with sparkling eyes and a charming smile. She was verbally quick and witty. Her future husband being very quiet, almost somber, and one to watch the party more than participate in it, seemed the opposite of Annie. I had always respected him because of his musical talents and because his silence was intriguing. As the evening progressed, Annie and I found ourselves talking to one another on more than one occasion and later dancing together. Her future husband was sitting near us and did not seem to mind or want to dance. As the evening progressed, to all but the most unobservant, we must have seemed like a regular couple: we danced together, we joked together, we were together. But, at the end of the evening, they went home together, and I went home with myself. I was fine with that, knew it was right, had a lot of fun, and yet, was confused because it seemed like Annie and I had too much fun given her impending marriage. I did not want to give up the fun, got that it was right to let it stop there, but still wondered why I was not making progress in this lifestyle or relationships. My new religious denomination of therapy, self-knowledge, and self-awareness did not seem to be helping much.

I heard later that they did get married. Ironically, this was at a time when marriage was no longer a given, even in a committed relationship for young people in the counterculture. Maybe they were not as much a part of the culture as I might have assumed, or maybe they had a relationship I did not fully understand. Berkeley was not made up of one or even a few patterns of lives. I was not as aware then of the infinite variations of experience of Berkeley, San Francisco, or the Bay Area there might have been at the time—despite media attempts to paint it in one, broad stroke.

My experiences and reflections are the context for my understanding of it all. Others will have had a different view. For example, what about others who were part of sororities or fraternities for whom alcohol, drugs, and sexual freedom may have had a completely different character? Or, what about students focused on their degree program and the rest was background noise? What about those focused mostly on political and social change in the culture? What about musicians focused on their music and probably drugs? What about the pure hippies who bought into letting it all go for music, drugs, and sexual freedom and ultimately moved up to Mendocino to grow carrots? Thousands of contexts existed in one time and place; whereas, in a much different place, one might discern just a few patterns, all part of a stable continuity.

Remember, I cannot remember us ever having a party at the Milvia house, even though parties were a regular occurrence. Yet, one evening when we were all home, probably having some, or maybe a lot of wine, we ended up having this huge group hug on the narrow stairs to the upper floor. This was not characteristic for that house or these people. We hugged and kissed. With, I think, a little bit of embarrassment, we all then made our way to our rooms. The next day Joelly informed me that she had knocked on my door later that evening, but I was asleep and did not hear or respond, probably because my hearing was so poor. She said she just wanted to be close to someone. I was honored and a little taken aback. I was not sure how to respond and maybe was too casual with her personal disclosure. Although I do not believe I understood it then, Joelly and I were as close as a single man and woman could have been without being either brother and sister or lovers.

A lot happened in such a short time back then. The young woman I first kissed came to visit with her sister-in-law. They assumed they could stay over, which given the times was true. We caught up; I was able to feel a little proud in that I lived independently in Berkeley while she was stuck, according to her, in a less than happy marriage in the Central Valley. My pride did not have much substance behind it. I was not really that happy myself. We connected quickly, we always did, but circumstances saved us from connecting too well. We seemed fated to just miss really connecting with one another. Around the same time, Daphne stopped by to visit. I don't think I had seen her for over a year. She seemed to be the same bubbly person I had fallen in love with. Somehow I could set the bad aside. Perhaps in an attempt to show I had learned to be more sophisticated, I kissed her and was surprised by her friendly but cold comment as to how we were clearly past that. I should have kept my distance, but you could have fooled me.

World Game

While walking one day, I saw a poster for World Game Workshop, an idea of Buckminster Fuller's. He envisioned that if world or business leaders got together and looked at the world creatively around major issues that we would advance as a whole, and we would have fewer problems.

He was a visionary and did not see why we all could not be the same. I was intrigued but would not have thought I belonged in a group considering world progress. However, Dr. Bold encouraged me to go to the meeting and see what was happening. I went to San Francisco expecting a group of business types and instead found a group of mostly counterculture types. The organization was not as intimidating as I thought. Fuller had laid out a plan for discussion, and we were going to follow it. I did not see how this group was going affect world policy, but it was more than I was doing. The group seemed interesting, I was not too intimidated, and I thought I might learn something.

I met one young man who became a close friend for the duration of the workshop and sometime after. He was different from most of my friends. He was tall and slender with frizzy, light brown hair, and a spacey look about him. We were compatible in the way we viewed most things. He did not live far from me in Berkeley, so we spent a lot of time together.

The World Game Workshop was fun and absorbed much of my free time for a few months. I learned that no one really knew much more than I did or even less in some cases. I could hold my own in most of the discussions, but I am not sure that anything final came out of the process. The organizers' motives were not totally clear to me. They arranged for Fuller to speak to us. They also ended up founding a successful waterbed company—waterbeds were only just becoming popular. I did learn that I had something to say, and in the right situation I could say it. Because of the World Game, I was immersed in the City again. All the meetings happened there in different venues, some near Van Ness and others in lovely, older buildings in Presidio Heights.

One week, my friend from World Game, I, and my Reichian contact from Etna decided to go to a Grateful Dead concert in Davis. We piled into my car and drove up only to find the concert sold out. My Etna friend was bold; she sidled up to someone—probably a guy—and got in. She then handed us tickets she got from others. We had a great time dancing through most of the concert in the front corner while most of the crowd just listened. I had not been to a concert for quite a while and really relished being back in that environment. We were a great trinity of souls that evening. Jerry Garcia was there in fine form, even though I had been ignoring him. I could still access the sense of that first acid concert in Berkeley even though I was not high on anything.

Still drawn to the High Sierra, I arranged another trip. This time it included my Reichian friend, my friend who helped me with my car, and Joelly. We all packed into my VW and got to the same trail base I had visited twice before. We were provisioned a little better to differing degrees. My car friend was more experienced and had more gear. Joelly either had done this before or was prepared for the trip. My Reichian friend was less prepared. We made it farther than I had ever gone and found a splendid place to camp past the reservoir along a creek. This was to be a two- or three-day trip. We had a good meal that night and a blazing fire. The night was very cold. My Reichian friend was so cold she needed to come lay next to me to get warm, nothing more than that. The next morning, she and my car friend were ready to turn back because of the cold. Joelly was ready to keep going. I wanted to keep going; however, my Reichian friend was older and I had always looked up to her. I made the decision to go back with them. I still remember watching Joelly going up the trail and thinking I should have gone with her.

During this time, I would also bring work home to do on my little table, but found myself frustrated as I was criticized because I was engaged in regular work and not some higher-minded effort. I was given more responsibility than I should have given my limited experience, and I enjoyed that challenge. My friend who was still completing school could afford to be more idealistic than I could or would. Somehow regular work for regular people in the real world was unacceptable. The discussions made me realize that I was different from these friends even though I liked them. Whereas, I earlier tended to ignore differences with the counterculture or those around me, I was now more comfortable noticing those differences and sometimes speaking up for myself. I was not like that earlier me who did not ever know what I thought or failed to express it.

About a year earlier, I had started therapy in the hopes that I would learn how I was inadequate, so I could be adequate, and my relationships would work better. Here I was with no better relationships, but something else was happening. Terry had encouraged me to try things like the World Game Workshop, which I probably would not have done otherwise. He did not discourage my thought that regular work was okay, that everything did not have to be ideal and in fact could not be. He had been encouraging me for a while to get my own place and be independent. Since first going to college almost six years earlier, I had always lived with others, whether in a dormitory, with my grandmother, or in the 11 various situations in Berkeley since. The Milvia house was great, and my experience there was as independent as I had been to date. Reluctant but optimistic, I started looking for a place of my own.

IV.

TRANSITIONS

Three and a Quarter Years

1.

INDEPENDENCE
3/71–9/71

Delaware

I took the challenge and found my own place just a few blocks away on Delaware just off Shattuck Avenue. It was an old studio apartment over a garage in a gravel parking lot. It was all that was left of what used to be a house. Small and strange as it was, it was mine. I was excited and lonely at the same time. I tried to maintain my social connections, but I was only gregarious within known boundaries. I visited friends and walked all around town and campus. I was not always lonely; I was where I wanted to be. Certainly, with Daphne, I was only lonely at the end. My life since had been filled with unstable intimate relationships but a fairly stable set of acquaintances even as I moved from place to place. Still, I really was lonely on my own; I knew I was happier in a steady relationship; the happy days of my early time in Berkeley were distant. I did not know it at the time, but with this move I was never again to live in a group setting except in a relationship or when I had a family of my own.

My reliance on therapy and Dr. Bold during this time was a substitute for a spiritual or religious connection. Trying to understand myself better was the most important thing at the time. My choice of a way out through therapy or the human potential movement was a good tool but a tool only, not an answer to my search. My embrace of the 60s in the Bay Area blinded me to what I would come to believe years later. At the time, I totally missed in the fog of my thinking that I had a strong faith and hope in things working out, and yet that idea was completely at odds with my worldview of philosophical naturalism or secular humanism. There was no room for a spirituality. The faith I had then is the same faith I have now, and it only comes from the spiritual, unseen reality. I was oblivious to the fact I was already in possession of the real source of my hope for the future.

Shortly after moving, I visited the campus art gallery one weekend. I saw a striking, slender, young woman with long, straight, very blonde hair. I managed the courage to start a conversation, which astonishingly succeeded. Maybe she was lonely and looking for someone, as well. She was attractive physically and in personality; we found conversation easy. Again, I am not sure how I was so bold, but I suggested a drive across the Bay and out toward the coast, and we were on our way. We had a wonderful day driving in the hills of West Marin, stopping to climb to a prominent rock along Lucas Valley Road to look out at the Bay. We continued out through redwood forests to grab some food at a store and had a picnic off the side of the road. The places did not matter so much as our conversation. Driving back to her home in the Oakland Hills off Park Avenue, we were very much focused on one another. She was different from me. She lived in a charming, craftsman-style house with quality furniture, not leftovers or free stuff. She had been married and was only recently divorced. She worked for a living in a full-time job, not part-time job as I did. Her ex-husband ran a service station in the City; they had come from Indiana, and the 60s culture was foreign to her.

Despite our different experiences, we were attracted to one another. She was wonderful. I was intimidated by her comfortable femininity and apparent sophistication. I tried to appear mature and masculine, but I was only clumsily assertive. I wanted to bridge the gap of our intimate experience and life experience, but I was aware of a part of her I could not reach. I suggested going to a concert. I did not go to them regularly anymore, but she had never been, and I was at a loss for something else to suggest. We went to Winterland in the City to see the New Riders of the Purple Sage opening for the Grateful Dead. The concert was terrific, but clearly, this was not part of her world—and not even much a part of mine anymore. At that concert, I realized that in some ways I was no longer the same and that I might not be able to bridge the gap with her.

While we had a good time together, too soon, I could feel a quiet distance. I felt very inadequate because I just did not know what to do. When this exciting romance ended in much too short a time for me with a call from her, I accepted it with grace though I was incredibly disappointed and confused. I was not sure why I could not get this right. She even thanked me because I was so gracious. I was matter of fact. I had some healthy distance from the pain, while still feeling it. I accepted the reality, even though I did not like it. I was wise enough to know I could not bridge the gap even though I really liked her.

William had a friend working on a local restaurant that was trying to open. One day when we stopped by, his friend had accidentally cut the cord off his power saw. Such was the well-meaning but amateur level of some of the new generation of craftsmen. They had to stop their project at the ground floor because the client did not have enough money to keep going, which was also in keeping with the by the "bootstraps" entrepreneurial energy of the times. Yet, the restaurant, Chez Panisse, very quickly well known, did open soon after, even if only on the ground floor at first.

I would still go to the same parties and get together with friends who lived in and about Berkeley. On one of these occasions, I was at a party hosted by a married couple I had known for awhile. While couples mostly lived together unmarried in the counterculture, many were part of the mainstream culture, were married, and found themselves bumping up against the counterculture. As the evening wore on, most of us were dancing in no particular pattern. As the small group thinned, I was left dancing in the soft light with my host's wife. I do not believe either of us intended to get carried away, but I did not stop myself even though I knew I was crossing a boundary. Dancing led to kissing, which led to more. We were very comfortable with one another and were softly drawn into each other's needs without apparent concern for the situation we were in. I, at least, had had too much to drink. Once again, the culture of the times said things were not as they had been, and old ways were not new ways. Many of us thought old boundaries were unimportant.

I left and began the drive home with the car windows open blasting cool air on my face. Only a short distance down the hill, I had an instantaneous and horribly clear awakening and sense of how far off I—we—had been. The alcohol eased judgment, and the tenderness of the moment was clarified in a stunning blast of that fresh air blowing current ideas out of my mind. I realized that no next steps could be easy or even possible. I did not think about the word repentance, but that would sure have described my mindset. I do not remember if I slept at all. I had no answers and knew I had made a huge mistake. It was not because of anything to do with my friend's wife except simply that we should not have been so naïve. I do not believe that at the time I understood how selfish or self-centered I was.

The next morning, while still anxiously processing how in the world I was ever going to face them again, my friend called. Without apparent anger and very matter of fact, he said that he knew what had happened, that they had been up most of the night talking, and that we needed to talk. I think I said I had blown it, was actually relieved to end the anxious processing, and agreed we should talk. While we had always been direct and could communicate well, we had never been in anything like this situation before.

The situation was a little more complicated than I have indicated. My friends had been together for some time, and while they had lived in the same environment I had for the last few years, they had not been a part of the counterculture. They were not hippies; they did not live in a commune. They were a married couple living in close proximity to a culture that seemed freer. From the perspective of when this is being written, it may be hard to picture that the breach of sexual and relational norms were only just beginning, rather than being widespread in the culture as they are now. They had been struggling in their relationship and had even talked about whether they should separate or open themselves to other relationships. Although his wife did mention this to me, I do not think they could have thought this was the way to start that experiment.

Their talk about living a new way and the reality were different. They were drawn closer together, not farther apart; their relationship was challenged by the standards of the culture and their reactions to what the new culture felt like. He did not see me as an enemy, and somehow we remained friends even though I have not seen him for awhile. He was responding as the times dictated—much as I had in my own relationship struggles—as if it was no big deal, even though he must have been grappling with more traditional reactions. I could try to excuse my role in the context of their struggle, but that was a blessing; I simply should have known and acted differently. Any excuse on my side, was just that: an excuse. I was unanchored or unmoored to what I deep down knew was right. In the same old fog, I was simply clueless and directionless. I thought of myself as a good person with a sense of commitment to right action, but I had been easily distracted by my own pleasure and the misguided influence of alcohol.

I shared this experience with Dr. Bold. I am sure now he was wondering whether I was getting much from his help. He reminded me that my friend could have literally gotten away with murder. I knew I was wrong, I knew he was right; yet, the total import of the sacred bounds of relationships was not clear to me even though I had been shown repeatedly that the new culture of relationships did not work. Indeed, I had been hurt by it regularly myself. That was more than just social training; something deeper did not work. I did not think about it at the time but much later would recognize that my worldview was full of dead-end streets and no answers. I was learning to be more assertive, less passive, and take risks, but the moral compass was not there. When I was passive and took no chances, it was not there either—I just did not get into such compromising situations.

While I had moved on from the intense involvement in the live music scene from '67 to '69, I still went to concerts from time to time. The Avalon had closed, but the Family Dog periodically had concerts on the Great Highway off Ocean Beach and Golden Gate Park. I went to one and happened to run into my freckled friend with the unattached lifestyle. She was still with the same guy in their version of a relationship! She came over to visit, stayed a night, and moved on. I again felt like we had some kind of relationship and enjoyed our time together, but it was so confusing. She lived in another world that I suppose was consistent with one part of the counterculture—a part that might seem acceptable in the abstract, yet, clearly not in reality. The Playboy philosophy, although it had nothing to do with the counterculture, proclaimed this same sexual freedom as a "healthy" release of constraints. While I could sense it did not work, I was too foggy in my thinking to put two and two together.

At some point during this time, I got really sick. Rather than lay around in my studio, I went home for a short while. My relationship with my parents was good, but I could not confide in them. I could not express my interior reflections or anything of my therapy or relationships. The pleasant care I received was offset by an excess of caution on my part.

Neighborhood Action

While living at my little house, I was for the first time called into a kind of leadership I had not experienced before. I was approached by a young woman who lived in the house behind mine. She had received a notice that an apartment project was planned for a combination of properties including the one on which I lived. She was trying to raise opposition as she felt the little, two-story shingle houses were more appropriate. I agreed to come to a meeting of neighborhood people at her house to see what this was about.

Most of the people seemed to be opposed to the project because it was big, it was stucco, and they did not want to see things change. I did not feel the same way, even though my place would disappear if the project was approved, but I thought it was worth getting involved, making sure proper processes were followed, and maybe helping in some way. Others were interested, as well. This was a time when neighborhoods were just beginning to develop their sense of political strength within the city. We went to review plans and the application. The general drift among the group continued to be unfocussed opposition, much like with the Dana house during the rent strike.

I found a weak point in the application and one that I could support openly. This was a big building proposal that should have been able to comply with regulations. Yet, they were requesting a variance from regulations for their building setbacks along Shattuck Avenue, a main thoroughfare. They wanted the building closer to the street so they could have more parking, and therefore, more units. While most of the group still arbitrarily disliked the project, I was able to convince the young woman, another neighborhood organizer, and others that opposing the variance was a more legitimate reason to oppose the proposal. According to the regulations, a variance should only be granted if a special hardship existed with the site. None existed; they just wanted to build to increase the number of units. I tried to argue that stucco was just a construction material, often used in quality construction, but many associated it with cheap construction because it was often used on the sides and backs of "tract" homes in the suburbs from which they came.

We worked on our message and presented our arguments in an orderly fashion at the planning commission hearing. Some of the commissioners supported us, but we lost the vote. I had gone to routine hearings before but never one with conflict. The applicant, my landlord, had her case presented by her attorney who was focused and well prepared. I was particularly incensed by some of his suggestions that I was only opposing the project because I lived on the property and might have to move. I was beside myself; I verbally confronted the attorney in the stairway. He very professionally did not take the bait. I went home and smashed a wooden chair. I had not expressed this kind of anger before. Maybe therapy was working a little, but clearly I did not have much control of my anger. I liked that chair and it was the only one I had. I was simply buzzing with righteous and obsessive indignation because the commission did not worry about the real reasons for a variance, and the attorney got away with personal attacks without addressing the issue. Maybe this is what those who were really political during those times felt. I was a fellow traveler, but I usually did not have strong feelings. Even though I was against the war; I was not AGAINST the war. I knew the issue was very complicated.

Eventually, I calmed down. We could still appeal. The city council had only just changed that year, and for the first time a moderate conservative council had at least three progressive left members, one white and two black. This was a turning point in the politics of the Berkeley City Council. I think partially because of my suggestions, we focused our presentation on the fact that no reason existed for the variance and that granting it would have negative effects on the streetscape. The young woman who first approached me and I alternated in providing the narrative to a slide show of good and bad situations. Others commented, as well. The appeal was sustained. The project needed to be redesigned to comply with regulations. I was the only one directly affected by this success and ultimately had to move.

I thought I was attracted to a young woman in the neighboring house during this time. The young woman with whom I was working on the opposition was probably more appropriate and may have even been attracted to me, even though she had a boyfriend. But, by now, you have figured out how undiscerning I was and idolizing relationship with foggy, not clear, thinking.

One day while out walking, I ran into the girl to whom I had been attracted but was too afraid to talk to from the earlier Dana house trip to the Santa Cruz Mountains. I was still attracted to her. We walked back to her house, and I had no problem talking with her now. I was lonely but more able to be assertive because of therapy. I flirted with her in a very forward manner. She at first seemed fine but then got her senses about her. I knew she had a boyfriend she was living with. Although I had met him briefly during the project opposition, I did not know him. Once again, my foggy thinking, greater assertiveness, loneliness, and no guiding principles from the counterculture, left me sadly acting without a clue. I went from not even being able to approach her when I was attracted to her and she may have been to me, to being able to talk somewhat with her as a real person briefly during the project opposition, to running into her again, conversing comfortably and then, thinking I was showing myself to be experienced and sophisticated, showed myself to be inexperienced, unwise, self-centered, and foolish. I did not fully realize this at the time; I thought I had handled myself well by respecting her setting a boundary. I missed that I should have set a boundary first.

Therapy was helping me with my lack of assertiveness but not with my foggy thinking, partially because the culture and attendant worldview did not provide guidance with a solid foundation. With my married friends, repentance was immediate; this situation was not as obvious, so it took me longer to fully recognize it.

Joelly and I visited on a few occasions. She was struggling with relationship issues as I was but in different ways as she had a steady boyfriend. That struggle was the case for most of us, though we did not know it. Most of us were just starting to step out of that long transition between home and the world that university life and its extensions had given us. Joelly had moved out of Milvia but was reflecting on her commitment to her longtime boyfriend and just where did that all lead. We talked very openly and vulnerably, but we both held back, as well. Really though, in that conversation, we talked more closely than I probably would in an intimate relationship at the time. The easy intimacy—meaning the easy move to a close physical relationship, then sexually intimate relationship—did not necessarily lead to more conversational intimacy in the relationship. Joelly and I did not have the baggage of an intimate sexual relationship, and yet, we were close enough to have those conversations.

About this time, I had the opportunity to buy a sports car my cousin was selling. The car did not fit my image of myself like my VW bug did. It was an MGB with a convertible top and a roll bar, as if it was some kind of race car. Nonetheless, I bought it. In addition, I decided to have my long hair cut more stylishly by professionals at one of the places in San Francisco advertised on the popular FM radio station. I had not cut my hair or beard since first coming to Berkeley in late '66. I cut my wispy beard as well and just left sideburns. While I was not aware of this at the time, a lot was changing. I was more comfortable being a little outside my student hippie persona. I still did have wire rim glasses to fit the hippie image though.

I continued to walk a lot in the evenings, sometimes visiting friends, sometimes just walking the Berkeley streets of which I never tired. Berkeley was, still is I suspect, a wonderful town in which to walk: downtown, the flats, the campus, North side, South side, College Avenue, wonderful old buildings, changes of landscape, interesting shops, and people watching. I was glad to be on my own, but I would rather have been with an appropriate woman. On one walk, I ran into my quiet, guitar playing acquaintance from the Dana house and his now wife, Annie. We exchanged pleasantries and that was about it. They were together, I was alone, and that was okay.

Some Sunshine

Surprisingly, one morning while getting ready for work, not long after that meeting with Annie and her husband, I noticed her walking by on the street across from my parking lot. I saw her again on another day and then saw her return as if she was coming from somewhere down Delaware Street, even though I knew this was not where she lived. I was incredibly intrigued. I went out on one of those mornings hoping to run in to her on her way back so I might talk to her. I had timed things well and ran into her a block down Shattuck. We resumed our easy communication with one another, and she agreed to my offer of coffee at a café on the corner on University. We talked for quite a while. I learned that she and her husband were no longer together, that she had broken off the marriage, that she was living with her girlfriend down the street on Delaware, and that she was returning from a therapy appointment. Sunlight, bright sunlight, was streaming into my life. Nothing had changed yet, but I was not lonely. Annie and I had such an easy attraction to one another, or I thought we did so confidently that I did not even question or worry about whether she felt the same way. Just as at the party, but without wine or heightened socializing, we talked on and on. I asked on more than one occasion about her relationship with her husband and consistently got answers that it was over, although I believe he may have hoped that the therapy would help her come to her senses. I suspect that when I had run into them near my house that they may have already been separated. They had not been married long. On our way back to our houses, we stopped briefly at mine, and I approached her about going out. She said yes, and while I did not doubt she would say yes, I was incredibly thrilled. I was attracted to her from that first night we met and danced.

I was affected by the culture even though I approached my relationships in a very traditional way, expecting commitment and continuity. When I was not in a relationship, I was hoping for one. I felt better in a relationship than on my own. I had respected the boundary of her relationship with her husband. With Annie and her husband, I knew I was only a friend, and if Annie and I had anything, it was simply a dormant attraction that needed to stay dormant. Our attraction had gone farther than it should have in a very open and public way, but it was only that with nothing hidden. With my other friend and his wife, I also knew I was only a friend, but the situation let me forget the boundaries. Ironically, with Annie and her husband, I would have needed reckless determination to have broken that boundary; yet with my friend's wife, because of the sensuousness and privacy of the moment, I needed more determination and willpower than I had to not recklessly breach the same boundary.

Yet, on my first date with Annie, I started to confront being seen as an enemy in a way that I had not been or had not recognized previously. We went to Keystone, a club that had live music on University just around the corner from our houses. I do not remember the band, but the place had decent groups, inexpensive beer, and good atmosphere. Annie and I danced and talked together like when we had first met. Our personalities fit as if by design, and we had the momentum of a future together. My friend from Grizzly Peak who helped take apart my VW engine was there with his new girlfriend. I ran short of money at some point in the evening and he let me borrow ten dollars with a measure of coolness. I did not take notice; I was in another world with Annie.

However, the next day when I went to his girlfriend's house where he now lived to return the money, he left no question that something was wrong. Even though she barely knew me, she greeted me quite cordially and chatted as she packed books for their move to West Sacramento; she was going study to become a winemaker at Davis. However, my friend, who was making some repairs to his car, did not stop what he was doing to take the money or acknowledge me beyond a few brief grunts. I left feeling the ice and that something was off without knowing what it was.

Within only a few days, I got a call from my artist friend with the therapy connection. She wanted to talk to me about my relationship with Annie. I agreed to get together, but even on the phone she strongly suggested that I should not be with Annie. I tried to tell her that Annie's relationship with her husband was over. We did get together over some food at the tiny, ancient courtyard movie spot on Euclid. She was quite emphatic that I did not belong with Annie. She insisted that Annie's relationship with her husband was just struggling and that, as I had guessed, he believed she was coming back. She also said that he thought that if they did not get back together, Annie and I might end up together. As if it made a difference, I naively told her about meeting Annie because she was living on my block and of my repeated questions regarding the status of her marriage before ever asking her out. That was not enough. She said I did not understand; I had inappropriately crossed a definite boundary. I thought I had respected that boundary by asking directly and more than once, but, obviously for others, I had not. I understood how others might take his side. It did occur to me that they had married—couples did not need to marry in our culture; yet, they had. But even so, the relationship had come apart in a very short time. While I knew their relationship was over, I did not press Annie for reasons that were not offered and knew she had her therapist for whatever she was working out.

With Annie, I could not understand what I had done wrong. Her husband was an acquaintance only—nothing like my married friends. With them, I had crossed a significant line in relationship and knew I was wrong. We dealt with it and moved on much sobered. I did not go to Annie's husband to discuss my interest because his relationship with Annie was already broken. They had dealt with it, although maybe not each with the same understanding of the finality. However, his friends were sympathetic to him, which left me in an untenable position. I could forget my unquestioned attraction to Annie or forget a group of social friends. I was very saddened to think that another part of my Berkeley life and life in the new culture was dropping away, but the decision was not hard, and I felt secure in it. I knew her husband was in pain, but that would not be fixed by me dropping Annie.

Annie was only temporarily staying at her friend's house and now started staying more regularly at mine. We socialized a lot with her friend and her boyfriend. Right from the start, I felt they accepted us as a couple. One morning, not long after Annie and I had gotten together, as she lay sleeping, Joelly stopped by to check in. Joelly and I talked for a moment before I identified the sleeping young lady, who was probably feigning sleep. Joelly handled the news without showing any surprise, which she must have felt. Joelly was not a part of the other group enough to have cared, although she did know Annie was married, and I did not have time to explain the circumstances. All things were just as complicated as they have been for centuries. Sadly, I had very little contact with Joelly after that.

Very shortly thereafter, as a result of my opposition to the project on my site, I was served with an eviction notice. I accepted willingly. Annie and I looked for a new place to live together. My life was in steady transition.

2.

LIKE MARRIAGE

About 9/71 to 3/73

Ungentrified Ninth

Annie and I got along terrifically and were both involved in building our life together.

She and I and her dog found a place to rent in the flats on Ninth. It was situated below San Pablo Avenue and south of University Avenue, which runs from the center of the university straight down to the Bay with a view of the bay and San Francisco. Unfortunately, our house didn't share that view. The area below San Pablo, while climbing slightly away from the Bay and the Freeway, is relatively flat. The Victorian was in fairly poor shape with a lower floor that had been a garage and storage area, which had been converted to a living unit. The ceilings were a little lower than normal and the floor was concrete covered with vinyl. The living room was narrow, being adjacent to the single car garage. The kitchen was spacious but had only one window overlooking the narrow side yard. One bedroom was to the other side facing the yard to the south, and one was to the rear with a bathroom at the very back. We painted the unit to make the place feel clean and comfortable. We were easily pleased, or at least I was. I found a classic, six-burner gas Wedgewood stove for the kitchen, as none was provided. With my other minimal furniture, we had a home.

The neighborhood was poor but stable. I had not lived in a neighborhood quite like this since the original Alcatraz studio I shared with my friends from Cal Poly. We were not the only white people but close to it. The area was near to light industrial activity; in fact, we backed up to an industrial building. Only a few blocks farther down toward the bay, the properties were all industrial. A well-known local bar, Brennan's, and a landmark fish restaurant, Spenger's, were only a few blocks from our house. That neighborhood has not changed much in the intervening years since the early 70's; however, only a few blocks away on the north side of University Avenue, the neighborhood changed dramatically with its conversion to an area of boutique shops and restaurants. Customers come from all over the Bay Area. Even the houses in the area have been upgraded. Maybe more than any other area of Berkeley, that area has changed the most since those days.

Annie and I had similar interests and had fun together. Socially we met up with her best friend and her boyfriend and also with Eddie and his wife who continued to be steady friends. We had a good life in our little house together. Financially, we were challenged; I did not make much money. I encouraged Annie to help by getting a job, which she did somewhat reluctantly. She was a very bright woman, brighter than me, but had not finished college, so her job opportunities were limited. She found a job in Oakland and made friends with co-workers there. We went on a backpacking trip with those friends and went on others to Monterey and Nevada with Eddie and his wife.

We made a trip to Los Angeles to visit Annie's family, as well. I am not sure what they could have thought of me since she had only gotten married a short while ago and was now living with me. If they had misgivings, I could not detect them. They lived in San Pedro, and her father worked in the shipyards nearby. Her mom seemed a little somber and out of place in her environment. She liked to write poetry and had eyes that just naturally made her look very sleepy or dreamy. Annie's brother and sisters were normal suburban kids. They were not counterculture kids nor was Annie. I enjoyed the visit and felt included in the family.

My relationship living with Annie was more like a marriage than my relationship with Daphne had been. Daphne and I never really lived together until after our crisis, and even then, having a room in a house for a short while was not the same. Slowly, almost imperceptibly, the shape of my life was changing. Annie and I had our own place and now were both working to support our life. She continued with the therapy she had started at the breakup of her marriage. While she was bright eyed and enthusiastic much of the time, she could also be somber. Perhaps she was frustrated that she was not using her intellectual talents, realizing her job was below her caliber, but not motivated enough to change things. She had never lived the basic hippie life I had; she had always had basic needs met by someone. She was struggling with something internal that I never fully understood. I kept trying to encourage her. Her job, while boring, was better than doing nothing and provided us some financial freedom.

I continued my therapy with Terry and still had the same job in Oakland. We visited my family in addition to visiting her family in LA. We went on trips together; spent time with friends of hers and mine. Our life was different. Instead of going to parties, we were getting together with couples for dinner, a trip to Pacific Grove, or a backpacking trip in the Sierras. I finally got into the High Sierra back country when she and I got a ride in on horses that got us past the difficult climbs. The area was stunning with exposed gray granite and a myriad of small lakes and mostly small conifers. We went out to hear music at a place by the Bay and have a drink; we watched television at home. We had a varied seemingly comfortable life.

For me, this was different. When I was with Daphne, we lived in a different world, although we did things with other couples. We were kids. During the time I was not with Daphne, I lived in the culture or was at school. Even later, when I was briefly with someone else, no other style of life had time to take over. My life with Annie was different. We were like a married couple even though we were not married.

The culture was changing and was no longer as important to me. The youthful intensity seemed to pass in reality and for me. The political intensity of life in Berkeley seemed to have changed, as well. The Free Speech Movement of 1964, the Summer of Love in '67, People's Park in '69, followed by Cambodia in '70—markers of my time at Berkeley—seemed distant memories. Moving into the '70s was different. Experimenting with drugs was a thing of the past for me, even though general drug use in the culture and beyond was more widespread. I seldom went to concerts. I still liked the music, but going to Charlie Brown's and hearing the group cover Doobie Brothers hits while having a drink was fine enough. In addition, I still listened to FM radio some evenings with Daphne's DJ having taken over a prime slot. The ardent political/social justice folks seemed to be moving into the culture. The hearing on the building on Delaware marked the transition of the Berkeley city council to a more radical agenda. One of the planning commissioners who supported our appeal later became a long-term mayor, and one of our team became a planning commissioner. The counterculture was becoming just the culture, at least in Berkeley. I was progressively liberal, voted for McGovern in the fall, and had a poster on the wall afterwards that said, "Don't blame me, I voted for McGovern."

New Opportunity, No Opportunity

During this time, I started thinking about owning a house on my own as an appropriate first investment. I looked with my parents at property in Berkeley, but it was all too expensive. I looked in an inexpensive area north of Berkeley on the Bay. Point Richmond was a special place, passed by on the way to somewhere else and stuck in the town of Richmond, which had been having problems since its prime during World War II when critical shipyards were there. Richmond had not recovered; Point Richmond was different. It had a diverse population, not all black and all poor. It had a wonderful setting with hills right on the Bay and a separate village commercial center all its own. It also had lots of undeveloped property. In retrospect, I should have tried to buy as much as possible. As it was, I did not have the money to buy even one cheap lot. Because of inflation, dollar values mean little over time, but the lots were cheap even at that time. I found a duplex lot for $3,750 on which I could construct a two-unit building. I had $1,500 in savings. By borrowing some money from my father and uncle with interest at 13% interest (high at that time)—so that I could feel they were not just doing me a favor even though they obviously were—I was able to purchase the property and still had money in the bank so I could apply for a loan to build.

I was excited about this new opportunity. I do not believe Annie ever shared my vision. She was either not as thrilled about the location, not really ready to leave Berkeley, or not as ready to think about our relationship in terms of moving on together.

About this same time, she brought home a cute, little homeless dog from work. Our family already consisted of Annie, me, and her dog. I have never been too attached to animals, maybe because my pet parakeet dying when I was young was traumatic; however, Annie's dog was special. She was attentive, well trained, smart, and just as good as a dog could be. I liked her a lot. Still, I did not think we needed another dog, especially one that was not house trained—not trained in any way really. Our budget could not handle veterinary bills for one dog much less two. For the first time, we were split on something, and our relationship suffered. Annie agreed unwillingly. I was fine because I got my way, but Annie was upset, and I could not fix it. As I thought about the house project, she became interested in poetry readings.

In an unbelievably short time, our close spirited relationship of over a year ended with her declaring she wanted out. I do not know whether she had already found a replacement for me, I did not ask and did not want to know because the change in her was so clear, cold, and final. I also still did not have the skills to try to bridge the gap. Although I knew we had disagreed on the dog and had different internal temperaments, I loved Annie and knew we had a lot in common. While I quietly accepted her decision, I was deeply hurt. I had not changed in that respect since my "gracious" acceptance of the loss of my art museum friend. This was a major relationship, but clearly I could not bridge such a distance.

The hurt was not the same as with Daphne. Trying to deal with Daphne exposed me to pain with which I was totally unfamiliar, pain too personal and embarrassing to talk about with any self-respect, pain that gave me no sense of a future. This was not the same. My heart was already scarred, the scars protected me some from the feeling, and I knew I could survive. I had been in therapy and still had the counsel of Terry. Nonetheless, I was hurt worse in some ways; I could just hide it easier. Because of my love for Annie, natural changes with age, and changes coming from therapy, I was committed to our relationship. What kind of wounds are those which when added to old scars that had desensitized the heart make the pain more bearable, yet are in reality more painful?

Like with other relationships, I did not try to change the outcome. Annie did not ask for something we could work out or change. I did not ask either. The impending doom in feeling things were not quite right followed by the confirmation, made me feel my only option was to move on. My experience with Daphne had taught me that I could not change the inevitability that she wanted something or someone other than me, so applying that logic to Annie and me was easier. I was too hurt to ask if I could do anything, if we could do anything. We enjoyed so many things together and seemed made for one another; yet, that all vanished as if it never existed. I had thought we were growing into something more that both of us wanted. Most of our social interactions were with other couples in committed relationships like ours. Out of respect, I had stayed away from asking what had happened with her husband and how a marriage could fall apart so quickly, but here in just a little over a year, we were falling apart, or rather, Annie was getting out.

While I was able to leave, I was sad, apprehensive, disappointed, jealous, and surviving despite having the most important part of my life cut out. I enjoyed my work and the friends with whom we got together, I had real plans for a house, I appreciated the things we did, but the context that held it all together was the relationship with Annie. I believe that our relationship was balanced and healthy. Annie had cut me out in a way that was different from Daphne, but the pain was similar even though I should have been experienced enough now to not be hurt. "Oh, really". Within a relationship, I felt complete and satisfied. Take that away, and the missing context became a dominant concern.

As I packed up to leave, a neighbor with whom we had spent some time while living there chastised me for leaving without saying goodbye. He thought we were both leaving, and realizing his error, he backed off entirely. Annie was keeping our apartment with the things we, mostly I, had done to make it livable. I could have asked her to leave, but I wanted to move on totally.

My life was heavily tied up in the relationship. That was my main idol. I was so immersed and lost in the culture that it did not even occur to me that I might reach out to God or pray even if I was not sure why. I had bought into the vision that I had to learn to know myself better.

Therapy was a part of that; I did have some solace in that regular connection. Within the relationship, my search for more meaning was not as important because I thought in a way I had attained my goal. I had not looked any further as I became comfortable and had faith that things would work out. I still thought I was finding myself even though I felt quite lost and in a fog when the relationship vanished. "Found" must be just around the next bend, but I did not seem to be getting there.

3 .

SITTING IN LIMBO

4/73 TO 9/73

Lonely, Lost, and Disconnected

A friend from work offered to let me live in a house in the Berkeley hills for free—back to free rent for me. The house was a rental of his that was vacant at the time. I moved, I went to work, and I started helping my friends and the contractors build my house in Point Richmond. But I was numbed, and the good feelings of the new venture were dulled by my pain.

My younger brother came to live with me at the time, and I know I was not very good company. I was not mature enough to be the big brother I should have been and far too private to have a closer relationship with him. By that time, I had been in therapy for almost three years and felt I was making progress in my "human potential," but I really did not have a clue. My positive self-image was only very tentative; my confidence was low, and socially I was not in comfortable territory. I no longer had my Dana and Grizzly Peak friends, or at least thought I had lost them when Annie and I got together. I respected that boundary, whether it was real or imagined. I was not going back. I was tired from working on the house and keeping my job. I spent many evenings watching the Nixon Watergate Hearings, which was a curious distraction. I was in a new world and not able to share that with my brother, even though he was in a new world too, being on his own away from home for the first time. I know now he could have used a mentor. When I ultimately had to move, he ended up moving to a cheap motel. It never occurred to me to offer him a space in my new house. Even at the house in the hills, I was not sure I was comfortable having my private life on display. I felt I was conducting myself in a proper manner, but my therapy and lifestyle were not things I shared with my family. That was true whether Annie and I had broken up or not, but now without Annie, I was definitely floundering. I was on my own again, without the support of my friends or a relationship. The only stable support I had was therapy with Dr. Bold.

While I tried to get out and meet others, I did not seem to have a clue. I am not sure how but I connected with some younger students who played volleyball one night a week at one of the beautiful, old seminaries on the south side. I also joined them for evening get-togethers and an outing to Lake Arrowhead, a beautiful lake in the mountains outside Los Angeles. But I felt hopelessly out of place. I just did not have anything in common with them even though they were nice people. They already had relationships, were moving through school on their chosen paths, and did not seem to have any, except very peripheral links with drugs, music, politics, or communes. Actually, I no longer had any links with any of those things, but they were part of the Berkeley culture I had been immersed in. The house in Burbank where we all met for the trip to Lake Arrowhead clearly belonged to a wealthy family. The whole family appeared to be quite healthy, as well: parents respecting children; children respecting parents; all focused on their responsibilities. I expect that most of them have been very successful in their lives, careers, finances, and personal relationships. Had there been a young woman in the group to strike up a relationship with, they would have been fine friends; however, without that bind, we just did not have much in common.

I pushed myself to go on a backpacking trip into the High Sierra in the same area as before but farther than I had been. I went on my own and was exhilarated even though I was alone and perhaps a little apprehensive. I did not even have a tent. The beauty and splendor were breath taking. Of course, I had no clue at the time because of my foggy thinking and confusion that the experience was a glimpse of the unseen, of God.

I did manage during this time to keep my job and get my house built. I went in to work early in the morning, put in half a day to keep ahead of things, then went out and to join the contractors already working on the job. I had purchased the land, gotten the permits and the bank loan, and now was actually seeing the house built. Still, I had an internal sense of emptiness because of the breakup with Annie even in the midst of my sense of accomplishment.

While I started the therapy for personal growth, I learned that the process might not be about what I thought, or rather, things I thought might change or need to change were not as important. I thought I was inadequate, not as badly as I did when the relationship with Daphne failed, but inadequate. Nonetheless, I sure hoped I would not continue to feel like relationships did not work. In a relationship, I felt complete. Out of a relationship, I definitely felt something important was missing, but was something also missing in a relationship that I did not notice? Couldn't life be a little simpler?

Point Richmond

After several months of work, my house was completed. I moved my basic furniture and was happy about finally having a place of my own. I had gotten to know the community some during the work and now got to know it better by living there. For the first time in over six years, since that transformational first walk on the Berkeley campus, I was not connected to Berkeley. I had lived in that environment longer than anywhere else in my life. I was no longer connected to a group house, no longer connected to a surrogate family of friends, and no longer in a stable relationship. I was on my own in a different way. I had a work environment, I had the continuity of therapy, and I had contact with family and some old friends like Eddie and Peter.

Although I knew I was in a new state of independence, I did not fully understand it. I was in a fog. I still believed having a relationship was the most important thing in my life. I still thought my therapy was mostly to help me with that. Maybe the world had other things to offer. I was unaware of how meaningless it all was, even though a brief reflection on my worldview of secular humanism should have revealed it.

I was clueless in my search for love. One would think I might have learned something from therapy, experience, or simply intuition. I could look out the window from my new house and see the fog roll in from the Golden Gate, across the Bay, and form a wall along Cutting Boulevard right into the El Cerrito/Albany hills behind. Everything south was in the fog while Richmond to the north was usually clear. That natural fog was different from my foggy worldview. The physical fog hid the landscape for only a time and would clear. My thinking was like that fog in that the ultimate reality: the overall context was hidden, and all that was clear was that which was close at hand. The fog did not clear. I was busy and getting better at surviving, in bits and pieces, like working and earning a living, but had no goal except a relationship. That was my idol, what I worshiped, and had been for a long time. I was so sure of myself. I was trapped in the fog of my worldview and the culture.

I could walk in the new neighborhood, but it was a small area with not that much going on. There was a good local bar; however, I was barely cognizant of the fact, that while I enjoyed working class groups maybe even more than student groups, I was unlikely to meet a young woman with whom a relationship would work. I did meet a nice young woman, but even I could tell we were very different. She was companionable, and we spent some time together, but nothing more was really appropriate. I should have been happy with that instead of thinking I did know how to pick women.

Backgrounds seemed to make a difference. I did not seem to be getting much guidance from therapy. I was definitely less meek in general, more independent and assertive. But in relationships, except for being able to step forward, I was not very discerning. Clueless would be one description and lost in a fog another.

To keep busy and try new things, I went to other events that interested me. In this vein, I attended a talk by Jacques Cousteau, the most famous sea life specialist of the time who appeared on public television shows. The talk was held at the Masonic Auditorium on Nob Hill in San Francisco, which must have held thousands of people. This was the same auditorium where I heard Bob Dylan play in '65. A lot had changed, and yet not much had. Then, I knew what I was attracted to, and I was not disappointed. The concert was an introduction to that genre of live music and interesting people in San Francisco. It was a romantic dream, but I got to live my own version of it. Now, I was working to understand myself better by serious and sometimes hard introspection and had less positive expectation for what came next. Some or a lot of my naiveté was gone. I knew why I was at the Masonic Auditorium in December 1965. Now, in the fall of 1973, the lines were blurred between what I found interesting in this talk and what I thought I should be interested in. I did not know myself well enough to even know my own interests. The fog was just not clearing.

Nonetheless, I happened to sit in that huge auditorium next to a young woman who initiated conversation. Prior to the start and at opportune times during the talk, we exchanged comments here and there. Her name was Carolyn. She was attractive and lively—not reticent about pursuing the conversation. Actually, we talked quite a bit. I learned something about her, and she learned something about me. She knew about my new house and where it was, but I did not venture more. I was not very discerning, as usual. I had not felt connected eye contact as with Daphne, nor had the conversation been a soul match up like at the party with Annie, but I had known many other young women with whom I felt attraction where the first contact was more subtle. While leaving and wondering whether I should have asked for her phone number, I ran into her again on the steps outside the auditorium. I asked then so I could invite her to my open house party. Was that serendipity, God, or did she take the initiative again?

I do not know. I do know I was glad it happened and for all my inner searching I did not think beyond the moment. Despite trying to be more in control, I still mostly went with the flow and was rudderless in the current.

The party to celebrate the completion of my house was a success and a failure. It was a success in that I was able to invite many older friends, neighbors from the hill house in Berkeley, and, of course, Carolyn from the talk. It was a failure in that while being a good host, I was not experienced enough to watch how much alcohol I drank. I drank too much and then was sometimes silly in my choice of words. Then, on top of that some of the guests were having some hashish on the balcony, and I had to prove my maturity by having a puff or two. I got none of the intended benefits; instead, shortly thereafter, I got sick and spent part of the party vomiting in the bathroom. I maintained my hosting to the end but was aware that I was not who I should and could have been.

4 .

NEW WORLD

9/73 TO 10/74

Marin and the City

Even though I behaved foolishly at the house party, somehow I did not scare off Carolyn. In fact, she stayed longer, we talked more, and she spent the night. I never asked whether she had too much to drink, as well. The next morning, I did not feel that well. I am not sure how she felt, but she agreed to my suggestion that we walk down to the village center and have breakfast. Carolyn was an attractive brunette of medium height and had a very expressive face with a great laugh and smile to go with it. I, also, noticed as we walked that she seemed a little older than me and more mature in the way she carried herself. She knew what she thought, she dressed more maturely than most of the women I had been around, and was not laissez faire in her manner. I thought the local greasy spoon we went to had character and made for good people watching, not to mention great food. I think she thought it was tacky and full of oddballs. Same place, different perspectives. I noticed those differences without too much consideration and focused on getting to know Carolyn better. I liked the adventure of a new world. I think she did as well because I would have been that for her. We were interested in similar things and found one another intellectually challenging.

Although somewhat subdued that morning, Carolyn had a wonderful, bubbly spirit. She was only a year older than me, but far more mature. She had never been a part of the '60s counterculture. She had gone to school, gotten her degree and teaching credential, and now taught school. While she had been in relationships with men, she had never lived with one and had never married. She was Jewish, and like Daphne's family, hers was primarily cultural or secular but did observe holy days and meals. Unlike Daphne's parents, hers were relatively wealthy. Her father was a well-known San Francisco attorney who was the principal of a good-sized firm.

As we began dating regularly, actually becoming boyfriend and girlfriend, I found my world changing dramatically. The relationship context I needed and thrived on was in place. The emptiness of losing Annie went from a firm, lingering substance to a vanishing vapor. Daphne was only a painful memory although her DJ now had a prime slot so I got to hear him regularly! The loss of my connections with the Dana people was a thing of the past. Although I missed some of those connections, I was in a new world. I had my own house, which was different from shifting rentals, and I was drawn more to Carolyn's circle of friends and activities.

Carolyn lived in a very pleasant but ordinary two-bedroom apartment in a large complex on the other side of the Bay in Marin County. Even including my new house, which was actually a two-unit duplex, none of the thirteen places I had lived for the last seven years had been ordinary. My parent's home was ordinary; my dorm at Cal Poly was very ordinary; but my grandmother's attic, my first shared rental, my laundry porch, sharing a studio with two others in a tough part of Oakland, moving deeper into Oakland, and on, and on, were not ordinary. I had lived an extended college, hippie existence and was sort of stepping back into the "real" world. I was not the same as when I stepped away, and stepping back was not going to be easy.

In addition, I was being drawn into a new community. Marin was physically different from the East Bay. Development was far more intimate and less urban. Driving in by way of the serpentine Richmond-San Rafael Bridge, Mt. Tamalpais dominated the scene with layers of tree-covered hills and single-family homes spilling right down to the Bay. Daphne and I had gone to one of the first music festivals on Mt. Tamalpais in '67. Peter and I had gone camping in the dampness at Pt. Reyes on the coast. I had taken that wonderful drive with my art gallery friend out to West Marin through the redwoods, looking back on the Bay from high above Lucas Valley, and then further on looking down at Tomales Bay, the long finger of the Pacific marking the San Andreas Fault and pointing to the epicenter of the 1906 earthquake. Daphne and I had spent more of our time in San Francisco, the Peninsula, and that coast. My years in the East Bay were lived in the flats, worked in the hills, and along the Estuary separating Oakland and Alameda.

In addition to physical distinctions, the community was different. Berkeley was a university town and had been for a long time. Pt. Richmond was a wonderful, diverse community but substantially working class. Marin, at that time, was more diverse than it is now, but was still upscale compared to where I had lived.

At some point, I spent so much time at Carolyn's that I moved in and rented out my unit in Point Richmond. She had never lived with anyone nor had a relationship like ours. Carolyn and I had a comfortable life. We worked, had dinner with wine in the evening, and got together with her friends. We took part in local Sierra Club activities with which Carolyn was already associated. We participated in local environmental campaigns even though as I did so I had that old feeling that some people wanted to stop too much, control too much, and were too angry. A new county plan had been passed that was going to stop new freeways and major housing developments in West Marin. Yet, the group wanted to pass a water moratorium so no new water meters could be issued. The idea being that by controlling water, development in most of the 11 jurisdictions could be controlled without changing each community. No water meant no new construction.

While we were living there, George Lucas was filming *American Graffiti* on local streets. Even though he was a relative unknown then, I was familiar with him because his first film, *THX1138*, had shown in an art theater in Berkeley earlier. This movie of all things was about the same type of nowhere place I had lived in the Central Valley and the kind of cruising street my friends had dragged me to. As I watched the movie, which was quite popular, I was struck by the conflicting emotions of pride because that was generally where I was from and confusion because I had thought it was nowhere, and now it was somewhere because of the credibility of the film. Yet, the protagonist escapes from the constraints of that place—a kind of nowhere place. I would have thought that then, as well; however, now as I write this many years later, I do not. Nowhere can be anywhere, and somewhere can be anywhere. Grounding in reality is what matters.

Carolyn and I did so many things that were so different from the way I had lived. I was invited to her father's office Christmas party at Bardelli's, an old-line Italian restaurant near Union Square, not long after we got together. I did not own anything that could be called business casual: not a suit, nice slacks, a sports coat, a white shirt, nor even regular shoes. I had a suit when I graduated from high school and had worn nice clothes to church before that, but since coming to Berkeley seven years earlier, I had never worn anything even close to dressy and thought I never would. I wore casual shirts, pants, and boots. Really poor ones would be used for dirty work; better ones would be used for regular wear or nicer occasions. I had absolutely nothing appropriate for a party in a fancy San Francisco restaurant. I went to purchase some shoes, trousers, and a shirt and cringe to think back on the situation. I did not have much money. I bought dress boots, dressier trousers, and a wool shirt. I had no clue what to buy. Nothing I bought fit together. The lawyers, young and old, were all wearing dark suits, white shirts, ties, and dark shoes. My shirt was casual and rough textured, tucked into slick, orange-brown slacks the texture of which did not go with the shirt. The boots may have disappeared a little. Somehow I survived. While her world was quite different from mine, Carolyn did not seem to mind. One on one, I could converse quite adequately with just about anyone, but I tended to stand to the side and observe as I had no experience with this world.

We traveled more than I had before, going on a trip to New York first. I saw it in a completely different way than I did with Daphne. We went to nice restaurants, I saw more sights than I had seen before, and I bought a suit. The suit was not an ordinary cut and color but rather a designer fashion at the time called a safari suit in a beige color. I was still not ready to be ordinary. We went to museums and other sights. On another trip, we went to Atlanta and New Orleans and experienced the South. I really enjoyed it; I think we both did, although the heat and humidity of our room in the French Quarter was unbearable. Carolyn was a great travel companion.

Culture, Not Shock

We also went to Mexico. This trip was different from my first real trip to Mexico in that little van during my time at Dana House. Carolyn and I went to the Yucatan. We went to regular tourist ruins, like Chichinitza and Uxmal, and also Dzibilchaltun, which could only be approached by second class bus and a long walk down a dirt road. We traveled well together. I could not have done it without her—partially because she spoke Spanish but also because I could be more confident as a part of a team. I do not think she would have taken on some of the challenges if I had not been an optimistic supporter on her team, too. The different language and culture were challenges. After the Yucatan, we went to Mexico City. We had not booked transport into town or a place to stay, but it all worked out. We spent several days and saw all the major sights. I also got to see a pick-pocket at work in a crowded subway car but could do nothing to stop it. It was as if it happened in slow motion. I could not believe what I was seeing at first, then realized it was real, and the perpetrator was moving on.

On the way back from Mexico City, our plane landed on a remote Pacific Coast beach. A huge Air France jet was parked there, and we picked up a bunch of passengers who had attended the opening of a new resort. After we took off again, I realized we were sitting just a few seats behind

Herb Caen, the columnist whose books and columns had been so instrumental in my understanding and image of San Francisco. After landing in San Francisco, we had a very regular chat with him at the airport, as there was no one else around. A taxi strike meant things were not running normally, so we had a lead in to conversation. He even offered us a ride home. We demurred as we had a ride already. Our conversation with him was quite ordinary, and he was very approachable, relaxed. I found it quirky to have formed so much of my impression of San Francisco, which ended up being very accurate, from this source and meeting him in such a simple, routine situation.

We sometimes went to the symphony in San Francisco because her parents had tickets. Because her father had "bought" a table, we occasionally went to political dinners, including the 40th birthday of Willie Brown, a prominent black politician, attorney, and, later, mayor of San Francisco. Many notable people were in attendance; her father was part of this world; we were simply table fillers. During music and dancing after dinner, we bumped into Herb Caen again. He had not forgotten us, but his demeanor was a little less open. We were alone with him before, but now he was in a large venue with the "A" crowd and at work. Even as confident as he should have been and unconcerned about his image at that stage in his career, I think he still needed to be on. It was a subtle but noticeable difference. On another occasion, we went to a fundraiser at the St. Francis Hotel for Jerry Brown's first campaign for governor, again as willing table fillers. I sat next to a judge who was the original Governor Brown's brother and the future governor's uncle. He was a really easy person to converse with on what I remember being very regular topics. Just a few tables away sat the well-known star of a TV cop show based in San Francisco and farther away another movie star in his prime.

We were invited to dinners at her parents' West Marin house and shared meals with notable New York lawyers of famous people. They were fine company, although they seemed overly impressed with themselves and name-dropped regularly. Carolyn's parents did not come off that way. I was comfortable with Carolyn, and I was impressed with the environment I was exposed to. However, I was an observer of something I did not feel a part of in that milieu. Really though, nothing about it was exceptional except that the people were successful and had made names for themselves.

I never connected well with Carolyn's father, and I missed some chances to connect better with her mother. I could not make the transition from my world to theirs. I felt of a different class and culture, and I was not ready to give up my affinity for the counterculture. They probably saw it as rebelliousness and were partially right. They were of a more upscale class than I was, but they had not always been. They had started out very poor. They were intellectuals, and, I think rightly, they were protective of their daughter.

While Carolyn and I got along well, I felt that we argued too much. I was not used to that. Maybe it was an attempt at communication, but it felt harsh and often seemed unimportant. I thought maybe she wanted me to move into her world faster or more than I could. I resisted for many reasons. Perhaps I was not mature enough to respond any other way. I needed to feel I was making my decisions in some way. Yet, on earlier occasions, she actually seemed to look down on the work I did as not "idealistic" enough, much like my friends from Milvia house. I was still seeing

Dr. Bold and Carolyn agreed to try therapy but did not take to it. She probably thought it was weird; I thought she did not want to look closely at herself. I was reminded of that brief early impression that we were really quite different. Even though this relationship felt and was more like a marriage than the one with Annie, I started to feel that even with all the good, the arguing and disconnection were harmful. I felt I was not the person she wanted me to be and felt pressured to change who I was. Much later, as I began to understand my unrealistic expectations of finding true meaning in relationship, I realized my doubts were partially driven by that solid chunk of foggy thinking.

On one occasion, my parents visited us, and we all had dinner with her parents at their West Marin weekend house. I thought it was a pretty pleasant evening. However, Carolyn informed me shortly afterward that her father did not want to have dinner with my parents again. I acted as if it did not matter, but it did. I could feel a tightness in my stomach. While her parents were very accomplished, I felt they had very narrow and inconsistent standards, even if something awkward had been said that I was unaware of. They were fine at other gatherings with too much drinking, odd conversations, and nude swimming; whereas, dinner with my parents and perhaps too much alcohol had crossed some invisible line in the sand for them. While we had not talked directly of next steps that I can remember, I certainly thought about us in that way in the background. This now became a real barrier. How could that work?

Added to my existing discomfort, this new factor seemed to be a tipping point. I had a disturbing feeling that I would be better off ending the relationship. I felt terrible. Carolyn was not a bad person; we were not incompatible; but something was not connecting, not getting better, and

I did not know how to fix it. Even though I ultimately left Daphne, she basically gave me no choice but to live with an unacceptable relationship; Annie dumped me without any explanation and just pulled away; painful as it was, I only understood being left, not leaving. This would be different for me and difficult as the relationship was basically good.

About this time, Terry and his associate started offering some independent classes in the type of therapy they did. These were actually classes for therapists or those studying to be therapists. Ever since first picking up the Reich book in the bookshop, I had been interested in the "how" of therapy. It was part of my nature, and I thought any new knowledge could apply in regular relationships. I felt nervous about showing up since I did not really have interest in being a therapist or pursuing training and assumed the others would. Dr. Bold did not discourage my interest, so I started a basic course that he taught once a week in the evening. I was also doing something independent of Carolyn and hoping for some answers.

The class was very intimidating. At least half of the class of 14 or so were practicing therapists learning a different technique. Some like me were in therapy and looking to understand better, and some were looking to become therapists. Some were about my age, but many were a few years older. Many were accomplished at talking in the group; I was not. Nonetheless, I kept going.

This coincided roughly with the end of my job of over four years. I was at loose ends again. Things were shifting on their own, and I felt I needed to make a change but was so unsure of myself. I was so buried in concern about the relationship and what I should be doing that I never got to wondering whether something was missing in my secular worldview that somehow still left me in a fog.

5.

SURPRISING CHANGE

10/74 TO 12/74

Certain Uncertainty

Moving out was very difficult because of my mixed feelings. I felt the relationship with Carolyn was not going to work, but my confidence was low, and I had never broken up with anyone in a long-term relationship. Even though I had a sense I needed to do so, I was really shaky. I was stepping out from the best relationship I had known. I still did not like living alone and did not understand or feel comfortable in the singles scene. I had no guarantee things would work out and would not spend a lengthy time on my own.

Because I had rented out my duplex in Pt. Richmond, I found an inexpensive apartment in the poor area of town about five minutes away and made the move; however, optimism, hope, and excitement were absent. I was in limbo again. I tried to get used to being alone again. Being in Marin was not the same as being in Berkeley, and I was not the same person I had been. My life had changed. I did not feel I fit into the world of Carolyn and her family, but I was no longer a hippie student either. I did not know what I was anymore.

I earned money doing a few odd jobs. I went looking for work, although I did not have experience job searching since my previous job had lasted four and a half years. I qualified for unemployment for the time being.

I continued therapy and the therapy class I had started attending. Both continued to be a source of growth and stimulation. At first I did not think of the class as a place to meet someone but decided one of the four women who attended might be an appropriate match for me. She was an attractive, relatively quiet Jewish girl whom I felt comfortable approaching. I had no definite sense of attraction as with Daphne or Annie, and I did not have the benefit of talking time to establish mutual interest as with Carolyn. All I had was our mutual involvement with therapy and my cluelessness. Appropriate or not, the relationship did not develop, which made attending the class awkward. I did not focus on the other three women in the class: two because I was not attracted to them and the third, who was an attractive blonde, because I immediately formed the opinion that she was involved with someone already. She brought homemade cookies one night, and that provided a risk-free chance to talk to her. I thanked her for the cookies and was pleased with myself that I said something. She reciprocated by complimenting my sweater.

The class itself taught me more about people and how they relate than about therapy. I knew Reichian therapy from fairly long, personal experience. In the small class setting, I was somewhat surprised by the positions Dr. Bold put students in, especially those who were not in therapy. He did demonstrations of the technique with different students as the "patient." I was impressed by those who agreed and relieved that he did not call on me. The older and experienced therapists asked questions and responded with ease in class. At first, I was totally intimidated, but as the class went on, I felt comfortable talking some; however, I was much more comfortable speaking during the informal time we all spent waiting in the foyer for class to begin.

By this time in my therapy, I was a lot more confident and surer of certain things than I had ever been. I arrogantly thought I was in less of a fog than I now know I was. I could voice opinions, particularly when I realized that—in my laymen's simplicity—I knew more about the therapy and what was happening than most. I understood physical armoring and how it limited emotional expression and how breathing could break that down because I had experienced it. I knew how to access the sadness and anger beneath. I did not understand everything fully or its ultimate limitations at that point. That was far in the future.

Unexpected Connection

All the class members would have liked a little more of that foyer fellowship with one another, if only to understand better what we were learning, but not until one of the last classes was the suggestion made that we go out for coffee afterwards. As I remember it, everyone came along. We went to a pizza place on the back side of Presidio Heights near the Presidio Theater. The place had few people in it, so we were able to push tables together to sit in a group. Finally, some of the concerns of those who were not in therapy and the knowledge of those who were convened in a way that brought the group together and opened up the conversation. Unlike my discomfort talking in the class, this format was far more comfortable, and as one of the ones in therapy, I could speak with some authority.

Our conversations meandered around, and while sitting next to the young woman with whom the relationship had not worked out and the attractive blonde, the blonde asked if we were together, meaning a couple. Obviously, she had observed something. The conversation came to an awkward pause. The question was direct and personal but not offensive so much as embarrassing because our "no" said we were not—though we had been maybe, but we were not. Somehow the conversation was able to survive and move on to where we all lived. The blonde, whose name was Allison, lived in Berkeley, but she was very interested in Marin because she wanted to move from Berkeley and had heard that Marin might be a better area for her. I asked her a few questions about what kind of a town she wanted to live in, listened to her answers, and even though I knew only a little of the various towns in Marin, I named one which I knew from experience and descriptions could fit her desires. At the same time, from nowhere I can identify I thought to myself, "And I am going to live there with you." I did not think more of the thought as it seemed so odd but did realize that I was attracted to her. I still had not totally given up on the other young woman and, in fact, gave her a ride back to her car that night. Terry had taught me to be comfortable being direct and accepting the results. I would have found it helpful to have a good manual to follow.

The next week was the last class, and once again, we all went out for coffee afterwards. This time, I gave Allison and the tall, young man traveling with her back to Berkeley a ride to the bus terminal. In the intervening week, I had in my time with Terry gotten some feedback and an idea about the possibility of approaching her. As I dropped them off, I asked for her phone number, even though I was not sure of her relationship with the man she was traveling with. Everyone had a phone number except her apparently, so I only got an address. While I had hoped for an easier way to make contact, I was thrilled. She was a very attractive woman—no, actually beautiful. I could not really explain how I had almost missed her. Now as the class was over, I maybe had a chance to see her again, and I had a sense that she might be interested in seeing me.

I knew from our group conversation that she sold handmade leather crafts on the streets in Berkeley and San Francisco. At that time in the early '70s, a whole new set of industries was arising out of the counterculture of the '60s. Young people with artistic ideas were making their own products and selling them on the street. Most were cutting edge members of the love generation, and ironically they were also the epitome of entrepreneurial capitalists. A lot of that same irony went on with concert promoters and music groups who made big money from the culture, not to mention the drug dealers. This street vending was similar but on a much smaller scale, one more in sync with the culture.

Over the weekend, with excitement and apprehension, I looked through the craft booths in both Berkeley and Fisherman's Wharf in San Francisco but did not find her. Early the next week, I dressed up to look for job but really meant to try to see Allison. I needed an excuse for why I was in Berkeley even though I had driven the distance from Marin just in hopes of seeing her. I pumped myself up to go to her address and knock on the door, unsure what to expect. She lived in a nondescript duplex on Ashby near Telegraph, one of the busiest intersections in town. Even though I had some confidence because of her offering her address and Dr. Bold's encouragement rather than dis-couragement, I was extremely apprehensive and nervous as I knocked on her door.

She answered, and her shock appeared even greater than my nervousness as we clumsily started a conversation, both trying to appear as if we were totally at ease and encounters like this happened every day. While I recall the scene clearly, I do not recall what we talked about. She made a pot of coffee, served herself a mug, and offered me none. I met her five-year-old, tried to talk to her even though I had no experience with young children, and wondered that she seemed younger than five by her very rudimentary speech. After a short while, we decided to go for a walk up the street to a park, chatting all the while. We talked more at the park while the little girl played. After a while, her daughter took off all her clothes and continued to play; Allison said and did nothing, so I took my cue from her and acted like this was quite natural. I felt it was odd but then again, nothing was really considered odd in the late '60s and early '70s. In any case, whatever we were talking about cemented a sense in me that this young woman was intriguingly different from what I thought. Obviously, she was not involved with someone else.

I was attracted to her in a new way. I had been around her once a week in a small group for at least two months but had missed her or ruled her out. Yet, ultimately, the attraction was somehow different and deeper from the start. I was in unfamiliar territory, still taking a step at a time. We were seeing the same therapist, had the class experience in common, and we had socialized in the group setting of the coffee shop. However, we still had a lot to learn about each other.

Our conversation flowed easily. Allison was supporting herself and her five-year-old on her own. She had been on welfare but had recently gotten off it by selling her leather goods. This had meant that previously she had to get up in the middle of the night sometimes, go out on the street, and sleep in her sales spot so she would have it in the morning. She would sleep with a knife to protect herself. Only recently, Berkeley had instituted a lottery system for spots, so things were a little better. She wore little or no make-up, did not shave her legs or armpits, and did not even clip the hairs on a couple of moles on her face. However, I really did not notice or found them part of Allison's appeal. She had a powerful yet subtle beauty, much more complex than the beauty of a model or movie star. She was tall and slender. Her features and manner were naturally formed for a perfect picture every time. Her demeanor, somewhat somber and not the least flirtatious, was focused, mature, and a little ethereal. That may have been reinforced by her blonde, unaltered eyebrows and fair skin. She carried her life experience in a way different from any woman I had met before. She was only twenty-five, yet had been supporting her family, which earlier had included her husband, for over five years. Most young people of the time delayed adulthood; at least a significant part of hers started at age 20. I recalled that during one of our therapy classes, she cried quietly but openly through part of the class. She did not hide how she was feeling.

We made our way back to her apartment and made a date to get together the day after Thanksgiving. We quickly became inseparable. We got to know one another effortlessly. We could talk comfortably with one another. She came over to my apartment with her daughter and fixed dinner for me as if we were already a family.

I helped her with her sales on the street. This was a world I did not know. Since I got together with Annie in late 1971 and we were forced to move to the flats on Ninth Street, I had not walked the streets of Berkeley. Just before Christmas in late 1974, Telegraph was a veritable bazaar with stands lining the sidewalk for blocks, and there were more stalls on Shattuck. In the City, the same thing happened in the Fisherman's Wharf area. I was mesmerized. Where did this all come from? The feeling was a natural extension of what had been going on in the culture. At that time, much of the work was original. Later, some vendors resold other products—an informal shop on the street. Allison created leather goods with original, hand-carved designs: belts, wallets, journals, and the like. I had never done sales but easily dropped into this new world and the crazy hope for a lottery-won vendor spot. Sitting behind the stall and feeling the tempo of sales or no sales was exhilarating and exhausting.

Dramatic Change

I know I was being open and vulnerable, and I believe she was, too. We did not hold our selves back. We were attracted to one another and quickly decided we had found something we both had been missing. We were talking next steps and long term from the start. Where did this come from? We communicated at a level of intimacy that was surprising given how recently we had met. Within no more than a couple of weeks, we had decided to marry. Marriage did not come up often in this new culture, even in long term relationships, and we had only just met. We bought custom made silver and jade rings from a street vendor friend of Allison's. The decision was not shocking to us because we seemed to be so meant for one another. Most of her street sales happened during the holidays, but she stopped in mid-December so she and her daughter could be with her parents in Michigan. She may not have been there, but Christmas 1974 was wonderful.

Such a dramatic change was hard to explain. I was never in this same position with Daphne, Annie, or Carolyn, all of which were serious relationships. Where was the almost year and a half drifting in the fog between Daphne and Annie or the more than half a year before I met Carolyn? I had not even adjusted to being alone and recalibrating, and I was already in a completely different place.

The decision was calm and measured rather than animated and hasty. We talked about it a lot. We talked about our future together; we talked about kids and family. Surprisingly, this decision was obvious and easy. Yet, how could it be so obvious, so fast? How could it make sense? Allison had a daughter with some obvious learning challenges, and she was supporting herself and her daughter at a financial level that covered the basics but not much more. I had no job and was receiving unemployment. I still owned my house but had to keep it rented to pay the expenses. I had been moving away from the '60s culture and into the regular world for at least a couple of years. In fact, with Carolyn, I had been exposed to an even bigger world that had me back in the City more than I had been since '67-69. Allison had been and was still a part of the counterculture, in her business, appearance, and where she lived. However, she was different in that she had the responsibilities of a family. That was a kind of maturity I had not experienced before. Thus, while it might have appeared that with this decision I was stepping back into the counterculture, in fact, the decision was a surprising forward step. Was I not ready for that bigger world and its challenges? This was a big world with an instant family and responsibilities, bigger in a different way. The appearance may have been counter-cultural but the reality was traditional. Something powerful was going on.

The transformational character of the decision was like when I first walked onto the Berkeley campus after struggling with the decision to leave San Luis Obispo. I had no doubt about that decision nor did I with this one. I did not have the perspective to know what was different with Allison, but I knew the feeling. With Allison, I had no doubt, no desire to hold back. I intuitively evaluated something differently. I was ready to make a commitment. Allison, with a different background and experience, found herself at the same place at the same time. Love was part of it, so was attraction, age, compatibility, and where we were in our lives. We also had a common cultural "religion" in our therapy. Another huge part of the experience was that I knew she wanted to be with me as much as I wanted to be with her—nothing tentative, not just be with me for now, but to be with me from now on. She seemed to like me just as I was. This was a part of love I had not solidly felt since the early times with Daphne. Even though my supposed secular worldview did not have room for faith and hope; I definitely had both. I trusted that this was a good decision. I just continued failing to connect the dots of the inconvenient fact of where that faith and hope sprung from.

I started this relationship from a better base than ever before. Daphne and I were young; I had no experience. Because I was so attracted to Annie, I ignored the question of why she broke from her husband so soon. Carolyn and I had common interests, which developed into a good relationship, but we did not start out with mutual, long-term goals drawing us together like with Allison. I do not think successful relationships require the feeling Allison and I had on getting together, and certainly, false or temporary emotion/passion had not been very successful for me before.

Allison and I started looking for a place to have a home together. In the spirit of the times we planned to live together. We could not marry right away because she had never bothered to get a divorce from her husband despite separating from him more than two years prior. In those times, these things just did not matter. We looked for some place to rent in Marin as we had discussed in the first coffee shop conversation. We looked all over the county at numerous places. Nothing quite worked until we were approached by a man painting in the unit next door to one we were viewing. His unit was available and was perfect for what we had in mind. Even better, we could afford it. We have never fully understood why it ended up being in the exact community I had suggested to Allison in the coffee shop, although that community did suit both of us more than others might have. And, I failed to mention that when I thought, "And I am going to live there with you" back at the coffee shop, I learned later, she thought the same thing at the same time. Where did that come from? We did not know one another at all. However, Allison had noticed me, even while I had ruled her out as taken. So, was a very undiscerning guy all of a sudden picking up very specific signals on his radar that night? I think not, nor do I think serendipity explains it. In addition, this was the only place in the community I had mentioned at the coffee shop, and yet, that was it. So, was this now serial serendipity?

Starting a new life with Allison seemed like all sunshine. The fog seemed to have drifted away, but it was not gone completely, as I was going on faith and feelings, not understanding. We were different in many ways. She had left home in Michigan immediately after high school because she felt verbally abused and controlled by her mother. Her father was a doctor, and, while they were poor while he went to medical school, the family was very comfortable by the time she finished high school. She had five brothers and a sister. She had come out to San Francisco "with flowers in her hair" shortly after graduation and a short time in Flint and Detroit. She only stayed in the City briefly before moving to Hollywood where she was part of a commune known as Rivendell House (after Tolkien). She ended up back in Ann Arbor where she was associated with various known countercultural music types and working as a waitress to support her family. After that, she moved out to Oakland to live with Michigan friends. Because of her quick exit from home and then having a family at 20, college had not entered the picture for her. Shortly after returning to the Bay Area, she had moved to Garberville in Humboldt County to live on some land her friends had. It was a very basic existence, not unlike my earlier commune visit in Mendocino County.

Unfortunately, her young daughter got a very serious case of pneumonia, so she was back in Oakland sooner than expected. During that time, her husband, who had followed her out even though they were no longer together, connected with Dr. Bold and suggested him to Allison. She did not have the money but asked her father if he would pay for the counseling, and he agreed. She later told me of some of her own disappointing relationship experiences, and that for quite a while before we met, she had decided to be alone even though Terry was encouraging her otherwise.

In one of our conversations about People's Park, I learned that the main organizer had invited her to coffee and hoped for more. She accepted the coffee but demurred on the more. We both had enough life experience that even with our differences, we could sense a core common vision of our life. That would prove to be not quite as common as we thought at the time.

V.

SEEKING REALITY

Twenty-Five Years

1.

MARRIAGE WORLD

12/74 TO ABOUT 9/81

In the Culture and Not

As I stated earlier even though Allison and I planned to marry almost from the start of our relationship, we could not for over a year because she had never legally ended her previous marriage. She had not found it important before we met. In the spirit of the times and our desire to do for ourselves, Allison wanted to make the change without an attorney. Using a book, she managed it, but that took her a year to accomplish even without roadblocks of any kind.

During that time, I continued with various jobs, some very informal, some more formal. Eventually I found a regular job in an office. Allison continued with her crafts, selling on the street and in crafts fairs. We would sell together when I could join her. All of it was exciting. We were in love, and the future, irrespective of our limited financial means, looked bright to us. We had faith and hope: a confident expectation that was inconsistent with our secular humanist worldview, but we did not know that then.

My friend, Peter and his wife, lived in Marin, as well, at that time, and we would visit them. They now had not only her three kids but also two of their own. Visiting them was always interesting. They lived better than we could hope to because of their financial situation, and their kids had complete run of the house. Somehow they handled more disorder than we ever could.

We still felt very much a part of the counterculture, Allison, perhaps, even more than me. She taught me to appreciate a part with which I had never been involved. She was into health foods, much like the Dana house people had been. She was also a really good cook. We started our own vegetable garden. I had grown strawberries and pumpkins in Colorado and helped with squashes and pumpkins in the Central Valley, but I had never actually tried to grow a vegetable garden. She was into trying to follow natural ways to stay healthy. She continued to use very little make-up, did not shave her legs or armpits, and wore clothes that were often hand done or hand modified. I was taking a step forward being responsible for a wife and child, yet was stepping back some into a purer form of the idealism of the '60s counterculture without the drugs and free love. That idealism was really an attraction to freedom, independence, and flexible, individual autonomy within the context of responsible participation in society. We paid our bills; we worked for our little bit of money; we were not angry at the system; did not feel we were owed something. We just wanted to live our life and were generally upbeat.

At first, we had a lot of time together. I only had part-time work and Allison worked at home making her crafts. If she went to sell, I could go with her. Later that year I got a regular job that gave us a little more secure living, even if it meant less time together. Even though we argued little, had plenty of time for physical intimacy, and a deepening relationship, I was still somewhat clueless as to my role and responsibilities in building and maintaining what we had. Much of great literature, when focusing on relationships, studies the difficulties of a man and a woman coming together in a relationship. They are not fairy tales; yet, in many ways, they mostly end with the same "happily ever after" ending, which is the true fairy tale.

Allison became pregnant before we could marry. Not being concerned with marriage before children has become common in the culture, in general, but was not so at the time. However, among those like us, it was common, and that was the world in which we lived. We had committed to one another early on, and marriage was just a formality as far as we were concerned.

Finally, a little over a year after we got together, Allison completed her divorce process, and we planned our marriage a few days afterwards. We really had no ceremony. We went to the civic center and were married by a court commissioner with his assistant as witness, then went home to our little apartment. Our stated purpose in having no other ceremony was that all that was unnecessary and silly. While I was ready to be married, was in love with Allison, and committed to her and our relationship, I was still much too shy to have desired to have a ceremony and be the center of attention. I do not know but suspect the same may have been true for Allison. It was just not on our radar. It did not even occur to me until much later that my parents might have liked to have had a part but I was too much into the culture of "this is a formality" and maybe this is "all about me and not others" to have caught that.

Buying tickets on credit and faith, we planned a honeymoon trip to Hawaii. This was to be our first big trip.

Neither of us had been to Hawaii. I had never really been anywhere by plane that was not part of the mainland. Allison had lived in Switzerland for five years when she was young, as I had lived in Japan for a little over a year when I was even younger, but had never taken a trip like this either. We were excited. We planned to see all four of the main islands, so we would know where to go in the future. Our trip was characteristic of who we were at the time or perhaps more who I was. Allison tended to follow my lead. We had planned inexpensive places to stay and rental cars on each island. But, because of the great expense of eating out, we planned to eat in our hotel rooms most of the time as if camping. In the entire trip, we had one outside meal: breakfast on the day we left. We saw Honolulu, drove all around Oahu, saw the wonderful steep green hills, the cane fields, the beaches, and the ocean on every side. We toured all of Maui, driving the entire lower half even though we were not supposed to, seeing the change from the tropical east side to the desert-like west side, camping in a park where the wind blew so fiercely it blew metal utensils right out of our dishes, and seeing the volcano crater, steep and forlorn. We loved Kauai, staying one night in a camper near Hanalei with the wind building in the mountain and attacking with such fierce intensity that we thought everything would be blown away; yet in the morning, everything was normal. We saw the falls, the canyon, the Na Pali cliffs in their steep fantasy, splendor from the bottom and the top in their precipitous drop, the Alakai Swamp in its wet, lush density, and the beaches and fields. Kauai had less development, more wildness; that was why we loved it. We saw Hawaii with its lush gardens, volcanoes, mountain campgrounds, ranches, and striking coastline at Kona. We loved Kona. It was developed, but it was not large, and it was just so stunning.

Our trip fed us greatly. We survived the struggles, the ongoing stress of possible financial setbacks, the tension of traveling with only basic comforts, and the extra work of having a child with us. Allison and I had been a family with her daughter from the beginning, and she naturally joined us on our honeymoon. We did not even think about another way. We went home exhilarated, returning to monthly payments to cover the cost of the tickets and other expenses of the trip and to savor the memories.

More Family

We had gotten married in late January, 1976, gone on the trip in mid to late February, and by the middle of May our baby was due to be born. We had been taking classes in natural childbirth and had an obstetrician who was a proponent of natural homebirth. While in times not that far past, babies were born naturally and at home, the practice was not the common American experience at the time. You went to the doctor, you went to the hospital, the father waited, the baby was born, the staff did whatever procedures were standard, the baby went to the nursery where the father could see it through a glass window, and at an appropriate time the family went home together. Even with my experience with the counterculture, I would have chosen that same way to do things if it were not for Allison. She really believed in doing things differently. Because of her confidence, I had confidence. Dr. Bold, in addition, believed this was a better way. He and his young, second wife taught a class in natural childbirth to us and two other expectant couples. That combined with the obstetrician, midwives, and most importantly, Allison, led me along the path.

As it was, when Allison knew the baby was ready, things went so fast that only the midwife arrived in time. The doctor came after the birth. Our son arrived "in a caul" as the water bag did not burst; the midwife had to puncture the bag causing him to shoot out in a rush of water. I was in position to hold him as he came out but with the rush of water missed him, and I think he bounced once on the bed before I caught him. My life changed instantly. I do not know how to express it exactly; I knew I would be a father, but actually being one changed my world. The birth of our child was completely different from thinking about it. A concept became a reality.

At that time, a subtle but powerful shift happened in my introspection. I was still immersed in my worldview—my denomination of self-awareness and its icon, relationship. However, I now had that relationship, and it had lasted and felt like it was going to continue to last. I had inherited a family, and now we had a child together, as well. My concern subtly eased because of that, which then left room for other cares of the world: money, prestige, and career. Much of this was natural because of the added responsibilities. Before that, I was focused on a relationship primarily, and those other cares were very secondary. Having a solid relationship and extra responsibilities, in my worldview, I had reached a goal, like climbing a mountain. You could say my life was more balanced, or you could say I was still foggy in my thinking as this was the extent of reality.

We were both still seeing Terry fairly regularly and getting his advice. Sometimes, I would disagree about something. Rather than debate, he still had that wonderful way of saying, "Oh, really," which meant we will see. I still usually came around to his view in time. Some of his advice was focused on us individually and some on us together. I am not sure we always had them properly separated, but we were poor, in love, and enjoying life. I was as happy as I had been, so much so that I did not notice the subtle shift and that I had not really found ultimate meaning. I was just too distracted to notice yet.

We continued to be very much in love and were responsibly committed to our relationship and one another. We seemed to have similar ideas about where we were going, although we did not specifically make goals and plans as that would not have fit our hippie like lifestyle. However, we talked about having lots of children, maybe eight. I was back in the counterculture to the extent that Allison worked in that environment, we tried growing our own vegetables, raised chickens for eggs, read books on natural this and that, bought much of our food at health food stores, and generally dressed and acted like others in that lifestyle. We did not use drugs; I had never done so except when "experimenting"; I think Allison may have smoked marijuana long before our relationship. We had never been particularly political, although we were progressively liberal. Our relationship was a traditional marriage even if we didn't look it. We were totally committed to one another, did not have ideas of open marriage—which was getting lots of media attention then, especially in Marin, flirting with others, or any of the other sexual innovations of the culture. It was odd how those ideas of the counterculture seemed to have crept quickly and quietly into the mainstream.

Nonetheless, we had much to learn. An upheaval like with Daphne wanting to be with other men was highly unlikely because of our commitment to a common understanding of love and relationship. Our ability to communicate or weather personal issues was dramatically unlike how easily Annie and I were blown apart. Allison was not as outwardly effervescent as any of them, but she was just as fun and very mature—not, perhaps in worldly ways as Carolyn was, but in an independent way from having struggled for so long. From the age of nineteen, eight years earlier, she had to deal with a pregnancy, a child, a husband who was unable to keep a steady a job, supporting her family, and finding financial independence.

On occasion, she did have a sense of sadness about her as well; she wanted us to be together all the time. We needed to work out how our day to day life would work. At first, Allison wanted to support me so I would be around "and drink beer and eat pretzels," an image only as I did not even like beer. Because of my limited work with odd jobs, we were together a lot early on. When I took a regular job for a while, Allison was less happy. She really wanted or needed me around. When I was on my own again, starting my own business at home, she was happier. I walled off an area in the garage such that she could do her leather work on one side and I could do my work on the other. Those were really good times. I would go out for appointments, but my work was at home, and when she did not need to be upstairs, she was in our garage workspace doing her work while I did mine.

We sometimes struggled on how to make an important decision in our family when we differed and both of us felt strongly. This was challenging when it happened, but most things we could readily resolve. We had to smooth some other edges to our commitment. We had no arguments and few heated discussions. Issues of money, responsibility, and the order of our life together were worked out easily.

I had to reduce my desire and comfort with greater order and get used to a more relaxed style. Part of that was Allison and part was our daughter who was not going to be that orderly whether I wanted it or not. Allison had to get used to greater order than had been her custom. We seemed to settle comfortably in the middle, and that was probably better for both of us.

In some ways, Allison was more rigid in her beliefs about relationships than even most non-counterculture folks. I still had three or four copies of popular magazines that had photos of naked women. These were not pornographic magazines; in fact, some were quite benign. She threw them away. I did not understand and was angry because they were mine. Allison was beautiful, most would agree, but like many good-looking people, she did not think or could not think she was beautiful. She felt quite threatened or worried about me. Separately, she had strong feelings that I should not need even one copy of a magazine like that. Allison would call me on a glance at a woman I had not even noticed. I could not understand the level of jealousy or anger. We had to work it out, although I did not understand the poison of the culture still in my veins. Much of the sexual freedom of the time was supposedly for the benefit of women, but really men benefited as most of the "freedom" would be of interest primarily to them. While I was fully committed to the relationship we had, I was still drawn to the culture within which we lived. I saw no harm in a little vicarious pleasure at that time.

We complemented one another well. Allison actually lived within the 60s culture more than I had; yet, by the time we were together, she was unyielding in her morality. I agreed with her but was vague on the edges. However, when it came to issues with authority, she reluctantly yielded to me usually because I dealt with it easier. I was growing more aware that much of the culture's rejection of authority was adolescent.

Still, I did not fully understand the difficulty of maintaining a relationship. I did not have a clear picture of us as a couple and as separate people. I had that image in previous relationships, yet, real long term relationships only survive in that reality even if it is not understood or noticed. I did not really have a clue and was still in a fog. Even with therapy and our solid relationship, I did not recognize the foggy thinking.

Moving from ill-fated relationships that lasted a year or two to one that was clearly moving toward lasting much longer and with the additional commitments of family requires deeper mutual commitment. That reality often gets lost in the activity of living—financial challenges and commitments, commitments to children, general obligations. Mutual growth and recognition of boundaries require response and change and continued commitment to the union. That union, that thing that is the couple, had to take priority over the individual without losing the individual.

Because our relationship was young, recognizing and respecting boundaries was not on our radar, perhaps masked by the new, exciting, changing nature of our relationship. The relationship boundaries for the early years mostly had to do with resolving conflict or building the ability to commit to being a couple instead of just two separate people simply choosing to live together. That commitment to the union before the individual is crucial. Being vulnerable in that commitment is crucial. Unfortunately, we lived in a time and a place when the commitment to the individual, the self, was on the rise, and a commitment to marriage and monogamy was under attack. The counterculture of "love" or "free love" tended toward sexual love rather than relational love. We were more traditional or old-fashioned hippies; yet, we found ourselves in a county of striving, successful, mainstream men and women for whom boundaries were breaking apart in relationships much like the counterculture model.

I continued working odd jobs, got some consulting work, and was around home. Allison made her crafts, sold in crafts fairs as far as Santa Cruz. We were together a lot and loved it. After Thanksgiving, we would sell together on Telegraph Avenue in Berkeley whenever Allison got a spot in the lottery. It had been ten years since I first walked on campus from this very street. I had moved on and away, and yet here we were selling custom leather goods with our kids in tow. We were poor and loved our life. While changing in many ways, we still looked the part of a young hippie couple with young kids. We were living out that original vision as we had seen it.

We started our daughter in a local Summerhill-type school based on A. S. Neil's school in England. We read a lot about education systems with various approaches, especially those with less authoritarian/disciplinarian structures than traditional models. Those school connections led to trying to start a school with others; ultimately it did not come together. We had a plan, looked at sites, and interviewed teachers, but then the other key couple changed their mind, and we had to give up the idea.

Finally, we started her in the local school but found that she needed help even though she was starting a year later than others in her age group. Allison had a hard time accepting the feedback and structure. She worried about the potential damage and emotional trauma. It was a hard time, but we met some truly dedicated helpers. Allison got involved with local pre-school play groups with our young son.

By that time, I had more consulting work and did not think that a garage office would continue to work for meetings and the like, so I looked into renting a small office close to the freeway. I found one not far from home, but Allison was sad that I was not at home. I was not any less in love, but I was excited to embark on something new that could improve our life. She saw something changing that she did not care about or like. I learned later that she cried most days. I succeeded in getting more work, so our financial situation was not as precarious. Allison was able to think less about selling crafts. We continued to go to fairs occasionally, and she geared up for the holiday season, a prime time for sales.

In early 1977, I found an inexpensive piece of property for sale near where we lived. Our dream was to have a house of our own built. The prices were high in Marin for existing homes, and my original house in Point Richmond was not really appropriate. It was too small, and we liked the area where we lived now. Before that could happen though, we watched housing prices in Marin double. I consulted a real estate agent, and soon after he found a very inexpensive house to consider on a secluded lot in our town. It was actually the cheapest house on the market in Marin at the time. The house had many benefits. The first was for us to have a house we could afford. The second was that the property, while in town, was on an ample lot with many trees and privacy. The third was that while much of the lot was steep, creating much of the seclusion, the top was flat with yard area and great exposure to the sun. Finally, the house could be remodeled over time; the site had room for additions when we could afford improvements. When I first described it to her, Allison was not particularly keen, but when she saw the site, she understood immediately.

The property had significant problems that would have discouraged others. The house was small, poorly constructed, and largely unfinished. The long, steep, unpaved driveway, barely passable in good weather, was completely impassable in wet conditions. The house was not connected to the sewer and had a very marginal septic system. Those were some reasons why it was so inexpensive. This opportunity happened before our financial condition had changed much. We had to borrow from both sets of parents to make the down payment and could only buy because the owners financed the purchase. Thus, we did not need to qualify with a bank, which would have been difficult given both the condition of the property and our financial condition. We made the purchase and moved in November 1977, about three years after we had first met. I think Allison's father was worried about the wisdom of their loan when he came to visit and saw what we had bought with his help. At that time, California prices, particularly Marin prices, were far higher than in most of the rest of the country. Allison's parents owned a large, charming house on a beautiful lot in a nice town in Michigan that was worth less than ours cost.

Our house was not much. It had no landscaping except the native trees and bare rock ground. Deer were prevalent where we lived, so landscaping had to be natural, deer resistant, or protected. The previous owners had a plastic rose against a power pole, and the deer had even eaten that. The site was at least cleared of the junk car, trailer, and other rubbish the previous owners had accumulated. The house had one bathroom with a metal stall shower, the bottom of which was rusted, a tiny sink, and a toilet. The second bathroom had a concrete floor and roughed in unfinished walls. That was it, no plumbing fixtures. One of the "bedrooms" had almost no windows and none that opened. The "garage" had a gravel floor. The kitchen had metal cabinets with a built-in sink and an uneven, concrete floor that had not been done professionally. The place had originally been built as a weekend place for people from the City but was constructed amateurly at best. The previous owners had raised five kids there and were retiring to the foothills of the Sierras. Even with the negatives, we were thrilled. A positive part of the counterculture was still with us. We had a place of our own with room to raise a family, have our chickens, maybe do some landscaping, and be close in and yet very private.

We had looked at other land farther out in West Marin with beautiful redwoods and greater seclusion. Yet, that was true seclusion that required traveling to do anything. With this property, we had the best of both. We were blessed even though we did not know to use that word then. Even when much later, things were financially better and we could have moved to something more valuable, we never did. Even as I write this, we have not moved. However, we have changed a lot, and the house has too.

I was feeling better about myself—certainly a little prideful and maybe too pleased with myself for living in Marin—although I was recognizing more and more its arrogance and excess of pride. Like with marriage and a family, I felt like I had climbed an internal mountain and achieved something. I still did not recognize that I was in a fog, and ultimate reality was nowhere to be found.

Changes

Our therapy continued. I went less often as things were developing. Allison continued to go regularly. In conversations with Dr. Bold, I found my political attitudes changing some over time. When I moved to Marin, I was a very progressive liberal, almost radical, though I was never an activist. I was not angry and was always more moderate; I thought things were more complex than others apparently did. When I moved to Marin and was immediately thrown in with the Sierra Club and others pushing for a water moratorium to stop development in the county, I participated and helped do bumper stickers. However, even then, I was thinking why was this necessary? Marin had that year passed a landmark county plan that limited development, stopped freeways, and preserved agricultural land. Couldn't, or rather shouldn't, local jurisdictions get to decide? I did not realize I was moving into a community that while appearing completely different from Berkeley was just as progressive in terms of environmental issues and growth, maybe even more so.

I mostly read national news through *Newsweek*, as I had since high school, which gave me a general feel for events and context. In addition, we watched some television news. Nixon had resigned in 1974 just before we met. I thought Gerald Ford had done an okay job being president and was fairly moderate. I was really a Democrat or a "declines to state" independent by this time. When Reagan ran against Ford for the 1976 election, I was very anti-Reagan, stemming from his decision to send the National Guard in to People's Park. I did not have much respect for him. Thus, I changed my registration to Republican just so that I could vote for Ford and against Reagan in the California Republican presidential primary. I do not recall how I voted in the presidential election as I was not that comfortable with Carter. Only four years earlier, I was clearly for McGovern who was to the left of either of them.

While I was interested in politics, I was mostly ambivalent. I more and more felt that less government regulation and more personal responsibility and freedom was better. I was seeing some of this in the tight control in our local communities in Marin. I felt the Vietnam angst and verbal assaults on America by some Americans had been over-done, especially on the Democratic side. The comments expressed more about the people themselves than about our country. I seemed to be hearing and seeing things differently than the apparent majority of the community around me, but ironically what I heard and saw in that community was significant in leading me in that opposite direction. I thought my views more consistent with the culture I thought I had joined. I seemed to be shifting, and so was the culture.

From the time I started therapy, I no longer read much fictional literature, new or old. I tended to read non-fiction, mostly psychological or educational such as Perls, Jung, Piaget, and the like. From when Allison and I had gotten together, I had continued to read almost exclusively non-fiction but mostly history and natural history. Now, for the first time, I started reading some more conservative writers, perhaps initially at the mention of Dr. Bold, but mostly because I was trying to understand this sense that my political mindset did not really fit with what I actually believed. I did not know why because I had thought myself settled in a radically progressive position since coming to Berkeley in late 1966. Terry had always been much more conservative than I. Early on I found some of his more traditional, matter of fact views somewhat reactionary. Over time, as our relationship grew, I changed and understood him better, and I usually realized he was right. "Oh really."

My views changed as I began to see less freedom in my old views. I was open to listening, and I found that the ideas in my conservative reading fit my view better. I was now finding that, except for things like sexual attitudes, language, and dress, more regulation and less freedom was the norm in the counterculture and the culture. The basic difference seemed to be a belief in less government allowing more freedom, less regulation, and better results (conservative) and more government controlling things to get better results (liberal). Neither was perfect; however, I had not previously allowed any room for the conservative viewpoint. Similarly, my reading on environmental issues still spoke to a concern for conservation but not the radical environmentalism of Berkeley and Marin. Again, it was as if government control could somehow create a better result—except that government control seemed to mean less and less freedom for people to have places to live and work. I would not notice until much later that this softening of my "faith" in the secular physical dogma did leave me more open to the metaphysical at a later point.

By the time the 1980 election rolled around and the choice was Carter or Reagan for president, I believed Carter was not a very good president and that Reagan was the only choice. I believe Allison agreed. This was a huge transition, and I realized I was being drawn in the opposite direction of many of those living in our community. Reagan was seen as somewhat dangerous and crazy. We still had many of the characteristics of a hippie lifestyle, but our political views were more conservative because of the aspects of personal freedom and less government control. I found that very consistent. In Marin County and the surrounding community, very few people would have agreed with us. And, very few to look at us would have guessed our views were different from theirs.

Financially, we were freed up enough to allow us to plan a significant trip to Europe for the first time in the spring of

1980. We had taken smaller family road trips and a trip to visit Allison's family in the Midwest. They were good trips, and the costs were reasonable. Part of the reason we could make the European trip was that our Italian exchange student from my senior year of high school had come for a visit and invited us to come to Italy, so the costs would be modest. We would have a car to borrow and places to stay for free most of the time. Our primary cost was the airfare.

The trip eliminated some of the mystery of Europe and added to it at the same time. We spent our time mostly around Milan and the Italian Riviera with visits to Pisa, Florence, and Venice and day trips to the Lake District. We loved the country and found that even when not with our host we could get by with little or no understanding of Italian. Allison had lived in Switzerland for five years until she was about seven, so she had an image of Europe. I found that because of the language and cultural differences along with the rich history, Italy took on a richer sense of mystery and attraction at the same time. We got to live like locals in Milan and in our hosts' small, rented house in a tiny village with narrow streets above Imperia on the practical, rather than touristy, part of the Riviera. We already loved Italian food but now even more so with the regional varieties of pastas and sauces. Our young son ate chunks of fresh parmesan cheese like candy. I had only known parmesan cheese as something sprinkled from a canister on spaghetti. We loved the trip and hoped to go again.

Our second son was born shortly after our return from Italy and four years after our first. Allison no longer needed to supplement our income with her crafts. Along the way, my work had progressed such that I was making more money than I had been, although it was still a very modest amount. However, our lifestyle did not require a lot of money.

I helped with volunteer projects and ultimately with local committees; Allison helped at our son's pre-school program. Although our therapy had focused on only paying attention to our own family, I was drawn outwardly to involvement with the community from my earlier experience in Berkeley. Allison was more introverted but seemed to be drawn into this, as well. This was a time of starting work, independence, growing financial security, involvement in school and community. Any extra funds, we invested rather than adding elements to our lifestyle.

My consulting business had grown as well. Allison continued to miss the time we had together when we first got together. Dr. Bold and I decided that I could manage on my own without therapy, and a couple years later, Allison felt comfortable stepping out on her own, too. We had been really happy for a long time. I had that relationship for which I had longed. So, what came next? We were entering a plateau in our relationship. We did not know how to move forward. Nothing was wrong, but something was missing. The plateau was not only in our relationship. It was in our life, from my perspective. I had a good relationship and family life. We had a little more money and a house. I even found a little self-respect. As I hit that plateau, my foggy thinking seemed to grow. The sense of a firm foundation under my feet went soft. The problem was always there but hidden by those icons of achievement: relationship, family, financial security, greater prestige, pride, and arrogance. None of my goals were tied to a real framework.

2.

BEGUILING QUAGMIRE

9/81 TO 4/88

Lost and Arrogant: Family
and No Understanding

I felt like I had climbed a hill and reached a plateau. I had
no specific goals except a lasting intimate relationship but
a lot came with that package. Life was becoming busier
than it had been and that plateau did not seem to be a firm
resting place on the way to something better. Instead, the
glittering distractions of the culture or the world and the
infirm footing I felt as I started to bog down seemed more
like a beguiling quagmire than a plateau. My foggy thinking did not help. As things had been good and better, I less
reflected on the fact that I had no clear basis to think so.
In addition to the fog, I had really been in a quagmire the
entire time. I just thought I was firmly moving forward on
some solid footing. I was not at all.

As our oldest son started school in the fall of '81, we
owned our home, were financially a little better off, had a
couple of other investments, and were feeling pretty good
about ourselves. We had taken the major trip to Italy, my

first to Europe, and felt like we had arrived. We were passing out of the phase of our life when we really struggled financially. Given our simple life, any extra money was a major windfall. We were somewhat caught up in the status of Marin. We still lived fairly frugally compared to many around us and were critical of the self-important, almost arrogant, attitude of some in our community. We could criticize it at home and still had the comfort of knowing we were a part of it—a not so subtle form of hypocrisy.

That feeling of pride, a little comfort and a little arrogance, carried over into our life in general. I certainly thought of myself as a nice person with high ethical standards, and I believe we, as a couple, thought of ourselves that way. We felt we were separate from our cultural environment, but we were affected by it at the same time. We were no longer hippies; yet, we kept most things fairly simple, did not spend extravagantly, and did not need showy toys to prove our worth. The Marin community was becoming more and more expensive to live in, the economic milieu was shifting more and more to people of wealth with the middle either pushed up or out, and the poor crowded into the Canal Area of San Rafael or were forced to commute.

Economically the environment was wealthy and seemed focused on money. At the same time, a curious variant existed in which the attitude prevailed of appearing not to care about wealth all the while actually having wealth and truly caring about it. This attitude was complicated. Generally, an expensive car was a status symbol; yet, purposely dressing down became a fashion early in Marin before it became a fashion everywhere.

Our arrogance carried over to our family. We thought our child was special and wanted the best school for him. In applying for an inter-district transfer, we were turned down at first but soon were granted one. We had already tried "free" school, meaning Summerhill-like, and fairly "free" pre-schools. Some of our focus came from consulting with Dr. Bold who continued to hold very individualistic viewpoints. We were still counterculture in many ways and proud of it. Nonetheless, we were ready to try the public school system, which our daughter was also enrolled in.

When I first moved to Marin, I was involved with the environmental community. I now found a distance between my own, conservation-minded views and those who saw enemies of the environment all around. I could not buy into the anger. The area was the home to a wealthy hedonism while at the same time denying it. Jokes were being made about the place even in the national media about hot tubs and peacock feathers. We thought it was truer than not; however we, like many I think, did take some pride in being a part of it, as well: proud in our denial of pride.

Most people had good intentions. They wanted to protect the environment; they wanted to help disadvantaged people; and they believed the government could best do this. Some simply did not want change. Environmentalism became very complicated such that it was not possible to be environmentally responsible and support any development. Development of new or expanded roads was opposed as growth-inducing and damaging, and new housing became more and more difficult to get approved. Prices for houses escalated in part because supply was so limited. Fewer and fewer families had adequate income to qualify to purchase a home and commuted to work from farther and farther. Others definitely had to have two incomes to stay. As more people commuted to work in the county, rather than from the county to San Francisco, the traffic got worse. As more and more people sent their children to private schools or schools far from home, traffic got even worse because the children were driven everywhere. Disadvantaged people had to deal with the situation as best they could. The really poor would double up on apartments, especially in the same neighborhood I had lived when I first met Allison.

While I experienced only a few windfalls with my work, because we lived fairly simply and did not spend conspicuously, my work provided for some extra savings. I regularly invested. In addition, we could start paying extra for private school and got nicer cars (used). We made additions to our house, which did cost some money, but which we saw as improving our home and an investment in itself.

We often took hikes close to home. Marin has lots of open space. We were particularly fond of the trails on the slopes of Mount Tamalpais. Sometimes we would go to the beach in West Marin or drive in the hilly agricultural area there. It was vivid green in the winter and dry beige in the summer with dark, shady redwoods in some areas and groves of eucalyptus in others. We liked the natural beauty of Marin, but we liked every place we visited. The mild weather suited us: mild winters and warm dry summers with that wonderful fog to cool things off most evenings. Sometimes Allison and I would go to the City. We would occasionally take the kids to the Nutcracker at Christmastime. That was about as fancy as we got.

Dead Again

While we were children of the '60s, our connections especially to the music had drifted on. We did not listen to that much music, although if we did, it might be more country at that time. Van Morrison still resonated with both of us. Into this context, I found myself doing a couple of very mundane consulting jobs for the administrative part of the Grateful Dead who were based in Marin. As I was leaving one of the meetings with my contact in the converted Victorian that served as their office, I casually greeted a heavyset, older man sitting on a plain, wooden kitchen chair near the back door. He returned a friendly greeting. He had curly, bushy, gray hair and a beard to match—maybe someone's father I thought. He had a relaxed manner. I went about my way without a thought.

Only quite a bit later, my brain kicked in. Even though the internet was not a ready source of information then, I managed to figure out by going to record stores (yes, they still existed) that Jerry Garcia had gotten older and heavier and had a bushy gray beard to go with his bushy hair that had gone gray.

The encounter struck me, not as much then, but later when I looked back. If a person, even if a person only described in a magazine, catalyzed my transfer to Berkeley and the start of this "long strange trip," Jerry Garcia was that person. Here I was, long past that dramatic transition, but still in many ways living in the same fog. At a time when the Dead were long past those early days, as well, they still toured so much that they were one of the biggest grossing groups financially each year. Even though I had moved on in my interests, many people had become a vast crowd of "Deadheads." While I was not one of them, a part of me was and always could access an affinity for their music, best expressed in the person, voice, and guitar of Jerry Garcia. Yet, in a quiet unexpected moment while I was just doing some routine business, a seemingly regular guy, looking a little tired, the undisputed lead and an idol to many, was just hanging out at the office. In the context of performance, I had seen him many times at only a little greater distance. During a break at a Greek Theater concert, I had seen him carrying his baby with a look and demeanor that was more "proud father" than "rock legend"—very regular. This was different. Simple as it was, I had a glimpse of a different reality, a different person, and a sense of continuity I could not quite explain. He was always a different kind of rock icon. He had the charisma but did not ever, that I saw, have the need to "perform" outside of his music like so many others seemed to. The chance meeting at the Dead office was purely ordinary. We were just two people exchanging a greeting.

As with the music scene, Allison and I were both beyond even thinking about drugs. We had found only a few years before friends who had never been into drugs when we were younger were now trying acid for the first time. Everything had changed so fast after I first came to Berkeley. Drugs were almost unknown in my Central Valley town; yet, by the early '70s, they were everywhere. By the mid '70s to '80s, cocaine was very prevalent in Marin. Even though we were not looking for it, we knew others who used it. We tried it on a few occasions because it was available. I did not notice much. Maybe I did not try hard enough. I certainly did not understand how so many people, even acquaintances of ours, could blow through hundreds of thousands of dollars on cocaine. The social world was very odd. Drugs, especially cocaine, seemed to have little if anything to do with any hippie or countercultural lifestyle. They were part of the mildly or not so mildly hedonistic, affluent Marin culture.

I got involved locally in civic committees. I was feeling good about doing something and being a little bit important. However, the mindset of those who had been in the rent strike and had opposed the apartment building seemed to be the prevailing mindset in my community and much of Marin. Ultimately, something had to give. I had to accept it and do what I could or simply stop participating. I did not need to wait long: something I had been interested in went awry because issues I had specific information on were conveniently forgotten or ignored. I was idealistic and felt foolish and betrayed. I decided to no longer participate. My efforts at community service and giving back ended for a time. Some who hoped I would continue helping in the community were disappointed and did not understand the nerve this exposed in me. My reaction did not fit with the nice person they thought I was. I could and would have dealt with it differently later, but I was not there yet.

During this time, while visiting a local arts and crafts street fair, I noticed someone ambling down the street in a manner that made me immediately think of my friend, William, from Dana House. It was him. He lived in Portland, I think, and true to his artistic roots was a potter and sold his pottery at fairs. We immediately connected and met for coffee that week. I did not think of it too much at the time, but I was a bit full of myself. I was doing better than I had when we lived together, and I certainly talked too much about that. Despite my "self-awareness," I was defined by my mild success much like my hippie look defined me earlier. I had not made much progress. William was still in contact with Joelly, as well, so I gave her a call, and she came up from the Stanford area for dinner one evening. I was excited to reconnect with both her and William, but again I was too proud of our very recent financial gains. I was caught between who I had been and who I was or was becoming. In other words, I was lost. While that affected both meetings, it was not a miscue. It was a telling snapshot of my lack of understanding, my lack of grounding, and the limits of my search for meaning in looking internally. I was disappointed that a potential reconnection of more substance did not come to fruition with either, probably because of me. At even a simple level, perhaps at every level, the world is beguiling and confusing.

As my political mindset continued to change, I did not know how to connect that with my youthful endeavors in the counterculture. With each step and time, I found the progressive solutions I was surrounded by were increasingly restrictive and less in tune with the sense of freedom I felt on coming to Berkeley. The core freedom was not there. The cutting edge "new" was now the conventional, and conformity was enforced maybe even more than previously, especially with regards to "correct" thinking. What I had thought was a new way of openness was simply a new orthodoxy waiting to become orthodox.

My reading continued to slowly shift. I read a range of books that often were not consistent with my progressive Berkeley background; they were more conservative. I found *Newsweek* expressing what I knew to be opinion in the guise of news—furthermore, expressing opinions I no longer agreed with. I started subscribing to the *Wall Street Journal*, partially for a broader look at national and international news than I could get from the local papers but mostly for the editorial pages, which I trusted to be more moderate and conservative. Between that and a subscription to *National Review*, I found myself reading a mix of older and contemporary conservative writers. I found greater trust and greater hope and freedom in what I was reading than the progressive milieu in which I had been immersed.

My thoughts on abortion had slowly changed, as well. I found that in my reading I was seeing a broader viewpoint on an issue that I had previously assumed was settled. Abortion was seen as both a social and political issue—or socio-political as was becoming a more popular term. Certain social views were associated with a liberal or conservative viewpoint. Abortion fell into that category of partisan issues. Even before my political views started changing, my thoughts on abortion changed without having read things to challenge my assumptions. My Berkeley friend's rebuke was still remembered. Of course, I was now a father and that experience also changed the way I would think. In addition, medical technology had advanced so much farther with ultrasound images and life-saving care for premature babies that it was clear these were living beings regardless of any inconvenience for the mother and perhaps the father. The abortion rights position seemed to be renamed pro-choice to mask counterintuitively the inconvenient reality that each advancement of the medical profession made it less and less tenable to assert that abortion was simply a choice for the mother. While this continues to be a very complicated issue—unsusceptible to black and white one size fits all answers—I came to believe that I had been wrong to think it was purely a woman's choice.

I had voted for McGovern in 1972 and believed that was the right vote. Yet, out of the Berkeley hot bed of radical progressivism and into the surprisingly advanced Marin "no growth," radical environmental wing of progressivism, I was slowly finding myself out of step with those around me. Allison and I were essentially on the same page through most of this transition, though I might have been the instigator. We continued to find the conservative, less regulated and less controlled perspective more consistent with our understanding of our "hippie" roots than the tightly regulated and controlled progressive liberal viewpoint. We were a minority.

No Understanding

Nonetheless, I was lost in a fog even while some things seemed to be getting clearer. The culture was everywhere and powerful, beguiling strikes me as an apt adjective, much like Pinocchio at the carnival. I only saw Terry for a portion of this time, so I was on my own. Allison and I believed that our therapy had and was continuing to teach us to achieve greater happiness and satisfaction in our lives. I could be more confident in making decisions and could more quickly notice how I was emotionally affected by situations. Allison was more likely to be somber and cry than to be optimistic. Part of why our relationship worked was that we completed one another; we were not the same. However, Allison and I had some issues particularly with who would make final decisions in the family. In reality, we made most decisions together, but I had a desire to lead on certain decisions, and she had a desire to make sure her concerns were met. She sometimes felt I was not listening; or hearing while I thought she was not hearing or listening to my concurrence. We were off just a little, but it was disturbing to our otherwise placid relationship.

In addition to all the other liberating forces in the culture, women wanted their liberation and were throwing off the chains of traditional relationships. Allison was not a part of that movement, but the movement was so prevalent in all that could be heard, seen, and read. Resolving how we would conduct our lives and our relationship was an issue.

What was also happening was that I was hitting the limits of my worldview. I realized much later that I had hints of this with Carolyn but only hints. Now, I had a relationship, family, work, and a little more financial security. Therapy had taught me to deal better with situations and be less fearful. Fear at least came with caution; less caution in a fog without firm grounding was not necessarily better. Without a solid grounding, the desire for something more seems to be built in. Life and its busyness distracted me from my search and noticing what was missing. My icon was still relationship, and foggy thinking allowed me to ignore that I knew that was not real meaning. I was starting to see glimpses through the fog, not of true meaning or ultimate reality, but rather that all the other good aspects of my life like family, work, and security were not paths to meaning or answers.

My focus on work also detracted from my focus on my relationship with Allison. I thought we already had a great relationship. I did not fully understand that having a great relationship requires continued focus and work. I do not mean I thought I could do nothing; I mean I did not realize that just doing the same thing that worked so far was probably not enough. Finding a loving wife and a stable home life was a major milestone, but unlike achieving a goal like graduating from college, this milestone was achieved and needed to continue to be achieved with ongoing effort. Instead, it seemed like a compartment that was doing well, and as I still had not found that ultimate fulfillment, I focused energy on my work, career, and financial stability. I did what I thought I needed to do without knowing what that was. Should I change directions? Should I take a position with a larger firm in San Francisco and let my small independence go? Where was the meaning in working in a larger context, in more prestige, in more money? The culture was not a help—it made those things seem more important than my relationship with Allison and the kids. It was a real distraction that required intention to counter.

Thank goodness I was still somewhat of a hippie, and career and money were not that important to me.

We were hitting the dead ends of that worldview. Instead of reaching a firm high plateau leading higher, it seemed like a marshy bog of a box canyon. The fog obscured the fact that no obvious next steps existed in our worldview. How were hope and faith fitting in? Our openness with one another meant we were ready for another step, but we did not know how to get there. I thought maybe this was all there was.

I lost track of what was important. I was floundering. How could this be? This was what I wanted? Many in our community were wealthy and on the cutting edge of new concepts of spirituality, self-knowledge, relationship, and pleasure—self-focused endeavors. Ironically, mixed in with them were those on the cutting edge of health food, organic gardening, clean air, alternative transit, restricted development, and anything "environmental," which would seem to be focused on others but was also self-absorbed as others could not necessarily afford their flexibility. The counterculture of the '60s left a legacy of self-gratification.

I was lucky, or blessed, that during that time of confusion and distraction nothing serious happened to change my relationship with Allison or my family. When we first met, everything was so clear, but the world helps fog it up. I had a great relationship and a family and now we had a third son and later a fourth. Part of the growth through therapy with Dr. Bold contributed to my confusion. No, I was not as insecure and passive as I had been. When I was insecure and shy, I knew I wanted a relationship with a woman, and I thought about that in a traditional sense with a family. It was my idol. As I became more confident, I lost some of the fear, which actually was a helpful boundary in some ways. I thought being more assertive meant I was more in control when I was less in control. The culture provides so many distractions—career, money, and prestige—to destroy faithful relationships and families. I did not have any clear direction for the future. I wish I could say that I weathered that period totally on my own, but that was not true. I was blessed rather than wise, bumping from here to there. I was weak but somehow protected.

I was looking for some ultimate order that my worldview did not provide. So distraction was good—look away into the fog, embrace the fog. We were affected by status and symbols even though we tried to avoid them. Our energies were focused outwardly. We were not fully cognizant of the drain or where else to focus them or at least I was.

Even though both of us had been in therapy, neither of us seemed to know how to take our relationship or life to that next level. Allison went back to therapy. I occasionally went as well. I found myself exploring with Dr. Bold some of the confusion. I was learning to be more sensitive to Allison and not simply expect her to defer to me if we disagreed, and she was working on relaxing and letting go of the need to control, but we were still in a fog. Dr. Bold had mentioned on one occasion that his patients who were Christians seemed to have the easiest time resolving issues in therapy because they had a peace he could not explain. He also could not describe how that fit with the nature of Reichian therapy. I tried reading the Bible, and while I was intrigued and attracted, I was not drawn further. The mysterious, supernatural aspects still did not resonate with my secular worldview. Our life was good but very much caught in that beguiling quagmire of infirm grounding and foggy thinking. What was next? The purpose was not clear. Did you keep doing the same things and that was happiness? This theme hung in the background.

Other Distractions and Attractions

During one of my times of checking in with Dr. Bold, I discussed an investment I was working on at the time. A few weeks later, he asked me if he could invest with me. I was flattered and taken aback as I suspected that was stepping over a line in the patient/client relationship. He acknowledged that he had never asked or done this with a patient. Terry was many things; unorthodox was one of them. I proceeded to work out the details, and he became one of several family and friends in that particular investment.

My parents would come to visit often. During the time we were remodeling our house and living in Sausalito temporarily, they came to visit on more than one occasion. We enjoyed walking in town and showing them around. Sausalito is just north of the Golden Gate Bridge, perched on the side of a steep slope running right down to the Bay. There is a commercial area on the narrow strip along the bay with shops mostly for tourists. Beyond were yachts and houseboats docked in the Bay. Walking in town was an experience of steep step streets, wonderful gardens, and old shingle and Spanish-style homes, shops to peruse, and docks to stroll along, looking at houseboats and sail boats. Our place was one of the brown shingles just up the hill on Bulkley Avenue.

The work on our house progressed. My father had finally retired and came up to help with painting. He did not seem well. It was enough that he actually said something about it, which was unusual for him. Normally, he was the type to just grin and bear it. I called for assistance; the paramedics decided to take him to the hospital as he seemed to be having heart problems. He was okay after an overnight stay, but he was advised that his heart was enlarged and weak, which he already knew, and that drinking excessively could only do more damage. I knew my dad drank too much; however, I was not experienced or mature enough to insistently intervene. I wrote him a letter encouraging him to stop drinking and do whatever he could to improve his health. He did well for a while but did not have the willpower to stop on his own and was too proud to go to AA meetings or get help. He remained vigorous, although he would have occasional spells of passing out from a chemical deficiency. My mom left once for a few days because of his drinking; things changed for a while, then they were the same again. By this time my dad and I had a really good relationship but I still couldn't help him.

We continued in our good life. We were doing better financially. Our family was bigger and getting older. We had improved our house with more than one remodeling project into a nice home. I for one thought things were fine. I was not really reflecting, although through the fog I was asking some questions. Because of my less progressive and more conservative reading, I was bumping up against religious thought, really Christian. I did not notice at the time because it was often a part of conservative writing. I was subtly changing.

I was noticing, as well, that flaws I ignored—hidden in the fog—in the foundations of my secular humanist or philosophical naturalist beliefs kept sneaking into the clear with my reading. What was the basis for a moral or ethical life, and who can maintain it? As Paul says, God's presence and message have always been clear to see, we just ignore them. The best I could do was entertain more skepticism of my secular worldview. Why could not science and its laws be a glorious attempt to understand order in the universe, consistent with a divine creator? I had always been comfortable with having faith and hope, but how did that fit in?

Our life went on, and my father's health generally trended downhill. He could not have heart surgery, even if he would have agreed, because his heart was too weak. Three years after the incident at our house, he had a major episode and was in intensive care for most of a week. On one of the first nights, no one was watching, and in a medication induced stupor, he unhooked himself and started walking down the hall. My sister, brothers, and I all decided that was too much; we would stay at the hospital on rotating nights to make sure things went smoothly. That was a great time for conversation. Dad came home, but the prognosis was not good. His heart would get weaker over time until his body and lungs would not be able to expel fluids, and he would die. The diuretics worked, and he did okay, but he would never recover fully.

About a year later, my mother called us out on one particularly bad incident. Another medical practitioner came to examine him. The practitioner felt so many things were out of balance that if they could get some tests and rebalance him, he would do a lot better. We all agreed and bundled him off to the local hospital for the tests. As we checked him in, I noticed how poorly he looked in the wheelchair because of the swelling of his legs and the wear of poor sleep. It seemed like we waited forever for the attendant to come draw blood for the tests. By that time my mother had gone home for some food and rest.

We all chatted with Dad, trying to keep our spirits hopeful and his. The lab technician finally arrived and set up to draw blood. He had trouble finding a good vein; then, as he began to draw blood, a startled look crossed his face. The needle had been just enough of a shock to stop Dad's heart. He was there one moment and gone the next. I was stunned even though I knew he could die anytime. I had never been present at anyone's death. I called Mom to tell her and then cried quietly in the hallway. My father had died. I may not have leaned on him a lot, but his just being there was a connection with my upbringing and a support that would no longer be there.

He was a good man; he tried to do the right things. The kid who never wanted to leave the safety of Colorado's San Luis Valley was gone. The kid who in his early twenties coming out of the Depression did not have enough money to go to college but enough to buy a house for his mother, brother, and sisters was gone. The kid who was devastated when his younger brother and closest friend was killed in the war and who felt it should have been him was gone. Gone was the Colorado boy who was not that courageous but took great risks in the war and two tours of duty in Korea.

For all my father's trying to stay out of the spotlight or leadership, he was a model of what it means to do things for others, to help and to give generously. His funeral was proof. The church was filled with not just relatives but people he had befriended and people who knew what he had done for them or others. It was surprisingly moving. He was such a regular person. We were all very involved; we insisted that the service, while religious, not be too religious. We let others give the testimonials even though we probably should have. At the grave site, we stayed to put the dirt in the grave afterwards—not just a handful, shovels full. The whole transition was too profound for words.

3 .

GOD AND UNDERSTANDING

7/88 TO 2002

Spiritual Awakening, Again

A few months after my father's death in 1988, my mother was planning a visit on her way to see a friend from the war who was terminally ill; sadly, her friend died, so her plans changed such that she would be visiting us on a Sunday. As on her other visits I did not mention earlier, I planned to take her to church services. This was important to her, and I thought I should make the effort. Our previous experience was much like my experience in San Luis Obispo: the church was a place to go to a worship service without any other connection. On one visit, only a few people attended the early service. We would have obviously been visitors; yet, the priest spent all his time at the door talking to one parishioner until we finally left. Our second experience at the same church was much the same. The church was beautiful and situated in an upscale small community. If I was to think only with my pride, it would have been a great place to go to church, although at the time I had no spiritual motivation.

On this particular, visit my mother suggested going either to San Rafael or to West Marin to a church where the new bishop for her diocese was from. I found this intriguing. I did not know there was a church in West Marin and knowing how sparsely populated it was, could not picture how a bishop could come from such a place. I had gone to West Marin often over the years. Even in my early visits, I like most, was drawn by the open hills with green grass in winter and dry, beige grass in summer, the beautiful stands of live oaks, and pockets of redwoods opening to the coastal areas. My family and I would still go there for hikes, to the beach, or just for a drive. However, I did not think of it as a place of regular connection like a church.

As usual I planned for us to go to the early service, which was usually a short, basic worship service. This allowed time to get on with the rest of your Sunday, with religion as a compartment of life. My two middle sons joined us, and we made the drive out through the redwoods toward the coast. The church was up a long drive on a spacious, wooded property that appeared more like a large, older house more than a church. The parking lot, while seemingly ample, was surprisingly quite full. We made our way up and were directed around to a side door as the service was already started. We stepped through a small door into a very small side chapel off the main sanctuary that provided extra seating for the service. The place was absolutely full.

Although I did not notice it immediately, only on reflection, the instant I stepped inside I was aware of a quality of light and the sound of the folk hymns; they were inexplicably different and powerful. Added to that was the smell of incense, which I had not been accustomed to in church since Wisconsin. My entire being was watching, listening, thinking, feeling, and present. The thinking part was not sure what was going on; the feeling part was transfixed, not yet transformed. The light and sound filled all the empty spaces. This early service in the middle of nowhere was full of people worshiping with a spirit unfamiliar to me. The music, which was often missing from early services, featured acoustic guitar music sung in a folk style. Everyone sang. The priest, soon to be bishop, was portly with a round, radiant, and expressive face. The spoken parts of the liturgy were not just words to be quickly dispatched. They were prayers full of meaning and spoken with feeling. I found myself completely open to whatever was happening.

The sermon was not like any I had ever heard before. I was moved by the spirit in the services in Hales Corners, but perhaps I was too young then to fully understand that I was hearing something significant. This priest's voice and delivery provided the perfect match to his radiant countenance and his conducting of the service. Insignificance, with his gifts, might almost take on significance; however, this sermon was significant on its own. He told of a conversion experience of someone who became blind as the corneas of his eyes peeled away and yet came to a conversion understanding in that moment, a real blindness like Paul's. He said God would peel away blindness when and if necessary so that we understand what we could neither see nor understand before. I had no question that this sermon was directed to me. I was overwhelmed; somehow I was back to whatever infusion of faith I had in Hales Corners. Even though I had done nothing and had shelved my faith in Christ, I was completely back as if I had never been gone, as if no time had passed. The questions regarding the supernatural mysteries in the Bible, those things that seem to defy rational explanation, were answered without any need for exposition. I could—and did—now accept those metaphysical mysteries. I could not have given a scripturally based witness of my faith in Jesus Christ and God and the Holy Spirit, but my faith was restored in a manner so complete and instantaneous it defies explanation. I knew. I knew the answer to my searching for meaning and reality. I knew that Jesus was the Way. I was transformed, or I was linked to my early spiritual awakening. Just one hour earlier, I would have said that I was too practical and pragmatic for this type of spiritual experience. I would have been totally wrong.

As I tried to comprehend what was going on and how exactly it happened, I realized that the instant I stepped through the doorway everything changed, everything was different. The plane of the doorway invisibly separated one way of seeing the world from another. That doorway was truly significant for me. I trusted what I felt. The general trend of my life toward more traditional and conservative viewpoints from the more liberal days of college seemed now to have turned on its head with a powerful new sense of reality. My experience was not unlike the short tax collector who climbed a tree to see Jesus. He was curious but not really seeking, nonetheless his transformation was instantaneous—not drawn from prayer, meditation, reflection, or trauma. My unquestioned conversion experience had happened in this casual service with contemporary almost popular music, which almost certainly meant the church was as liberal as everything else in our community. Oh well. God leads, and I could accept that even though I did not know where he was leading me.

We went down for coffee time in the fellowship hall after the service and were greeted by numerous friendly people.

We got to speak to the priest, and I was very embarrassed when my young son informed him that this was the best service he had been to, and he had been to three. At the time, he was about seven, so three services was clearly not very regular attendance. The priest said that was nice with the same easy, infectious confidence that radiated from him during the service. It was impossible to avoid the gentle power of his character. I learned from others I spoke to that I was completely wrong about the place. The character of services had changed dramatically since I had stopped going to church 21 years earlier. The prayer book was different; the casual service was an option; folk music was an option; and the liturgical formality was somehow more expressive. While this was often associated with liberal churches, and this denomination was in general liberal, this church was not. The priest was leaving the very next day for the national church meeting that happened every three years; he would be questioned because some opposed his installation as bishop due to his traditionalist views. A great movement was on the brink of approving women as priests and making that the established doctrine about which everyone was to agree. Supposedly, the opposite view was treated equally, but not really. The national church had been getting smaller for years. The change in the prayer book had caused an exodus; this issue was causing another. The old mainline churches were losing members in general, while the evangelical churches were gaining members. The mainline churches tended to follow liberal social trends, and the evangelical churches tended to hold to traditional views. The approval of homosexual relationships was gaining momentum, and the approval of practicing homosexual priests was right behind. The priest soon to be bishop was traditional and gifted at sharing his views. The local church was popular because he had established a retreat ministry that attracted many some of whom then traveled great distances to come to church each Sunday. Unlike most churches that drew their congregations from the immediate vicinity, the majority of this church's members traveled at least half an hour to church—some as long as an hour and a half.

This spiritual experience was so uncharacteristic an experience for me, subtle in its own character, and, yet, a powerful transformational force. The experience reconnected me to my earlier faith; however, I was no longer a seventh grader, had been essentially AWOL in between, and did not have much understanding except for that unquestionable faith in my heart as the fog cleared. Truly, my life was different from that moment forward. I approached everything differently, meaning I did ordinary things differently, thought differently. Still, I had a huge amount to learn and needed time to understand more fully this sense of peace. I had a lot of ingrained secularism to sort through. Not unlike with therapy where emotions get translated into physical armoring, secularism was so long a structure in my approach to life and meaning that I would need to be patient if I wanted to grow into this new reality.

Allison was the most affected; she could not understand what was going on. I could explain the experience and the feeling of transformation, but this was so unlike me—or at least, the me she thought she knew. She could accept that this was something I felt strongly about, but she could not understand why I could not go to a local church instead of driving half an hour to this one. I could not explain this to her because she was on the other side of a thin but significant boundary between the physical and metaphysical, and I did not yet have the tools to explain. The transformation for me somehow gave me the wisdom not to force the conversion on her.

Because of my lack of understanding of what I had been drawn into despite the profound sense that my search had been answered, I immediately and enthusiastically threw myself into study. I was no longer a seventh grader. I was an adult who had been searching seriously for answers for a long time, had gone down many wrong paths, and had been distracted, even beguiled, by worldly concerns. I knew the instant my wake-up call occurred what it was, and that it was real. Nonetheless, I did not know the simple descriptions of my faith at that time. I realized I had always had a faith, which I now understood intuitively was tied to a belief in God through Jesus Christ. I could accept and believe the unseen, the supernatural, the spiritual, the metaphysical which I set aside 21 years ago. I was no longer a rational, secular humanist. I was a rational Christian for whom the supernatural was rational, not some kind of magic, myth, or morphine for the soul.

Even though the priest did become a bishop, he served three more months before moving on. I kept going to the church, often with my young sons in tow. The transformation gave me the maturity to accept the disappointing fact that this incredibly gifted teacher had been a short distance from me for 19 years and I only showed up on the Sunday he was essentially leaving. What was I doing all those years? Why didn't I get a wake-up call earlier? I was only a few miles away. I must not have been ready. I started the boys in baptismal classes as none had been baptized. The interim priest, very traditional in his views, would come to our house once a week and teach. His lessons were instructive for the older boys and especially for me. At church, a number of people at first assumed I was a single parent. Allison only came on special occasions like Christmas Eve. I followed a whole new path of reading and learning. I found it easy to get involved in the church and a whole new group of people I did not know. I just did not hold back. One of the men asked me to come to a men's breakfast on a Saturday morning. I said, "Yes." I had never done anything like this. I found going to that event awkward, as these were mostly mature Christian men, and I did not know what that was. I could not talk the language yet, but I hung in there. I knew I was in the right place and on an important journey.

The Beguiling Quagmire

Since putting my active Christian walk on a shelf as I embraced first the counterculture in the church of secular humanism of Berkeley and San Francisco and then the denomination of the human potential movement, I had been wandering in a true mental fog for 21 years. I ignored my faith, sampled other spiritual options, tried to get by on good intentions, learned more about myself, tried to focus on marriage, family, and career, and still I knew something was missing. If this life was it, if there was no more, what was the motivation to do good when I knew consistently doing the right thing was unrealistic? The awakening was an experience of that "peace that passes all understanding"— the instant recognition of what had always been true and present but which I could not see or understand: a sense of belonging, being home. The invitation was open and broad; however, the path was narrow. The path was faith in the gospel message of Jesus Christ. I was not in control; I could not do good enough, and even if I could, where is the hope if this life is all there is? God so loved the world that he sent his Son to die for us for forgiveness of our sins and so that we could have eternal life. No other message of reality is like it. All other messages of reality depend on personal effort that we cannot maintain. I had already found those other paths lacking but did not change my ways. Only Christianity accepted my fallen nature, the inability to be consistently sinless, and provided the grace and mercy of Jesus Christ who atoned for our sins with his death and on which we depend.

The message is so profound in that it is so simple, and yet, so complex at the same time. Since my first quarter at Berkeley, I accepted that religion was more cultural and biologically based. We had needs. We lived in groups that had other needs, which led to society and religion. Studying anthropology, Maslow, and religion from a sociological perspective all helped firm up my new worldview. The supernatural aspect of religion was simply myth or protective thinking for the masses. I was so naive that even as I stood in a fog, I believed I could see clearly. I mistakenly believed then that God had to be proven from a rational standpoint and that could not be done from simply believing. That view was actually the myth—that this physical life is it, that we are accidents of nature.

I find that even now as I do some final editing of these thoughts that current, well-written books from sociological and psychological/philosophical perspectives trying to explain Christians or a life experience of peace like Christianity try to do it from a physical description, whether of actions and attributes or thought processes, missing that it is metaphysical first, and that is the only place to start. I understand how hard that is to grasp because I once thought that way. I believe I had an easier transition because I had an earlier "religious" experience, and I had actually found the tenets of philosophical naturalism lacking. Over time, what I read and the thinking that came from that, while not bringing me to a spiritual transformation in itself, broke down some of the resolve of my '60s adopted worldview, such that I was open in a way I did not understand or notice.

So, Christmas was what it had always been, but now the real meaning jumped to the forefront. God came to us in the form of a baby, fully human and fully God. The incarnation is unmatched. He is not just a person. I realized also that I had never completely let that go and I think lots of people like me have not. Christmas is learned in childhood and children get it and do not lose it at some level even if in the background. The narrative of the baptism of Jesus is unmatched. Clearly, others knew he was something different, and, at least, John knew he was the Messiah. His ministry is unmatched. No one did what he did. His statements about who he is are unparalleled. He cannot just be seen as a good, ethical teacher. That requires leaving out too much of his declaration of who he really was and is. As Lewis said, otherwise, he was either a lunatic or a boiled egg. Jesus' death, burial, and resurrection for us is supreme. No other narrative even comes close. No answer to the question of reality is so profoundly and simply stated, yet so deeply complex when carefully considered.

What happened in my awakening was an immediate acceptance of the metaphysical reality that the God of the Trinity, Father, Son, and Holy Spirit was the reality. Not a reality that needed to be proved but rather the true reality of reason. Coming from the perspective of God first is how I found it easier to embrace my faith and backfill all the missed years of understanding. That transformation is the hardest because the conventional wisdom of secular humanism is even accepted by many nominal Christians. I have come to believe that many secular humanists or philosophical naturalists are like I was, caught in that marshy bog or quagmire: not really atheists, not even really agnostic, not acknowledging Christianity, yet, having a faith and hope that only comes with Christianity. My indoctrination into secular humanism was broad, as I believe it is for others. Little room was left for religion, particularly Christianity. Everything needed to have a scientific basis first, and that had to be accepted. Anyone countering is a denier, forget responding to their comments. The metaphysical is just not part of the discussion.

Yet, the metaphysical is the total point. An assumption of the God of the Trinity first can explain the creation of the earth, life on earth, physical laws of nature, and the relationships of men, first with God and then among themselves. The unseen reality is more real than the seen reality. We accept that we only "see" a small part of the spectrum of light, but we do not accept that we do not see an unseen dimension even though the most profound societal icons have always been those spiritual realms, that is until the Enlightenment convinced us as a culture to let that go. The legacy of the Enlightenment has persisted, although we have always had John the Baptists stepping out of the "wilderness" and into the wilderness of our culture proclaiming that we should repent for the kingdom of God is at hand.

I have struggled to explain how to bridge that gap such that the metaphysical can be embraced and the unseen seen. I have found and felt that efforts to simply use Bible verses to disciple those caught in that big attempt to transform someone's belief from a position of rational argument are not heard. I understand that the culture does everything that way, so that strategy makes sense. For someone struggling with a trying situation, that might work better than for others as they are actually in a spiritual frame of mind already because of the those struggles, open to something else. For me personally, as I reflected over time, I became surer that many things happened that I could not explain. Nature and serendipity were not adequate answers. I was looking and had a whole lot of life without explanations that all of a sudden could be explained and further, a sense of the future that while not determined could be explained in that same context. I do not yet have a simple, fool-proof way to bridge that gap for others stuck on the "seen" side.

The circumstance of my experience coming just three months after my father's death was not lost on me. I was not looking for something to replace my father. I had a strong, direct relationship of mentoring with Terry for regular support. I was not searching with any more rigor since my father's death than before. His death had changed me though; perhaps I was open in a slightly different way. Nonetheless, I would not have even been in attendance that morning except for my mother, and she would not have been visiting if my father were still alive and in need of her care.

Making Up for Lost Time

While driving in the beautiful hills of West Marin one day not long after my wake-up call, I heard a particularly distinctive bible study program on the Christian radio station that I used as a study resource. The teacher had a strong southern country accent, his insights were clear and direct, and he made the Bible understandable. He was covering the book of Daniel at the time, which to me was and is very hard to understand without help. Only a few months before, my perception of this teacher would have been that he fit the stereotype of the simple, born again Christian fundamentalist from the south, incapable of creative thought—a simple, backwards hick. Instead, he was to become my first path to reading and understanding the Bible.

I had tried to read the Bible when I was younger but never got any help and lost interest. Mark was assigned during the sociology of religion class at Cal. I read it in the context of the class and would have been open for more but had no guidance. Reading the Bible as sociology or literature totally misses the point. That is secondary at best. Later in my searching, I would pick up the Bible and try again but could not get beyond the supernatural mysteries, particularly such rational-defying ones as standing on pinnacle of the temple. Now, I had faith, and I had help. I bought the books to go with the study, so that when I fell behind or missed a program I could catch up. I took the time the program took but read and studied through the whole Bible—five years. J. Vernon McGee with his Texan accent was a Godsend for me.

I was drawn into active involvement and leadership very quickly. I wondered at the time about being in leadership so soon and have since. I was picking up my faith tradition after being in the wilderness for 21 years. This was a small but thriving church. Why would they look to me as anything but a beginner? Even though I was flattered, I thought it was odd at the time. Churches and Christians are just regular people even though some, especially non-Christians, paint them otherwise. With the departure of the pastor for his position as bishop, the church had a need for additional lay leadership. So, in addition to serious study and immersion,

I was also involved in regular church activity and active leadership.

I clearly understood the shift in priorities now in my life. Christ was first, and my relationship with Christ was first. Other relationships, financial matters, career, and the like followed after that. Nonetheless, because of the activity at church and even just going to church meant that I still had to compartmentalize my spirituality. It would be that way for a long time. The pattern of changing "religions" from secular humanism to Christianity meant I immediately understood with crystal clarity that I had been on the wrong path, no foggy thinking. However, it did not mean I could immediately change the mental structure of 21 years and the impact of so many years of foggy thinking. It was so deeply ingrained; it couldn't simply vanish.

I saw my whole life differently and felt my search for reality was ended. I would take a long time to have the reality of Christ operate in me not as a compartment, not as a default computer program but rather as my whole operating system, the melding of my head and heart. I understood the real goal but the world and culture were still running on the old operating system. Now, as I write this many years later, I find the difference between my awakened faith and my current faith almost as striking as my original step away. The outward and inward expressions between then and now are striking. I did not have the confidence in my faith to discuss it calmly or not to worry if others didn't understand. I either stayed too quiet or got too hooked in conversations because I could not explain my faith coolly in a way that resonated with others.

Actually, my Christianity was a source of defensiveness. I was not well grounded for a long time, and our larger community was mostly not predisposed to Christianity. I would find myself trying to say who I was but unable to maneuver around the negativity. I mostly stayed quiet. Most assumed I was like them because they had an image of what a Christian was, and I did not fit it.

I conducted my life in a different way though; continued change and regular re-evaluation became the pattern of my life. Besides the Bible, I asked for and followed other reading to expand my understanding of this change in my life. A whole world of literature opened up.

Changed Priority, Ongoing Struggle

My relationship with Allison was easier and how to respond to her became clearer. That beguiling quagmire of cultural temptations seemed to dissipate overnight. Our relationship seemed better and easier with greater focus on one another. Christian focus changes things. However, the reality of the world and its beguiling ability to throw things off course was right at hand.

Terry had mentioned more than once that patients of his who were Christians seemed to have the easiest time accepting things and creating change; some of his patients had also become Christians. While other of his patients had become Christians in therapy, I believe Dr. Bold was surprised by my transformation. I was too practical to be given to wild, emotional enthusiasms. He asked many questions and seemed to be aware of the priest who had been the catalyst of my conversion. He did not discourage me in anyway, although I believe he did not fully understand.

My work was still about the same. We were somewhat caught up in who and where we were and what we had (a nice house, a good car, good schools, good job). I did notice at the time; however, I did not do anything about it. I was comfortable, and changing would require effort. My faith was somewhat still a compartment.

Late the next Spring, we were drawn into a very troubling issue at the private school two of our children attended. The issue involved teachers acting very inappropriately with students on an outing and the administration's desire to hush it up rather than deal with the parents of an affected child. Allison and I were so disturbed by it, the hypocrisy of this being a better educational environment, one founded by Christian families, when really the moral compass was broken. We decided to remove our kids from the school and were surprised that none of the other parents did the same. They may have felt the eventual responses adequate, or they may have felt they had no choice in order to provide the best for their children. I was angry; Allison was distressed—she had heavily invested in the school community.

Our plans had to change quickly. Allison did not question that we had to leave. This was a conversion experience for her; she embraced Christ and all that went with that. We discussed this change with our oldest son who was going to need to leave his friends as he entered the eighth grade. He took it well and started the eighth grade in a small public country school, which turned out to be far better than the expensive private school. We moved our second son to a local parochial school where we also started our third son. At the new kindergarten parent's meeting, we met a mother who invited Allison to a bible study. Ultimately, she became a best friend to Allison. Allison slipped comfortably into our church and immersed herself in the women's bible study group at her friend's church. She actually questioned my faith because I did not express it in the same way she did. I had not tried to convert her, while she could not embrace my conversion. I waited. I was disappointed that she did not see and understand my patience when the lights went on for her, but I survived.

We continued to be attracted to a more conservative viewpoint and reading. We saw this as consistent with freedom carried over from our understanding of our hippie roots. Now, that old viewpoint made even more sense as the gospel message turned out to be a way of life rather than a bunch of rules as we had thought previously. The way of life leads the behavior rather than rules enforcing behavior. We became more secure in our grounding, and the community around us continued in a different direction.

As I read, I was led to other writers by reference or mention. These works exposed me to many other works that challenged assumptions of my secular humanist or relativist worldview. For example, evolution was a theory that was and is taught as a fact, and anyone who questioned that was some religious nut case. I believed that; I did not question that. However, I now read numerous well-written books that raised serious issues with the "fact" (like Johnson and Behe). For example, the inconvenient fact of missing transitional forms in the fossil record to prove the theory; the improbability of complex structures, such as the human eye, simply developing through selection and if so not enough time had elapsed for the changes; and finally that an alternative answer of intelligent design was not inconsistent with the established record were not something of which I was aware. I read others I respected and found that serious people knew these inconsistencies—and more—existed, but it was not generally taught. I became open to a broader viewpoint: that the grand accident theory of our existence had many missing pieces and required a kind of faith to be believed in itself.

I found financial challenges easier to deal with even when they were pretty disastrous. We had more financial resources partially because we continued to live modestly. I still felt torn between consulting for others and the greater independence of individual investments. Recession led me to refocus on consulting primarily because of the reduced risk.

Because of my spiritual awakening and, in a subtle way, my father's example, I found myself drawn to service in the community again. While I had always felt that draw, my earlier experiences were too political and as such out of joint with my natural inclinations. This new involvement seemed a natural outcome of my explicit faith. I said yes to joining local organizations and being active. Many would do this for networking to develop their business interests. I only did it for service and stayed clear of more overt networking. I especially liked helping organizations that helped the needy, but I also liked business advocacy. Because of the political climate in Marin, business often got lost in that political climate as a barely necessary inconvenience. I started participating with my sons in their scout program, I participated in other local committees making decisions for the community, and I organized a few foreign exchange trips for kids. I also helped individuals in need. I became more comfortable and drawn to giving of my time and our money with Allison's agreement.

Another Big Transition

About three years after my adult conversion and a little more since my father's death, while both Allison and I were briefly consulting with Dr. Bold again, he suddenly found he had leukemia when contemplating an elective medical procedure. He canceled appointments and passed away not that long after. He was only in his late 50s. He had time to say goodbye by phone and even recommended associates, but neither Allison nor I could conjure up a vision of someone else filling his place. He had been a huge influence in my life for 21 years off and on. I was able to deal with life far more effectively because of him. Ironically, therapy was only a part of that, although that would have been enough. I will always remember him for his outsize personality and for modeling a way to carry myself through the way he talked about different things that would not be a part of traditional therapy. And because he was actually a partner with me in an investment (definitely outside therapeutic tradition), I had much more than a therapeutic relationship with him. I felt the loss like the loss of a surrogate father or older brother, but felt well prepared to carry on.

Family Education

Our educational focus for our kids continued to change. Our oldest son moved from the private school to the country school then to high school. While I tried to be involved in the high school, I found my conservative/traditional voice was not really appreciated. However, I was oblivious to my son's appreciation of the late 60s music groups. I had a little bit of pride as I could tell him I was there; yet, because I was still beguiled by the times, I totally missed the fact that I only lightly experimented with drugs when I was a sophomore in college and he was using drugs and alcohol when he was only a sophomore in high school in an entirely different world.

At the same time, our next son, bored with school, having missed a quarter of the year being "sick", asked to go on an outing with homeschoolers studying California history. They would be in the Gold Country of the Sierra foothills touring historic mining towns and panning for gold. He was inspired and asked to homeschool. I was skeptical but like with homebirth earlier, followed Allison's lead. We educated ourselves, found we were not alone, and moved forward with Allison doing most of the work. He was able to complete three years of school in two, making up for being held back at the private school because he was a boy born in September! He was prepared and looking forward enthusiastically to high school. As with our older son, we looked at all the options public and private, but he wanted to continue homeschooling. This was different from elementary school; his options for higher education could be affected. However, once again, we went forward. He was motivated and did well as a home schooler, and by now we knew from his brother's struggles that some of the greatest advantages of home schooling did not have to do with education. They had to do with avoiding the time focused as at our older son's school related to social attitudes the school felt compelled to advance even though it was a private parochial school. My efforts to comment meant nothing. With home schooling, we could be parents advising our children and focus on education. As our son advanced, he was able to take more rigorous courses at the community college. The focus at junior college was on education, not social engineering, the students were serious, and the teachers were skilled and intelligent. By the time he finished high school, he had credits equal to almost a year of college.

By that time, for different reasons, both of his younger brothers were home schooling, as well. Our third son was not highly motivated to do well in school and thought he was stupid; he was not. At the completion of fifth grade, the same point at which his older brother started home schooling, we offered him the option. His brother had been home schooling for two years at that time. Allison had the materials for sixth, seventh, and eighth grades, and she had the confidence of two years' experience. He made the decision to try with the option to return to school if he wanted. He was not as motivated as his brother, and was somewhat harder for Allison to teach because of it, but he never looked back once he found the freedom.

At that same time our fourth and youngest son started home schooling, as well, but earlier and for different reasons again. He had only completed the first grade, so teaching him would be different from anything Allison had attempted. He had significant problems learning to read because of dyslexia. The parochial school did not have resources to give him additional help. After seeing the struggles of our older son and how much of an easier time he had home schooling, the decision to send our youngest son to a public school just for the help was not very attractive.

The irony was that just about everyone who heard we home schooled our children and who was not a home school parent themselves worried about their socialization. They did not understand that most homeschoolers are involved in many other activities, come from homes with lots of interaction, and are not recluses. Conversely, none seemed to understand the negative socialization in school, whether public or private: social opinions taught by well-meaning teachers in addition to poor peer education on relationships, attitudes to authority, appropriate language of discourse, appropriate dress, sex, drugs, and alcohol. Home schooling will not work for most families; it is very hard work, but socialization is not one of its problems, despite often being the first argument brought against it.

Teaching our fourth son was a challenge. The other boys had a firm foundation from which Allison could build; he did not. While he could understand concepts fine, he could not read easily or well. He needed focused help with his work. The older he got, the more restricting his reading difficulties would make his education. However, Allison stuck with it, and he was very tenacious.

Notable Passings

In August, 1995, Jerry Garcia passed away while in a recovery program in West Marin just over the hill from suburban Marin where we lived. Even though his drug escapades, his willingness to be out there, were a significant part of my original attraction to the Bay Area, he was, by then, known to have a drug problem he had been trying to control for a long time. When we greeted casually, he seemed clear but tired. It seemed to me he must have needed to work all the time to support his in and out of addiction lifestyle. Ironically, because I had been to treatment programs with many relatives over the years, I had been to meetings at the facility where he had been making this effort. Even though I did not listen to much music at the time and certainly not much Dead music, I was deeply moved by his passing. He had been that original and iconic catalyst of my move and had been a regular cultural presence ever since. However, that one casual but intimate meeting connected me with the regular guy that was surprising in its quiet power. Much later, listening to some of his eclectic recordings as I edited this writing, I was struck by the breadth of his musical talent. I had missed that part of him even though it was there all along. He embodied the '60s culture that I felt I was a part of even though I was gladly an insignificant member.

He embodied the creative talent, almost crazy disregard for limits, and ultimately sadness of unrealized peace.

A year and a half later in February of '97, Herb Caen passed away. As with Jerry Garcia, he was not someone with whom I had a direct relationship except in a very momentary, casual, insignificant way. Yet, he had a profoundly significant effect on my whole initial and ongoing understanding of the City and Bay Area where I was to spend my entire adult life and had spent much of my childhood. I cannot describe the subtle grandeur of San Francisco and the Bay Area the way he did in his columns, but I can picture it all: Golden Gate Park with its surprises at every turn, the thin fingered panhandle, the striking glass arboretum, lawn and then trees, lots of eucalyptus with their peeling bark, on and on to the ocean, and the huge wooden Dutch windmill, the many hills particularly Russian, and Telegraph with their steep streets forced by the grid pattern, North Beach nestled between Russian and Telegraph Hill with its narrow streets and original Italian then Beat then Asian culture, Chinatown stuck between North Beach and the Financial District with a jarring culture shock of Asian color and architecture, people, and language, Union Square with great department stores and the St. Francis Hotel, Nob Hill with those iconic structures of Grace Cathedral, and the Mark Hopkins and Fairmont surrounding the old Olympic club building with views out to the Bay and Bridge depending on where you are, the Bridge, graceful, dramatic, and iconic connecting the City to the steep hills and cliffs of the Marin Headlands, and the Fog and Overcast always bringing a welcome coolness and surprising vistas: the Bridge hidden by fog, the City clear, but only parts of the Bridge showing, and that powerful, yet wispy fog, pouring down on the Bridge at the Headlands.

Still the World Presses In

My life was busy, and my Christian walk was more compartmentalized than I would have liked. I studied, I went to retreats, and I listened closely to sermons besides other worship and prayer. Even though I could articulate the priority of the gospel message before all else, it way easier said than done. So much of what I was doing was in direct response to that message: helping those in need, helping organizations that help those in need. Yet, the result was that the service and even the direct service at church combined with career, financial needs, and a family led to a level of busyness and preoccupation that did not allow me to access that greater peace in relaxing in God's will and then acting. Difficulties did not disappear. The world truly did press in; it was a beguiling quagmire even when knowing the truth. As I edit this about 15 years after first assembling some ideas and five years after realizing I needed to make clear that Jesus and God's will are first, I know my ability to access a sense of peace on a regular basis requires patience. Along with that, I am better and better able to accept situational results, good or not, for now.

VI.

CLARITY

Fifty Years

1.

FINDING ORDER

1967-2002

Genesis

When I first had the impulse to write, long before I actually started putting thoughts down, I was much younger and thought I should write about the late '60s and what a different time that was. There was seemingly so much cultural change coming into play with so many baby boomers coming into adulthood. Of course, I had not fully understood that part of that sense of change was not just the times but my own entry into adulthood. Nevertheless, I thought I had, if not a front row seat, a really good seat for observing the many interwoven threads of that multi-colored fabric especially as expressed in the Bay Area. Because I am not a writer, this was not much more than a thought.

Over the years, I saw the image of what I might write change. I no longer saw the late '60s as the same glorious time, even though it was a unique time. Instead, I saw that period as a time with good impulses and an amazing confluence of energy for change; yet, the impulses were often terribly naïve, in some cases more angry than creative and arrogant without understanding the impact of that arrogance. I saw my personal experiences differently, as well. I began to understand how that naïve, well-meaning sense of arrogance fogged my thinking and view of the time, my actions, and their real meaning in my life.

Even when I started this effort about 15 years ago, I saw the '60s counterculture without much analysis despite the years of distance and spiritual separation from it. Even though my adult reawakening of my faith had occurred quite a while before, I had not changed the narrative much. My foggy thinking about God may have cleared, but I had built in thinking about the world and my experiences that were still a structural part of my fogged in thinking. It took time for real clarity to develop and the compartmentalization of my life to breakdown such that the whole focus of the narrative changed.

I am glad the effort of writing had a long time to simmer in my mind and heart such that I could experience a different sense of order and wholeness. I had to see that sense as related mostly to my inner journey seeking meaning. Further, time was required for the gospel message, as a way of life, to permeate through the structures and compartments that had long built up in me and dissolve them into a whole. In a strange way, the changes caused by immersing myself in my Christian walk were not unlike and were analogous to my therapy much earlier, changing the way I saw myself and responded to life by changing the way I was doing things. Reading Reich's book was only an introduction. The regular work of therapy and immersion took time. I remember Terry once saying that real change from therapy would only manifest itself maybe years later. He was right about therapy, and I was seeing my Christian walk manifesting greater and greater wholeness and clarity over time in similar fashion.

While I suppose I could wait even longer to see if I see things differently yet—perhaps even coming full circle—I think not. My views have been gathering strength in their clarity, order, and depth rather than changing directions. I am no longer lost in a fog, which is not to say that foggy thinking does not drift in from time to time; however, I now know the clear skies are right behind the fog. My sense of reality is clear. Life is primarily relational, and my relationship with God has to be first.

Early on, my focus had changed and clarified from being about the times to being about intimate relationship and hopefully a long lasting relationship with a spouse, not a greater journey than that. Much later, I realized I was ignoring what I already knew. I was still caught in an old narrative and an old way of thinking. I had simply moved from idolizing the times to idolizing relationship. Writing the narrative helped me express my thoughts and thereby see the bigger context, which helped clear the fog and got my thinking out of the quagmire and onto firm ground. Ultimately, everything flows from a relationship with Jesus Christ and the Gospel message of salvation. Other relationships followed from and after that in importance. By leaving God out, I had still been idolizing relationship in a way and not prioritizing the most important relationship. Yes, the rest of the activity of life adds color and texture but trying to find meaning starting with myself, my spouse, family relationships, or life's daily toils is a dead end. Necessarily, the shifting focus of this written journey has meant I generated thousands of words that have been set aside as this narrative does not require them.

Although I now know a noun from a verb, I still found it hard to write. I came to this with no experience or training. Furthermore, I am not a theologian or apologist, politician or political pundit, sociologist, psychologist, or scientist. I am just a regular person trying to understand and see connections and find meaning. Our world needs those who are destined to stand out, but our society could not survive without the masses of "just regular" people for the standouts to standout from. Those regulars are just as important, especially in God's eyes. My "just a clay sculpture" from art class was not some kind of pejorative nor is "just a regular person." The reality is that those standouts are "just regular" people in other parts of their lives, like the bearded older gentleman I said hello to when on a consulting errand.

This spiritual search or confession narrative is written from my very regular perspective and only for a very few people. Having that limited goal has kept me going in spite of the challenges. Writing made me state things more clearly because I was forced to explore and put down my thoughts and ideas. Like any journey, each small step helped me write a little more completely, a little more personally, reflect, and take the next step. This helped me realize I was once again missing the spiritual—not unlike I did so long ago when I did my timeline—only now I knew the truth.

Moreover, by leaving out or changing names to protect others and by being anonymous myself, I found it easier to write more deeply about the foolish internal me because that was another character in the narrative, not me any-more. Do not misunderstand, I will always be me, but I am also no longer that me. Stepping outside myself has been an indispensable tool in fashioning this narrative. My mem-ory has been a blessed resource. Even now, any incident could be picked out of this narrative, and I could be there in the moment. I do not live in the past but can access it like a living photo album. Again, I am not that me anymore, but will always be that me at the same time. Over time, I have understood my thoughts and ideas much better, and in so doing I have understood my faith, as well, in a much more powerful way that is deeper and simpler and more profound all at once.

Countercultural Fog

When I came to Berkeley I naively thought, dreamed, and believed the counterculture would be the guiding reality, and an intimate relationship would be the fulfillment. I thought I was seeing clearly when in fact I was in a fog or in darkness or simply lost. Instead of putting childish things aside, I now see I was picking them up and embracing them. They seemed new and exciting to me, and those around me thought that way too. Maybe, because I had not cut loose in adolescence I confused this freedom as maturity.

Then, after being stunned out of my dream by a broken relationship and the ensuing confusion, I thought and believed with therapy and personal growth that I could learn to get back to the dream only to find that even though I was emotionally stronger and could more competently deal with life, something was still missing. That period lasted a really long time as I continued to embrace my worldview and the world that went with it. Finally, when my mental and spiritual fog cleared and I had truly "put away childish things", I knew that God and faith in God were the reality. True hope only lies in that reality. Intimate relationship was important but only after and within that relationship with God. Otherwise, relationship was simply a false idol.

The culture was no more than the temporal context within which that reality and those relationships were lived out.

In fact, I now believe the influence of the counterculture on mainstream culture has been mostly negative; yet, that is hard to convey especially to those who do not know what it was like before and who assume that the current culture has been as it is for a long time. Certainly, aspects like loose sexual attitudes and drugs have been around forever, but they weren't fully woven into the primary fabric of the culture as they are now. Much like with adding new ingredients in a cake batter, the new cake is different from the old, but still a cake. With experience only of the new cake, how do you understand the look, smell, taste, and texture of the old?. Even with experience of both, convincingly explaining the different experience of the old cake and new requires effort.

Unfortunately, today's culture, which is now so mixed in with the counterculture of the '60s that the boundaries have been either blurred or erased, has regressed from a general understanding or acceptance of an order that included some knowledge of faith and God to one in which God has become much more compartmentalized and marginalized than ever before. This erasure in the mainstream culture is so complete that even questions about God are not on the radar. A basic grounding in any metaphysical reality is often completely non-existent for many. I understand that because I thought that way myself even when I was really trying to understand. I had embraced the secular worldview so completely that the metaphysical was not in the picture. Intimate human relationships may be an idol for many as they were for me; however, with the increasingly direct, wide open sexual and gender culture even relationships have become more confusing. Beyond that, the culture seems to be absorbed with temporal life: career, money, success, prestige, recreation, diversion, food, pleasure—especially sexual—relationship, and family. It truly is a beguiling quagmire immersed in fog and not a plateau on the way to something better. The scripture for the worldview is media, politics, sociology, psychology, and science. Meaning is to be found in the pursuit of happiness. Examined closely, no foundational grounding will be discovered in this beguiling quagmire. Accidental existence ends in nothing or worse.

I found that only over time did I become more and more aware that I was ignoring the obvious flaws and inconsistencies in my secular humanist or philosophical naturalistic worldview that were all readily apparent. I believe many were and are like me: caught in that quagmire. Reality came from a big bang, an accident. Why? We had evolved over time, but the complexities of life and of individual organisms cannot be explained with an evolutionary theory that lacks transitional elements. There is no logic that can rationalize how that occurs accidentally. Why? Science or nature is described by laws and rules, but why are there rules? Societal conduct is defined by rules, as well. If all this ends in death and nothing more, why do we make the effort to conduct our lives well? We all know we are not capable of consistently doing so. Why do we have hope in the future? Where does that come from? It has no place. The beguiling quagmire is the dense mental fog of accepting as clear and real something that is clearly neither. I know I was not alone in living in that illusion.

While I was never a political activist, a true hippie, a druggie, or part of a free love lifestyle, probably no one was a pure adherent of the counterculture. Whatever I was, I was consistent. I liked the general freedom of dress, political views, relationships, and drugs, even if I did not feel the need to exercise all that freedom. I definitely looked the part. I was radically progressive politically without being ardently political. I believed in free relationships despite wanting one steady one. I experimented with drugs but never was attracted to using them regularly. I loved the music scene but never became a part of it. I went to school, worked odd jobs to pay my way, and enjoyed the company of really good people on their own journeys. I thought I was putting away childish things and thinking like a man, but I was convinced to choose embracing those childish things as I became a man.

Broader Cultural Fog

The post-World War II economy was one of expansion, faith in the future, and greater wealth at all levels. As such, the training of children of my age, following the example of Dr. Spock, was less discipline-oriented and more oriented to building the child up. Much of this was good, but it certainly played its part in the sense of rights and entitlement of young people that when mixed with all else created the environment for the changes in the '60s. An abundance of our parents, including mine, had lived through the Depression as kids and then the war as young adults. They had grown up with less flexibility and wanted something better for their kids.

Religious devotion, under attack for at least a couple of hundred years, had a revival in the late 1800s and a mainstream commitment to faith through the first half of the 1900s, but a continuing loss of numbers among the intellectual elite and because of other patterns of recreation, general wealth, priorities, and, perhaps, loss of understanding of faith and its role in life, religious devotion was not central to as many lives as had been true earlier. In addition, interest in other religions, particularly eastern, increased especially among those who felt something new was needed. Secular humanism had become the predominant default religion.

The use of mind altering drugs had always been for a fringe element of society. With some of the post war, pre-1960s Beat generation poets, writers, and artists, the use of marijuana in particular became more mainstream. Other more powerful drugs were written of, and the boundaries between the mainstream and the fringe were pushed further. With the '60s, at the time I became involved, drugs and experimentation were not common. That changed so fast such that in just five years or so marijuana and psyche-delics that had been cutting edge were rampant in small town America. Now as I edit this, cannabis is moving totally into the mainstream, so much so it is legal for recre-ational and medical use in several states. In the mid '60s as part of a distinct minority I would have agreed. Now, again as part of a distinct minority, I see a careless disregard for the potential, almost certain consequences.

Movies and television followed similar trends. Movies developed out of traditional drama and because they were presented to broad audiences were controlled by those producing them such that the content was not too provocative. The '60s brought about more graphic violence, more profane speech, more nudity, and more explicit sexual love scenes. Some X-rated pornographic films actually made it to the edge of the mainstream by the early '70s. My generation saw the start of the influence of television. The first shows were family oriented, simple westerns or dramas, or older movies shown on television. As the medium reached its adolescence, the content changed. Boundaries pushed first in movies migrated to television.

With the onset of videos and then their availability on home screens, meaningfully, nothing was off limits.

Music became more accessible with simple recording, inexpensive record players, and radio stations such that by the '50s, selling recordings was a big business. Popular music bought mostly by young people became an even bigger business. Radio was the medium, but then television joined the market with music shows. Music was the "air" of the youth culture and most often focused on the unrequited love between boy and girl. I do not believe I was much different from others in my preoccupation with that relationship. Songs got more suggestive, the performance was more than just music, and the message was aimed at younger and younger audiences.

Television programming, print media, fashion, and other aspects of culture all changed. Comedies changed from presenting families with simple humor to dysfunctional families with caustic humor. Print media and television increased the glorification of young idols. Print media pushed soft pornography under a mask of literate writing into the mainstream. Movies followed by pushing the limits of what could be shown and said. Fashion started taking its cues from youth and even the dark side of street culture. For all the ultimate concern with control by older people, the youth culture began its reign as the market leader, the real control.

Science became the reality, the rationale, of the secular worldview. Darwin's theory of evolution became a "reality" not a theory; it became part of the scripture of the secular worldview/religion while inconvenient flaws in the theory were ignored. And, of course, intelligent design, let's not say God, does not fit with this new religion. Ever since the ridicule of the Scope's trial nothing else has been taught in school. Physics and biology led the way followed by soft sciences less tied to the scientific method: sociology, psychology, and political science.

Darwin and Marx both published their culture changing works in 1859. The impacts were far reaching for both. Darwin's became the answer for the scientific underpinnings of life, even if it was not quite so. It took 100 years for Marx's ideas to move from theory thru practice—with the Russian Revolution and communist revolution in China—and they were still a real factor among many intelligent people in the '60s. Some legitimate questioning of the existing political structure, tolerated by the protection of free speech within that structure, led certain factions to assume extrapolations that were neither logical nor legitimate. Millions died under Stalin and Mao.

Ironically, George Eliot's *Adam Bede* was also written in 1859. While "just a novel," ultimate reality and relational life were clearly painted with exquisite detail that applied then and now; whereas, Darwin and Marx, truly cutting edge in theory, were part of a misunderstanding of life, the consequences of which negatively affect us even now. Eliot was a truly innovative person; yet, she wrote fairly conservatively and her work is not dated even now.

Serious conservative political thought ironically was developing concurrent with the counterculture of the 1960s. We made fun of it at the time. I do not any longer. I ultimately found in it a basis more consistent with my emerging belief that government was not going to fix everything, was not meant to control everything, and would not lead to a better society, which is not to say I came to believe that no government is an option nor do any conservatives I have read. Society needs government for protection, external and internal. The political differences are fundamentally the line between too much and too little.

Too much includes an insistence that others buy into the same agendas; conservatives seemed to be more flexible accepting differences. Those differences are also about how much government should push social agendas. I now realize that the political intensity and anger I witnessed in Berkeley seemed like religious fervor, just another denomination of secular humanism. I was drawn to the self-awareness, personal growth denomination. Others were drawn to the politics and social justice denomination. Environmentalism had a like character of religious dedication with its own doctrines. All were looking for meaning. I see this even today. In the political history of our nation's founding, the clear reliance on primarily Judeo-Christian principles and values are now ignored, downplayed, or denied. The real question is not just historical/political but more pressingly spiritual. The non-spiritual of secular humanism is in fact spiritual but does not take its source from the real source; thus, the whole conversation is skewed into meaningless babble, completely off track. Man solving everything on his own is not reality. Creating more laws to make people be good will not work. Making an idol out of planet earth with its own Armageddon narrative will not usher in the answers for the lost who seek real meaning, ultimate reality. It is a beguiling distraction and deception.

On abortion, my attitudes had changed early when I was first drawn to a more conservative viewpoint although the viewpoint includes more than conservatives. I never forgot the rebuke of my Berkeley friend and the clarity of that window into her experience. The issue continues to be very complex and difficult because two living beings are involved. It only seems less complicated early in pregnancy but certainly gets more complicated mid- and late-term. While the discussion is often political/social, I found much later, long after being immersed in the transformation of my life spiritually, that I was convinced the issue was primarily spiritual and only secondarily political/social. The pro-life side is predominantly (not solely) Christian sourcing beliefs and actions from God and the heart, not from legal statutes. They fight for rules to protect the unborn primarily. The pro-choice (abortion) side is predominantly secular humanist. The motivation for the viewpoint is primarily human-centered from the rational, legal, rights, and political/social perspective. Neither viewpoint is really based on science, both are spiritual; however, with each new day science exposes more clearly the tragedy of the one view.

Community and helping others (social justice) originally came from religious, primarily Christian roots. Now those efforts have become a part of the social justice arm of government, and in some cases now, Christians cannot participate because that is viewed as pushing a religious agenda and a breach of separation of church and state. Untethered from the spiritual heart, it does not have and cannot maintain the same moral compass. Disenfranchising those who originated the impulse and imperative to serve others is a master sleight of hand and deception. The deceivers will be deceived as the impulse is metaphysical-spiritual not intellectual-spiritual.

2 .

RELATIONAL ORDER

Family Relationship

Assembling these thoughts, the realization became clear that the relationship Daphne and I had with her parents buffered both of us from the wilder aspects of the culture during those early years. On coming to that awareness, I realized I should acknowledge their role with no thought of the time that had passed. Besides allowing me to be a member of their family, they were more than that; in fact, the network of odd jobs that supported me during my time at Berkeley primarily started with her mother. While they were a Jewish family, they were not religiously orthodox Jews; nonetheless, they were distinctly Jewish in certain habits, cultural/religious traditions, charities, celebrations, and on and on. They did not observe the Sabbath or dietary laws, but from them I learned a smattering of Yiddish, to eat matzah ball soup, gefilte fish, bagels, lox, and cream cheese, to celebrate traditional meals, and more. I even attended a wedding at the dramatic temple on Arguello of my childhood memory. I was seamlessly immersed and permanently broadened in my sense of family and culture. Daphne's father escaped Germany very late but did.

Many of his family did not. He was a calm man who was not bitter and who really embodied a "peace that passes understanding."

In considering that insight, I made contact and was fortunate to visit with both her parents. Her mother passed away only a year after that. I continued to visit her father who only recently passed away at 103. Shortly after reconnecting and first visiting them, I got a call from Daphne. She said she wanted to apologize. I asked for what. She said for everything. I did not ask what that meant but thanked her, while acknowledging that broken time was still about as dark as I had experienced. Life had changed for her, too. She told me her oldest son was about to turn 19, which was how old I was when we got together.

I was protected also by my other living arrangements that were fairly traditional and by long term friends in Eddie and Peter, who are still friends today. While I never lived in a commune, the Dana House was a variant of a commune and became a surrogate family as I stepped away from Daphne. The people were to continue to be an extended family in a broader sense until I was on my own and leaning on the advice of Dr. Bold. Terry was not "just" a therapist but clearly family, a surrogate father. With Carolyn's family, she and I were included in all kinds of events. The relationship was not the same as with Daphne's family, but it was substantive and in another Jewish family. Though, I did not feel they embraced me as Daphne's parents had; they had a protective barrier around their daughter, for which I do not fault them.

My family was always there, as well, but I was unable to lean on them for emotional support at the time. I did not know how. Even without that, though, I had a solid connection except for the short time I was estranged from my father, or rather we were separate because he could not apologize for something simple. We fully reconciled, and he was a support to me. My mother was always supportive during that time. My upbringing was good. I may have been too shy; I may have been upset with the many moves and bad schools; but that was not something they knew how to deal with. They did the best they knew how.

Self-Awareness

Therapy was not the path to fulfillment in life or relationship. Secular humanism was my denomination in which I could worship my idol, relationship. That was and will always be a dead end street for understanding reality because it ends in death, nothingness, or worse on the dark side of the metaphysical. However, do not get me wrong, beneficial personal growth can and will happen in the right conditions and probably most conditions. It did for me on more than one occasion, but fulfillment will not happen. In the context of faith in Christ, therapy is and will always be a potential tool for many working out relationship or coping issues. Priority and order are everything.

For example, much later, I sought out additional counsel as I was dealing with and had dealt with so many relatives with alcohol issues. Not unlike the first time with therapy, I thought I was going to learn one thing and instead learned something completely different. I learned that in some situations I was responding like a co-dependent, thinking I could avoid problems or uncomfortable conversations by accepting the emotional load and ignoring the problems—as if that did not have an emotional cost—rather than responding directly and dealing with whatever might happen. Once I could embrace that concept and act on it, many things improved. I gained insights into my earlier struggles and therapy. I have come to believe that my parents were both co-dependent personalities, trying to fit in, not stick out, and passed that on to me. Clearly, I am borrowing from recovery terminology, but the principle seems to fit. Further, my mother's parents may also have been co-dependent; I am less sure on my father's side even though I suspect the same is true. That possibility says a lot about why I was so fearful as a child and young adult.

As part of my childish thinking, I understood my world much like most adolescents even as an adult. Religion was a compartment. The family was a compartment. Education was a compartment. School, as separate from education, was the compartment of social life that occupied most of my thought. This social compartment included my friends, attraction to girls, social insecurity, music, and thoughts of being someone other than who I was. None of my thinking was integrated in any coherent way. That structure characterized the order of thought for me when I was young. Education is like work for an adult. It was my "job." All the way through grade school, parents were involved; however, at high school, they backed off or the adolescents asked or demanded that they do so. The community for young people centers around school, and teachers have huge role in directing or misdirecting them, as the case may be. I had no other mentors or teachers who added to my understanding outside of their subject. My parents were not a source of help. Their formative years had been different, and I think they believed, like most parents, that church and school taught most of what was needed. They were doing their best to get by. The schools were different then; they tended to teach the subjects more than prescribed views. By the time my sons were in school that was no longer true;

understanding and teaching social goals was a definite aim of curriculum for many teachers in high school if not grade school.

Concurrent with all this, the social world of boy/girl relationships was defined primarily by the music and only somewhat by television and movies. The music along with dance shows were about love. I was addicted to the focus on the boy/girl relationship because I was shy, had no girlfriend, felt I was odd, and did not have the courage to approach a girl. I did not have a clue that I was only too shy, but that nobody knew anything more than I did. I certainly did not know that this "truth" sold to young people was actually destructive to most. As I entered college, the music of junior high and high school and the focus of the social scene on boy/girl relationship intensified. That was the transition to my shift to Berkeley in 1966.

Intimate Relationship

Romantic love has always been problematic. When I was young, music on radio, records, and finally on TV became big business. For young people, most of the music was about romance. Much of literature is about the relationship between a man and a woman and the problems or solutions. Poetry and songs are mostly the same. Certain ideal patterns seem to work best. However, those ideal patterns get a fresh look every generation, as each generation knows better than the last, and ideal patterns are seen as old and outdated. With relationships, some change does seem to build chances for greater happiness and success; yet, other changes actually make that more problematic. The extreme protection of young women in the upper class prior to meeting young men that existed, at least in some parts of the English/American culture, 150 years and more ago may have helped some and hurt some, although in general that protection did serve valuable purposes of setting some boundaries. Arranged marriages are not much better, granting some protection but at a cost. Still, the level of protection of young women in our culture especially since the 1960s has deteriorated to an extent that generally few boundaries exist for young women and young men, and their future relationships have more challenges.

This pattern did not start in the 1960s or with my coming of age, but had been gathering strength for at least 100 years with the women's liberation movement among other influences. That movement was rightly correcting attitudes and rights of women that had been unbalanced, such as their general treatment in society and relationships; however, as with so many corrections, any movement can take on a life of its own with territory to defend, those leading can have different agendas far larger than the initial correction, and before long everyone forgets the vision or to evaluate whether some difference between men and women actually benefit both sexes and their future relationships. Thus, general liberation for women continued slowly, and liberation for men followed step. Behavior that may have only fit less cultivated and civilized men was brought into the mainstream. The 1960s, through a number of factors including new birth control options, provided a sea change such that long standing, edge sexual behavior became the norm.

With the popularization and acceptance of *Playboy* magazine depicting semi-clothed young women, articles of a general sexual nature, and the Hugh Hefner's extolling of a philosophy of sex free of a traditional monogamous relationship, this type of magazine was changed from adult soft porn to mainstream media. At the same time, sexual studies, vaunted as purely scientific and only later shown to be clearly flawed, purported to demonstrate that many people were living different sexual lifestyles, and monogamous marriage was not what it seemed. Add to those influences widely available birth control and the late sixties counterculture of free love and all was interpreted as progress away from repressed attitudes toward sex. Everything was turned upside down; childish things became manly things. The change was practically invisible from the inside because it was consistent with a way of thinking that had been developing for a long time. Now, soft porn is everywhere, and hard porn is available in everyone's home on the internet or TV. The only way to avoid it seems to be to not go there. But how easy is that for young men?

Dating changed. Dating in any circumstance can be almost as difficult as more involved relationships even though it may not include sexual intimacy. The personal relationship between a young man and woman establishes expectations for them and for those who know them. Unless they are completely detached, which is a different problem, their hearts are involved and a break will cause damage—the more intimate the more damage. Can damage be avoided? Mostly no, but the extent of the damage can be limited. Parents and mentors could play a much greater role, but instead the culture is the mentor. The schools now educate on sex and relationships, and everything is some kind of social science construct, totally missing the point. The parents have abdicated to the schools; kids will not listen anyway—they think they know better. They do not have that kind of mentoring relationship with their parents, and they also give into their feelings as they've been taught. Some parents may try, but too often the efforts are either from the perspective of authority giving direction or as a friend not giving guidance. The wisdom of proceeding slowly, developing knowledge of one another while always being conscious of the attraction of physical appearance, character, and care that may be love is not the usual path.

Everything has changed. With the shift in culture, sex, not sexual intimacy, has taken on prime importance such that believing in sex only after marriage seems weird. Of course, the culture says one must know that compatibility before thinking about a more serious relationship when in fact it is the other way around. I know I thought that was true and was led by attraction.

When I was younger, I made the mistake of thinking my parents did not understand, that things were changing, and that I was missing the boat. No way could I have communicated with my parents about attractions to the opposite sex. They were shy, and so was I. Patience never entered the picture. I was missing life and did not want to miss it any longer. I wanted to be a part of that adventure and hoped I might find some girl who could like me and want to be a part of that adventure, too. I could never approach any of the girls to whom I was attracted. I never realized that as a blessing. I was not ready. The experience with my attractive prom date was disappointing. I thought we would be together and did not understand her dating others. I never told her how I felt, and I am not sure it would have mattered. I was very lucky, at least for quite a while, with my relationship with Daphne. We were as committed to one another as anyone I knew and were able to travel the late '60s carnival together, skipping a part of the free love, no connections world. The alternative, although perhaps attractive in thought at the time, could not have been. It had and has nothing to do with what a relationship between a man and a woman should ever be.

Our relationship, ultimately, was based on our feelings, immaturity, and lack of preparedness. We did well for the times and our age. I thought we were fine and would not have changed anything, but I understand that I knew little about relationships and how they need to grow. I was incredibly naïve about the seductiveness of the culture. We were not anchored in a truly traditional relationship, and we were trying to live in a very untraditional culture. We had a traditional grounding or anchor point in Daphne's parents, and that base that let us explore our counterculture without being totally adrift. When Daphne moved to Berkeley and the volunteer job at the radio station, the protective boundaries started collapsing, perhaps purposefully on her part.

Because of my naiveté about relationships, the consequent damage was worse than it needed to be. My attempts to adjust were totally confused. I was disoriented like I was lost in a fog stumbling about. Of course, I was not aware that I had raised a false god in relationship and could not find real meaning and peace. I was stuck in the quagmire. I do not believe a real relationship can survive with shared partners and certainly not with one sharing partners and the other not. My time alone was not much better. I felt inadequate and was thrown back to my old shyness. Any boldness I had was in the context of a committed relationship. I had much to learn about relationships, women, and myself. Nonetheless, my sense of what was right and what worked was dead on.

For more than a year, my relationships just did not work out. I approached each desiring a long term relationship without exercising any judgement in entering a relationship. Expecting great results I intuitively responded to the person, my attraction, and I think they did the same with me. But, how could I expect a relationship with a married woman might work? Did I think she would like me enough that she would leave her husband? I did not consider that I was maybe justification for him to try someone else or payback for her for all his relations with other women. The therapy and Dr. Bold's advice was different from the culture, but not totally. I am not sure he even realized or felt as I do now that the whole premise was wrong. More experience was not the answer; it accumulates a different kind of collateral damage in that trust in relationship was subservient to sexual experience, probably more damaging to women than men, but damaging to both, nonetheless.

Even in my relationship with Annie, if I could have looked past the passion and attraction, I could have wondered about her mood, her hesitancy to work to help us financially, and her leaving someone she married in less than a year. It should not have been difficult to see potential problems, but I was in love and very optimistic. To the extent I was capable, I was not holding back; I was being vulnerable; I could be hurt because I was serious as I always was even if I was also drawn by my pleasure. I tried to live generally by the rules of the simplest and best stories, novels, movies, and television shows with strong messages of good and evil, right and wrong. Of course, I made mistakes along the way. For all my affinity for the new culture, a foundational, traditional impulse was still present. The failure of that relationship did not hurt as deeply as with Daphne; however, the hurt was significant because I understood more and considered our relationship one that would last and grow. It was like a marriage to me.

While I believe young people need to learn to be alone, I believe for most of us, our ultimate strength is in a committed long term relationship with a member of the opposite sex (marriage). In many ways, Carolyn was an answer to what had been missing in my relationships with Daphne and Annie. She was mature and accepted working and moving on with her life. She would challenge me on a personal level. She never gave me any reason to doubt her faithfulness. Her friends and family opened up a much larger world to me. Our relationship started with conversation and friendship but consistent with the times probably moved too fast. I was attracted to our differences; although, ultimately they were more than I could bridge. This break was hard for me, but I know it was harder on her.

I cannot explain the timing, but I was saved from that loss by the connection with Allison so shortly thereafter. That connection, even though much too fast to be prudent, had the benefit of a common "religion" of therapy and surrogate father and advisor in Terry. He could have stopped either one of us if he thought it was not right; he could have chosen to offer no words of encouragement when questions were asked. In addition, we were joining together with similar world views. More importantly, my attraction to Allison was profoundly deeper than I had ever experienced before such that we were both ready to move on with starting a family and our life together immediately. Allison, of course, already had a family and had been in a marriage. We were less the same than we thought at the time, which became somewhat of a challenge as our relationship developed; however, we also had a stronger attachment to the relationship than to our individual positions than I had ever experienced before. We were blessed in spite of ourselves. Nonetheless, I took a long time to understand that in relationships with the opposite sex, a better pattern really did exist and I was sometimes to blame for being impatient and assertive without softer edges.

I started therapy thinking I needed to become more sexually attractive and then my relationships would work. I bought into the idea that relationship was mostly about sex even though I knew better intuitively. I learned that Terry was working on something completely different from that, something bigger and less specific. He was working on my sense of myself and how I could relate to other people in a less fearful and more assertive manner. From that, a relationship with a woman could develop. Sexual relations are a subtext of the relationship, important only if the relationship exists. However, once it does, some focus on sexual relations, never necessarily sexual performance, is appropriate. Men and women in general really are different despite what the culture wants us believe. Much later, when I came back to my faith in Christ and when Allison followed a year later, most of our relationship issues resolved themselves much easier. Problems did not disappear; yet, their impact was muted by newfound priority in Christ, and we had greater clarity and calm in dealing with them because of surrendering to God.

Scripturally a serious intimate relationship can only be between a man and a woman. Out of that relationship and the process of growing to know one another through life flows the greatest gift God gives us outside of the gospel. An attraction outside of that is only self-centered, which cannot be good for the relationship. The wayward spouse and the other man or woman cannot be thinking about the relationship; he or she is only thinking about physical and emotional pleasure, which truly can only happen in a committed relationship. Dating, sleeping together, and even living together do not meet the standard. Dating and sleeping around to find the right person skips past what is first in a relationship. Sexuality took priority in a relationship according to the counterculture and later the mainstream culture, as well. It is important and the clue to some unhappy relationships, but it is just one part that has been glorified at the expense of the whole. The idea that sleeping together is necessary to know with whom you are compatible is a totally false narrative. It has almost nothing to do with whether the relationship will succeed. A marriage is the union of a man and a woman into one being, while still individuals, under God. The union under God is it; this is hard for humans to accomplish. We understand that our right hand needs to work with our left because we have one body, and if the parts do not work together, we have problems; yet, while we understand and say "union" in marriage, we have trouble applying it. Instead of being two people acting as one, we are constantly drawn to pursue our individuality and personal pleasures. This means we are not necessarily investing all our emotions in the relationship to protect ourselves, which ironically keeps us from the very thing we want. Intimacy is more powerful.

Even when I was foggy minded, clueless, and spaced out, I had at least a sense of this, a glimpse of the towers of the Golden Gate Bridge sticking out of the fog. I saw clues; I was weak. I chose to ignore those clues for immediate gratification and to avoid real work. This is not new news. I wanted to be with the young woman in my hometown because it made me feel good. It was a connection on the road to relationship and collateral hurt. I did not have a clue how living in the culture was going to get me to a relationship and, in fact, it would not. Further, I would not clearly understand this until taking the time many years later to reflect on what was going on in the context of all those core signals that were ignored. When the world governs, that is natural. The quagmire truly does beguile.

Knowing the best way to proceed means that when things do not go right, one can more quickly adjust to the right path. But, how do you know the right decision or path? God has to be first along with a sense of the primacy of the metaphysical, and all other affairs come after that. I believe in selecting a mate the decision will be obvious after developing a friendship then realizing it is more than that. The counsel of others is important: friends, parents, and other mentors. No formula can predict the answer. However, compatible spirits, a common worldview, shared desires for family and the future, and mutual interests help. Complete opposites can work, as well, one completing the other, although the balance of factors is difficult. Of course, attraction is important too: appearance, manner, speech, actions, and much more.

A relationship is not done at any point. Constant awareness—not in the sense of anxiety, but in the sense that a prize rose requires attention to disease, proper irrigation, seasonal needs for nutrients, and pruning—is critical for a healthy relationship. Praying and listening to God followed closely by talking and listening to your spouse are at the top of the list. Understanding that men and women are different is critical. Reading can help as long as the guide books and other literature are always seen as secondary and God leads. Sexual intimacy is important, although not as important as our culture has made it out to be. The misunderstandings with regards to sex are rarely fully explored, and the difference between men and women plays a big role. To put it simply, the woman needs to trust the man and the man needs to feel pleasing to the woman. The man is usually ready on a moment's notice and does not automatically understand the emotional character of the woman's desire. Almost universally, he has to change his nature; he has to take his time; he has to focus on his wife with more than just sexual desire. He has to lead and yet ultimately let her lead: let her lead the timing, let her choose to give if she feels right, let her be pleased first unless she chooses otherwise. The woman comes first getting in the car, entering the doorway, sitting at the table, and in intimacy. The woman's challenge is to truly trust her husband, submit to him, and, yet mysteriously, passively lead him at the same time. The culture has difficulty understanding that because its roots are part of a metaphysical reality, and the culture does not accept that reality. My experience has been that even with a very imperfect effort the powerful feelings in sexual intimacy are greater in time and with age, not less. I do not mean the natural desire is as strong; I mean the depth of feeling is.

REAL ORDER

Reality, Order, and Priority: Jesus Christ

All of culture, community, self-awareness, family, and intimate relationship is meaningless without a relationship with God. Yet, that most important of relationships is lost in the fog because of that beguiling quagmire for many today as it was for me. I thought I had ascended to a firm plateau in my life yet I was in a fog and did not realize I was bogged down all along. My experience is that everyone I know and have known is searching for meaning, which is a search for God. Some more, some less, but all searching, yearning.

Secular humanism provides no meaning when examined. My worldview was one of emptiness. I could only continue in my worldview because I did not focus on obvious inconsistencies and apparent answers from outside my worldview. Science is easily understood as man trying to be God and knowing everything. The culture ignores that we seem to be learning science can be an expression of God's laws. God is not excluded by science. And, science definitely does not exclude God as science has no answer for why this all happened from nothing and how everything developed by happenstance. Oh, really. Evolution is only a theory with great gaps that are not explained. Philosophy certainly does not explain why in that scientific worldview of accidents ending in nothingness a purpose exists for an ethical, moral life. Clearly, it does not matter.

My thinking was completely fogged in, and I was not walking on firm ground. It should have been more apparent to me as I found career, relationship, more money, family, some prestige, etc. just were never quite "it." That false plateau before reawakening to God and understanding was a time and place of dense fog and ground that was sometimes firm, at other times so mushy it was hard to walk, and at other times I was knee deep. The foggy essence was like one of those Kafkaesque dreams we have all had in which we are trying to get somewhere but never do. The dream just goes on and on and we never arrive. In the dream at least, we wake up. Life provides beguiling distractions and preoccupation, so that the scurrying about without a clear sense of reality goes unnoticed.

Atheism and agnosticism are more words for stopping conversation than firmly held spiritual beliefs in my experience. Few reject Christianity from an evidence-based position; indeed, most have no knowledge of the evidence. And still, just as I found inconsistencies in looking back at my beliefs, I saw them in those around me. These are the people of the vast cultural quagmire just like me, not really looking, not really paying attention, not really searching, but secretly knowing that something bigger is going on. They're too committed to the culture to admit it and too busy and distracted to take the time to investigate. That was me for a long time. Lost in the fog and thinking fog was clear skies because fog was my reality. Is there a way to shake out of that fog? How did it happen to me? I was so committed to the fog that when I spread out the different effects on my life on a piece of paper, spirituality or the metaphysical was totally missing, even though it very definitely had a place. As Paul makes clear: we have all seen the evidence of God all around us. We see it in special things that happen to people and between people. We see it in an ocean view, a sunset, a mountain scene, or a mountain stream. Deep down we all know that is God, not Mother Nature.

I put my faith tradition on a shelf and embraced the secular humanist worldview/religion on coming to Berkeley. The disillusioned time at Cal Poly had prepared me. The classes at Cal enforced that new, more sensible "religion." Traditional religion was studied as sociology; the Bible was read as sociology or ancient literature; I got it and it made sense; it was not spiritual. Then, anthropology threw in the Pacific Islanders and Maslow. Did Maslow have it right? When one is focused on God, do needs change? That was not discussed; I remember it only as food, shelter, and only then anything higher. Self-actualization is not possible without basic needs first? This seemed sensible, but how do the persecuted in a poor country get there? No atheists in foxholes and yet no God in any of this? It all made sense then; it no longer does.

How did age and experience change the way I came to see this? In a perfect world, parents act as God's representatives and communicate the message so that children become healthy, Christian adults. The norm, however, is not even close to perfect. Even Christian families get lost. The world is our environment and must be acknowledged. We live in it and are battered by it. I cannot blame my parents. They did the best they knew how and trusted structures like the church and schools as they thought they should.

I never understood the order of priorities. Starting with politics, sociology, psychology, or economics creates a seemingly sensible order but one that ultimately is incohesive and chaotic. Having an understanding that stems from disorder makes wise judgment very difficult. The culture has gotten so far from looking at God as the priority that those who do not see that cannot accept a miracle or leap of faith, and those that do often cannot communicate it because they understand God as an entity but not how He fits in the world—that He is everything. Every Christian should understand this as a part of their discipleship. Truly, the forest cannot be seen for the trees.

In the seventh grade, my spiritual awakening was real and was an experience of God through Jesus Christ. I was open and really believed. I do not think I ever had reason not to believe. It made sense. But, as I have tried to express often, no matter how real a seventh grader's awakening experience is, it has to grow just as with an adult. However, most young people do not have the same focus as they will in later years nor do they have the Christian mentors to keep growing. When I came back to the Lord, I sought out counsel and pursued my faith through any means at hand. I was mature enough to know I needed to learn and understand more.

Today, stating something that will resonate with someone who is not Christian is even harder than it was then. Secular humanism is more thoroughly entrenched in the culture. In many ways the counterculture was somewhat spiritual, influenced by Buddhism and other eastern philosophies; secular humanism was more rooted in academia. However, I have come to believe that over time, the counterculture mostly merged with the secular/humanist culture. Where we live, it is the dominant worldview/religion. Criticisms of Christianity tended to focus on myth, literalism, and the emphasis on the unseen, the metaphysical, and dismiss the "simple" thinking of believers. I was looking to learn and not very discerning so I was a perfect subject for conversion to secular humanism.

I remember how foolish I thought Hubert, the red haired, passionate, bible thumping evangelist at the Sproul Plaza entrance to campus was. Yet, I did watch. He was so passionate he would often spray a little as he exuberantly expressed himself. His evangelistic technique would never have resonated with me. But, at a crossroads in my spiritual life, he was a signpost I ignored right there in front of me. He was right; I was not. I took the wrong road and ultimately had to wander all the way back.

While I spent a lot of my life following the wrong roads and false gods. I do not regret the journey because I can now understand the transformation that took place. Maybe I will have said something that resonates such that the light of the gospel message can be seen. That message has little to do with church and rules and everything to do with the person of Jesus and the simplest and yet most profound reality in our world. I could not even entertain that idea when I was immersed in the counterculture and my new-found religion.

I thought I had been snapped back into a faith tradition in an instant when I walked into that church and heard that sermon in July of '88. I thought that for a long time. I now realize after reflecting for years that I was wrong. I believe I was and am a lot like many around me. I was just not paying attention. Or, rather, I was paying attention to the wrong things. The world has many beguiling distractions. Just outside my peripheral vision, my experience and reading were changing me in subtle ways. In addition, I had never lost my faith and hope from my original epiphany. My faith was like one of those little sponge rubber balls attached by a rubber band to a paddle board. My faith, when I was young, took off with the force of the paddle, but then it was pulled away by the force of the reigning culture. However, my faith was not gone, the band held. As the ball reached its limit and started returning, I was likewise starting to question true meaning as my secular humanism left a void. No amount of focus on relationship, family, work, or money brought fulfillment. Nonetheless, all this time I had a faith incompatible with my worldview. I was searching for answers as the ball travelled farther back to the paddle until on impact, as I walked into that church, I woke up suddenly and all was clear.

So, while I now realize my return to my faith was a long time coming, I did experience it in the moment. The sermon about a conversion experience was clear as a bell. Often when talking conversion or discipling, I have found Christians starting with basics of faith like the trinity, the authority of Christ, or key bible verses proclaiming those foundations. For me and I believe for others in the culture now, that can be a bridge too far. The concept of the unseen or metaphysical is not considered or understood as anything but myth or superstition. For me that acceptance happened immediately, but I was prepared through my long period of casual searching. Time had no meaning. Most will not find it that easy. Many do not have the benefit of an earlier conversion. Moreover, today, many have less experience with Christianity except to know some Christians, which can sometimes be worse than no knowledge. For many, getting over the barrier of the metaphysical is the first, huge step in conversion, and it is not easy.

Yet, the unseen is always present. At the time, I read mostly non-fiction. The unseen and metaphysical pervade the older novels, but I was not interested at the time. That sense of peace and goodness on the resolution of a well told story is an aspect of the unseen or spiritual. More modern fiction tends to lose that. I read mostly modern fiction during the dark days at Cal Poly; I do not remember a hint of the spiritual but rather darkness and hopelessness. Now with the secular "religion" of science, environment, and the like, the thought of the spiritual has been relegated to the margins or to tales of horror or science fiction; whereas the metaphysical, God's realm, is actually present in the most ordinary things during the most ordinary days.

As I started editing, Paul's admonition that we all know this resonated more and more, and I was sure most of us, including me, experience the metaphysical when we stand quietly at the ocean sensing the breeze, smelling the air, and seeing the vastness, or in the mountains with high peaks, a little snow in summer, rugged rock formations, trees in myriad shades of green, or travelling the Golden Gate Bridge as it crosses to Marin, watching the roadway disappear into rushing fog spilling off the Headlands before disappearing into the Waldo Tunnel. That sense is an experience of the unseen, of God. The inner sense is a yearning for God. The God of the trinity is the reality. The unseen, God's order, is what holds things together. Science is man's attempt to explain order by putting the pieces together, not realizing it can never complete the puzzle because it's missing the ultimate piece. The order it tries to explain is God. Science is not going to make things better; God will.

One simple glimpse of the spiritual presence can be observed in twelve-step recovery meetings where the spiritual without religion governs, and sharing happens without crosstalk. It's a forum for listening and sharing without judgment or response. Without verbal responses from others, something powerful happens: a spiritual connection. It is unseen; it is metaphysical; and it is noticed even by those having trouble with the spiritual. While not Christian in name, for some it may provide a stepping-stone, a tilling of the soil, like my reading of conservative writers did. Perhaps our culture could use a good twelve step program with lots of listening and no crosstalk.

Borrowing again from recovery terminology, a metaphorical and metaphysical elephant is in the room in our culture. The elephant is the lack of the God of the Trinity: Father, Son, and Holy Spirit. The culture is in denial and trying to create a workable reality to compete by starting with the pieces to understand the whole. The effort is a like a variation of the blind men trying to describe a real elephant: from physics, this, from anthropology, that, from sociology, psychology, philosophy, biology, and more this and that, but no reality, no elephant, no escape from the quagmire of man trying to be god.

When crossing a busy road with a child in tow, an adult holds on to the child and stays in the crosswalk for safety. The child, if it understands, holds on tightly, if not, less tightly and sometimes even lets go entirely. Nonetheless, the adult is always watching. Young or old, when we are cognizant of God in our life, we hold on tightly. When we lose track, we hold on loosely or not at all. If we are one of God's sheep, He does not stop watching for our safety. I can only conclude that I was blessed that God did not let go of me, even though I did not know it for a long time. I thought I had let go and that He had too, but that was one more thing beyond my control.

Recognition of a personal sense of faith and hope is a basic and powerful signpost of the metaphysical and should make acceptance easier. Many in the quagmire have a basic faith and hope that they never realize is inconsistent with their worldview. Similarly, many who might call themselves agnostic have that same faith and hope. True faith and hope are part of the realm of the unseen or metaphysical that is rarely considered. Once that realization happens, the possibility arises to entertain that something more than the physical and man's rationalizations might exist and to accept the unseen spiritual realm. Often, what happens quietly in the background is awareness that all the physical realm, supposedly the only reality, just happening on its own defies logic. As the questioning and searching continues, the refusal to acknowledge the unseen slowly softens. Serendipity gets to be a less and less adequate explanation for the unexplained. Love is often mixed in as "God is Love," which while scriptural is often conflated with romantic love; while, this can be a window to the metaphysical, it is not understood in the scriptural sense. In the same way, a generic God may be entertained, not the God of the trinity, but a lot more than no God. All can be openings to the reality.

Along with the sense that maybe an unseen realm might exist usually comes a sense that trying to keep control is not possible even with great organizational skills. Suddenly, the boundary-breaking reflections entertain the thought that God, or at least spirituality, might be worth investigating. This is still a long way from accepting the gospel message of Jesus Christ, but is an equal distance from entertaining no thought beyond the physical.

Christ is the only answer. Christ truly is profoundly different. He calls us to believe in Him. That's it, very simple, very profound, and very complex all at once. The inability to sustain that consistent effort in the culture or other religions is the harbinger of the search for deeper meaning. What I also believe is that many really do believe in a form of prayer even at a time when that, much like faith and hope, is not on the menu of secular humanism. At the stage of entertaining the unseen, prayer of some form seems to be more readily embraced.

Seemingly on a separate track, my conservative reading challenged some of my strongly held progressive secular humanist/relativist beliefs and broke down the solid wall of the physical. It was not direct and only became apparent on later reflection. Questioning that system of belief left room for another. Of course, many of the writers were in fact Christians, even though the writing was not explicitly religious or Christian.

Often, a trial—physical, emotional, or relational—will provide a breakthrough either in talking with someone, reading something, or going to a service. When I was in a true dark trial earlier, I was still too far from accepting the idea of comfort from another reality that was more real than the one I in which I was trapped. For many though, this while a stalling point, is also the first place where a more traditional conversion mentoring or discipling plan can work. I do not believe it would have worked for me as most of those plans are so patently manipulative that they set off alarms for recovering secularists. I have found it odd that some of those programs make no bones about the manipulation (the end justifies the means), which I find in conflict with my understanding of the gospel message as a free offering. Predictably, it turns a number of people off. No one path exists in the search except for the searcher to stay open, embrace a widening of the possibility of the unseen, and pray in any form. Brilliant men like Augustine and Lewis both worked diligently in their search; yet ironically, the tipping point for both was instantaneous and other-worldly. For the disciple, listen and pray for the will of God as to what to do or say. God is in control of what will be seen, heard, understood, and when.

Stumbling Stones

Certain parts of scripture that were not "realistic" were barriers to my understanding. From the outside and a position of searching skepticism, barriers are daunting until there is a willingness to listen openly. That is where I was thrown off in that first quarter at Berkeley. That is also where I see good secular authors trying to understand and explain Christians getting thrown off themselves by some imagery in the Bible, somehow blinded by looking from the outside in when Christianity is totally from the heart (inside) out.

Past religious experience can be a barrier. The general culture still has many Christian elements, such as the celebration of Christmas. I believe because even secularists celebrate Christmas for their children and children do not have a problem accepting the story. This is another of those instances in which Paul says we know and just pretend we do not. For many, Christianity is still a bigger part of their cultural heritage and maybe it was negative. For other religions, like Hinduism or Islam, the step may be bigger, although Islam springs from the same monotheistic root. The Buddhists I know are actually Americans who converted because of their attraction to the philosophy. Ironically, openness to Christ may be hardest for Jews even though the scripture of Christianity is the New Testament and the Old Testament together. Christians study the Bible from Genesis through Revelation. Christianity is an extension of traditional Judaism, at least as Christians see it. Christ is the answer because of who he was, what he did, and because he was anticipated. The first Christians were Jews. The Jewish religion changed forever a generation after Christ with the destruction of the temple. Yet, maybe especially, because of often outrageous persecution over time, the Jews have maintained a tight religious culture no matter where they have been in the world. Their religion is not what it was at the time of Christ, and most Jews I have known were more cultural than religious (meaning a powerful faith in their God) and largely secular. Yet, the religious culture sets a powerful barrier to considering Christ and the gospel message.

Some see Christianity as full of rules when the reality is there are no rules. Christianity is a way of life, a worship of Christ, and gratefulness for the grace of the gift of salvation. Again, what looks like dogma from the outside is really an attempt to live like Christ from the inside out. But, even for some believers looking for a pattern to follow, they often default to rules or legalism and lose sight of the core impulse of heart faith. Certainly when I was younger I defaulted to structure, and a legalistic approach was my only guidance. I have seen that tendency in churches even among very faithful people.

Church can be a barrier, as well. Church worship fosters growth and relationship among believers in fellowship and is an important part of growing in faith. However, church is full of imperfect people just like everywhere else (except hopefully they are working on their faith in a different way perhaps than the searching skeptic). People in churches come in all forms just like the real world, and they make mistakes that can be unsettling for the skeptic who might be expecting something superior or perfect. In addition, churches can create barriers in trying to distinguish their form of worship and leadership structure from others. Accepting the gift of salvation of the gospel message of Jesus Christ is so easy. Yet, fitting into the structure of some churches, which seemingly should only exist in support of the gospel message, is so difficult that the effort can be a real barrier to new believers and skeptics trying to escape the quagmire.

The Christian church has many forms and denominations most of which hold to the basic gospel message. Many, in defining themselves and their style, exclude others. The Orthodox and Roman Catholics argue about being the oldest and the one church. They split a thousand years ago, not over the gospel, but over details like the Pope and some wording. According to them, if you are not part of their fellowship, you are not really Christian. About 500 years after that split, Martin Luther and other religious leaders, along with the printing press, led to an explosion of "protestant" churches, again most adhering to the core gospel message but each with a different style and emphasis. So, what is the one holy catholic church? I think it is the church of the gospel of Jesus Christ, which includes all that hold to the gospel message. Is it helpful that some evangelicals do not think Catholics are true Christians, or that Orthodox and Catholics do not think others are? Oh really. Everyone cancelling everyone else out. Is that the gospel message? Is that scriptural? Is that how God sees it? I do not know, but I do not think so. That is the boggy, quagmire thinking inside Christianity that most wisely ignore. I understand how this could give a skeptic pause; however, my experience is that most believers find a form of worship and fellowship that mostly works for them, and the key word is mostly and leave the rest which is not to say the proper role of faith and works and direct access to God are not important issues. I am not a theologian, but I think God cares about the gospel message, the saving grace of Jesus Christ, and He understands the church of the gospel of Jesus Christ is fine even if the churches of man are just that and as such are flawed. The proliferation of forms of churches has spread the Word farther and reached more people than ever. I am comfortable letting God have control over the differences.

Early experiences can be a barrier to renewed faith. I grew up in a liturgical protestant church and find the liturgy very reverential because I was taught to see what the words meant instead of seeing them as rote prayers. Some are turned off by that form, especially evangelicals who cannot relate to the style and Catholics who had bad experiences in their youth. I find the Orthodox worship service the most reverential of all with the chanted liturgy and a cappella hymns. The incense helps, too. However, some of their traditions I do not find necessary, and I cannot take communion because I am not a "member" of their communion. The Roman Catholic worship is similar. While I prefer the liturgical style, I have found that breaking up scripture into several small readings in the service followed by a short sermon (that may or may not relate to the scriptural reading) is not the best for me, even though I spent years in that form. I do not easily reassemble those bits of scripture into a whole. I find a worship service that is based on expositional preaching from scripture in a fairly long sermon works better for me. I have learned to appreciate the casual music style of typical evangelical services. I have a preferred style, but I find nurture and reverence in most services I attend without regard to the denomination.

Richard Hooker's Anglican model of "scripture, tradition, and reason" as a foundational way to understand and explain the church provides a helpful way to explore these similarities and differences. I found it to be a useful tool until I became confused by the "three legged stool," each element being a leg, and I questioned how to find the balance between the three while I watched a current tendency for reason to regularly trump scripture. Some say evangelicals put too much emphasis on scripture and have no tradition. In some ways, the comment is telling in that some evangelical churches are so dependent on the star power of the pastor that they fail without him and his teaching; there's not enough tradition. However, the Orthodox and Roman Catholics could be criticized for too much tradition with their manifold rules that are based in tradition, not scripture.

Reason, the third element of Hooker's model, is very dangerous. Since the Enlightenment, reason has found God unnecessary because in its formulation, man is god. Reason allows strange revisions of scripture in light of current thinking. For example, everything that changes in the culture now can change the interpretation of scripture, just as scripture was supposedly affected by the culture when it was written 2,000 years and more ago. Never mind that a believer should be accepting scripture as inspired by God and therefore timeless. Never mind that the culture only just changed its views on certain social issues in the last few years that have otherwise persisted for most of those 2,000 plus years.

The organizing model of scripture, tradition, and reason is meaningful when in that original order of priority. We will develop traditions, and God calls us to use our reason, but problems arise when priorities get mixed up. Scripture should always be all caps, SCRIPTURE. That stands out for most Evangelical churches. For liturgical churches, scripture is also the foundation; however, tradition in their structures developed over a long period of time can confuse what comes first. In my layman's experience, tradition in Orthodox and Roman worship and belief can be seen as all caps, TRADITION, instead of just Tradition. My experience of mainline protestant liturgical worship is that while talking about scripture, tradition, and reason, reason in the Enlightenment form has such emphasis that it is all caps, REASON; whereas, it should be all lower case, reason, as the least important of the three. Scripture and tradition are present in the ongoing structure of the church, but contemporary thought and cultural influence have great sway, which represents reason. That leads right back to man as god. I find that Evangelical churches do have more tradition than tends to be acknowledged: services have a regular structure, they practice the sacraments of communion, baptism, and marriage, and most understand the danger of too much dependence on the pastor.

For me, Scripture has to be primary. Tradition is important, but only insofar as there is some worship structure and the sacraments, not manmade structures like buildings, leadership, or rules. Reason has gotten out of hand. Reason is important, but not as a change agent for everything new in the culture, or to question God's presence and authority such that we become gods ourselves.

While I have found myself on the traditional side of scriptural interpretation, I have found it easy and consistent to embrace others who have a different interpretation, especially if they treat me in kind. I have plenty of personal failings to work on without worrying about others. I am not in control; God and that other person can work on their walk. Many Christians take a more strident posture. I thought that way once; however, much like with conversion, a change of thought does not come from a debate. Do not misunderstand, I know what I believe, but can accept that others may believe differently. That is different from agreeing with them. This is particularly true in issues of morality in relationship, human sexuality, and gender issues. Unfortunately, the way these issues seem to currently play out in the wider world is that Christians must change their views to match the secular world.

While I prefer to focus on the light, scripture is clear that a dark side exists that is eternal as well. Secular humanism says that life just ends, darkness. At least, I can work on staying in the light although some Christians focus a lot of attention on the dark side. Knowing it is real is important, but I can remember going to a retreat focused on how young people are thrown off at secular universities by all kinds of teaching and that can include darker elements of music and film. Yes, but when I watched a video that had a clip from the movie, *Rosemary's Baby*, depicting Satan to help make this case, I could not convince anyone that this was just my roommate's carnie cousin playing a part to make money. They were smart, serious believers but they could not embrace that he was just the satanic priest from my sociology fieldtrip not a real Satanist. They may have been wrong but they were closer to the truth than secularists who might make fun of them because Satan does not exist. I did not make fun, but I was perplexed. Life can be so strange. The dark side exists but the light should be the focus. The quagmire is mostly dark and beguiling unless my priorities are right. It was there all along and is now as well.

I continue to be struck by the power of Paul's witness in the New Testament. He was a model Jew. He was brilliant and understood the Old Covenant as few others have, then or now. He acted on his understanding until forced to confront a new reality. Then, he became the most profound expositor of the gospel message. So much of the New Testament teaching consists of his epistles. The Four Gospels and Acts lead directly to Romans and the rest of Paul's epistles. So much of what I am trying to convey is simply a colloquial expression of that witness in bits and pieces as I have learned it over time.

The gospel message is simply the most profound message ever, very simple and very complex. Christianity is the only religion that says God became man (incarnate) and walked among us, both fully man and God at the same time. It is the only religion that says definitively: I cannot work for my salvation. And thereby, it is the only religion not based on a set of rules, contrary to popular belief, but rather a spiritual transformation and faith in Jesus Christ. The desire to live consistently with the teaching of scripture follows only from that. Patience, humility, faith in Christ, and following His lead govern. That God would allow His Son to die on a cross, to be resurrected, and then ascend after more ministry is like no other narrative. Christ's death, burial, and resurrection completely changes the Jewish culture from one that was inwardly focused to a new culture that was outwardly focused, including Jews, Gentiles, and all the earth, instead of only a small ethnic group. The sacrificial religion changed. Christ was THE sacrifice for our sins. Everything changed.

To paraphrase Paul, "When I was a child I talked, thought, and reasoned as a child. When I became a man, I put those things behind me." I lived stuck between those two verses thinking I was in the latter when I was totally in the beguiling quagmire and fog of childish things between the two verses. I believe others were as well, have continued to be so, and moreover, our culture celebrates it. Thinking that I would find answers in science, philosophy, psychology, or relationship, I got nowhere. With my adult spiritual awakening, I could see better but still dimly. As I continued to embrace my Christian walk, my clarity of sight kept growing. However, the ultimate clarity will be in the afterlife, face to face. I have to keep growing in my comprehension that I and all Christians live between this physical world and the metaphysical on accepting Christ. While it is easy to simply relate to scripture, church, and worship songs, they are only outward expressions of the inward power of abiding in Christ through the Holy Spirit.

Listening to God and following what is understood as His lead can be seen as not setting goals nor being proactive, but is truly active faith. Mistakes will happen because not all the leadings are God, or sometimes those mistakes serve His purpose. The absolutes He calls us to need to guide us. Love God with all your heart, and love your neighbor as yourself. Then, we step forward, trusting in Him. Setting too many goals is our fallible, human attempt to control results; setting no goals is not any better, being the sign of no faith or foolish faith.

I have come to believe that all the time spent trying to work backwards through philosophy and the sciences toward understanding life and meaning in life was foolish and silly. I truly was fogged in. I was wandering in a fog for a long time; I had it right that relationship was important but not as important as I thought; as I found a solid relationship I hit what I thought was a plateau when really I was in a quagmire and had been all along. Now, against the backdrop of my faith, working on whatever I choose from that faith perspective makes sense. I know I am not in control. I move forward looking for God's will. The culture including career, money, media, music, recreation, and political and social institutions are the environment in which life is lived, not the environment from which life is understood.

One Way, Any Place

After moving so many times when I was young, being uprooted, then moving so many times even in Berkeley/ Oakland, being unrooted, to being in one physical place for over 45 years, I found my roots and cleared my mind mentally, emotionally, and spiritually. I moved a long way internally in that one place. I know that one does not need to go anywhere physically, and physical location does not matter much. When I look at my life as a whole, I see that I did not move very far out of a fairly tight geographical area, the northern part of the Bay Area. The bridges of the Bay Area and the regions they connect define where I have lived for at least 60 years, and when I did not live there I was connected still because my family had lived there for over 100 years and still do.

All those places, the Peninsula, East Bay, Berkeley/ Oakland, Point Richmond, and Marin, a counter-clock-wise chronology, circle the City closely, but they are not the City, and for all its primary attraction to me as a young adult, and even now, I have never actually lived in the City. I never needed to. Just a day visit, walking in the Outer Sunset on Judah, seeing the Ocean, feeling the fog, or an overnight at a hotel near Nob Hill, walking up, walking down, from Union Square, to Chinatown, to North Beach. It is part of my blood, a variation on Herb Caen's City. In all that time, I have never lived more than about 30 minutes away. It can take that long to get from one part of the City to another. Further, that northern part of the Bay where I have lived gets the best of the blessed, iconic Fog, physical fog. It seems to continue to have a lot of the internal fog, as well.

While the Bay Area is where I have lived and experienced life and the setting for this narrative, anywhere would have been fine and could have been just as good. The late '60s, Jerry Garcia, and the counterculture were part of my journey, but were definitely not essential. The physical place and circumstances do not matter; the spiritual place does. The spiritual is not dependent on the physical. It is available everywhere and sensed internally. How do you get to that place and stay in it?

I now know generally how I found the right answers and got back to my faith tradition. I could not have planned my path. I can only define subtle shifts that worked together to open my heart for something more. Parts or maybe all of my journey may resonate for some. There is only one Way, the gospel message of Jesus Christ, but different paths may lead to that to that Way. Do not misunderstand: only one Path, Doorway, or Gateway, but many paths or journeys to get there. Some may have been Christians from their earliest days, learning from family, and guided in scripture by mentors. Many will not; many will start out in a faith tradition and drift away at university as I did. The culture of university teaching can be enough to draw someone away from faith.

Then, what are the other paths back? Some will seek counsel in dire straits: physical, emotional, and relational. Good counsel combined with teaching, fellowship, study, meditation, and prayer can bridge the gap back to faith and a belief in the unseen, the spiritual. For some, it will be an experience like I had against the background of real but ignored searching and a softening of the heart. Some may be open enough to respond to street corner evangelism with its many forms and techniques. My experience has been that these many paths and more work. I did not try as hard as Augustine or Lewis, not even close, nor do I think myself their intellectual or spiritual equal; yet, Jesus helped me find my way back. I cannot fully understand why He did not let go of me in the crosswalk when I let go. I hope to someday understand when I see more clearly on the other side. I pray that some of my stumbling and human frailty on my journey resonates. I am also so grateful to those who endured my presence in their lives. Those relationships defined my path.

Once open to that reality of one Way, some will find a mentor, some will read scripture and be part of focused Bible study, some will listen to sound teaching, and some will combine these measures. Study and counsel are important for growth. Despite all the cautions of stumbling stones and dysfunction, certainly a good church should be involved. Fellowship of some kind is essential. Church, the bane of secularists, is the usual answer. Church is the assembly of imperfect people making the same mistakes everyone makes; the secularist view of this as a failure of Christians to live up to the higher standard of the Way is a total misunderstanding of the Christian walk. Christians know they are imperfect and can only ask forgiveness, which is freely given.

The variety of churches with different worship and teaching styles is an asset. The number of denominations exploded such that now a 1,000 years from the first split, numerous choices are available. Not all churches stick to scripture and scriptural teaching of the gospel message of salvation through Christ, of his incarnation, ministry, death burial, resurrection, and the forgiveness of and atonement for our sins. Even where important doctrines are consistent, less fundamental doctrinal teachings of one denomination are not always consistent with another. To the extent that these do not counter the gospel message or scripture, I believe as a layman that they are relatively inconsequential. The professionals might not. God is in control. But, of course, that is the point. Because we are human, the differences become important. Again, while I am not a theologian, I believe the choices of worship styles are God given. Does God really grieve at the many churches given how they have spread the gospel? However, discerning denominations that have truly changed scripture and that gospel message to suit their interpretation is important and not that difficult. They do not belong among those choices.

I have been blessed to worship in many different styles: mainline Protestant, Catholic, Orthodox, and Evangelical. I find elements that resonate with me at each. While I prefer the liturgical services with the great tradition, reverence, and prayers in their services, I have come to accept that I belong in an Evangelical setting with expositional preaching from scripture as the main element of the service. I find that keeps me rooted in scripture. Importantly, I have found many good churches with good pastors or priests and good people, even if none are perfect. Going to church is an important element of my faith practice, not as a requirement, but rather because I need regular connection and reminders.

The relationship of the City and the fog are great metaphors for the clarity in my Christian walk. I understand the City and its fabric of hills, neighborhoods, and parks. On a clear day from the Golden Gate Bridge, I can see from the

Presidio across the Marina to Downtown in the distance. When life brings trials and tribulations like the fog, I cannot see as clearly for a while but I still know clearly how to complete the picture or what to trust until the fog clears and it always does.

As my spiritual walk has become more a part of my being, I am more comfortable with not being particularly "spiritual," instead feeling that the spiritual governs everything despite seeming ordinary. I am more comfortable being "just" regular, way beyond my embarrassment long ago of my "just" a clay sculpture. Scripture says God is the potter and we are the clay, the work of his hand. I can now be "just" a clay sculpture myself with more peace and far greater understanding than I ever had in that sculpture class so long ago. And, while even longer ago, on a beautiful day walking onto the Berkeley campus, I allowed myself to step farther into a dense internal fog thinking I was stepping into clarity and on solid, not boggy, ground, nonetheless I was then blessed to be led out of that fog to firmer ground and this less dramatic but truly more beautiful and glorious day.

9 781649 709073